T0287987

CANNIBAL CAPITALISM

CANNIBAL CAPITALISM

HOW BIG BUSINESS AND THE FEDS ARE RUINING AMERICA

MICHAEL HILL

WILEY

John Wiley & Sons, Inc.

Published by John Wiley & Sons, Inc., Hoboken, New Jersey.

Published simultaneously in Canada.

For general information on our other products and services or for technical support,
please contact our Customer Care Department within the United States at (800) 762-
2974, outside the United States at (317) 572-3993 or fax (317) 572-4002.

Wiley also publishes its books in a variety of electronic formats. Some content that
appears in print may not be available in electronic books. For more information about
Wiley products, visit our web site at www.wiley.com.

Library of Congress Cataloging-in-Publication Data:

Hill, Michael, 1971-
    Cannibal capitalism : how big business and the feds are ruining America /
Michael Hill.
      p. cm.
    Includes bibliographical references and index.
    ISBN 978-1-118-17531-6 (hardback); ISBN 978-1-118-19775-2 (ebk);
    ISBN 978-1-118-19776-9 (ebk); ISBN 978-1-118-19777-6 (ebk)
      1. Income distribution—United States.   2. Industries—United States.
3. Capitalism—United States.   4. Right and left (Political science)   5. United
States—Economic conditions—21st century.   I. Title.
HC110.I5H55   2011
330.973—dc23

          2011039742

Printed in the United States of America

10 9 8 7 6 5 4 3 2 1

TABLE OF CONTENTS

INTRODUCTION

There I was, sitting in bankruptcy court. It was all gone. It was over. Why? Why me? What did I do wrong? How was I going to take care of my family? My wife was six months pregnant with our second child, a little sister for our two-year-old daughter. Why did I put their futures at risk? How didn't I see it coming? I was all in. Everything I had was on the line, but it was all tied up in the "safe" haven of real estate. Everyone said the real estate market only slows, not stops. It was considered more stable than gold. In fact, land is the only property called "real," and yet there I was. The whole thing had collapsed. They called it a subprime crisis, but the whole economy was in crisis.

By 2008, the whole thing had failed. "Dog eat dog world" is just a figure of speech, until you are the one being cannibalized. It was as if the whole country had turned on itself economically; instead of growing through the pain, the pain caused a cannibalization of engines of growth in the economy. Small businesses like mine that produce tangible goods and services and employ regular people were sacrificed, while paper traders who amass vast wealth through the exchange of abstractions derived from the real economy were propped up as too big to fail. It was a panic—a panic initiated by the greatest fear of the super-rich—the fear that they might become a little less rich. For those a little lower on the totem pole, the fear was based on the near reality of losing everything.

Just a year earlier, I had won a Custom Builder of the Year award for the Greater Washington Metropolitan region, and my company was valued by an investment bank at $47 million. My homes were featured in magazines, and I was rubbing shoulders with celebrities. We were engaged with a venture capital fund to take the business nationwide and ultimately go public with a stock offering. I thought I'd realized my dream, but it all blew up in my face. Sales froze and I was stuck holding over $10 million worth of real estate that was "underwater," as they say.

I had to retrace my steps. I had to understand the market forces that drove my success, or the illusion of it, as well as its collapse—not just for me, but for everyone caught up in this economy. The old distinctions we once safely made between Wall Street and Main Street have proved to be fallacious. Our money may come from the banks, but the value of that money comes from the real economy of Main Street. When a business fails, they may say, "You win some, you lose some," but what is a game for some is life and livelihood for so many more. The forces that drive wealth creation and destruction, the flow of capital up and down the socioeconomic ladder, and even the trading of financial instruments that no one understands, govern our lives in ways not easily perceived.

I pored over census data, market trends, economic theories and reports, and book after book of analysis of the economy. In the course of my studies, I turned myself into a sort of blue-collar economist, not academically trained in theory, but well practiced in real-world economics and the art of business. I am a career entrepreneur. I have skills in a variety of highly technical areas and very broad work experience. I've held jobs ranging from janitorial services to research assistant in a solid-state physics lab, but my life has been business. To understand my predicament, you have to understand my background.

My father is a rocket scientist, as turgid as that may sound. This is significant only insofar as the end of his career shaped my view of work, money, and career. He had long dreamed of working for NASA, and that dream came true. He worked on the space shuttle before the time of its first launch. It meant everything to him—perhaps too much. He gave himself fully to the space program, and in the end, it cost him his family. Now, there are many details that I won't describe here, but in short, when he faced the life-changing choice between career and family, he chose career.

Ironically, a short while after my parents divorced, the space program suffered wide-ranging budget cuts, and he was laid off. He played by the rules and got a good education and a good job, but ultimately, his dream was empty. The illusion shattered. If being a rocket scientist—the well-worn cliché for any intellectual challenge—is a guarantee of nothing, then what is? I became determined to chart a distinct course. I would not live my life that way.

Think about it—my father's education and diligence led to a dead end, while college dropouts like Microsoft's Bill Gates and Oracle's Larry Ellison number among the richest men in the world. To me, it's strong evidence that something is very wrong with what we are all generally taught. "Go to school, get good grades, pick a career, get a degree, put your money in a bank, work hard for job security, buy a house, and retire to a warm place." It's standard fare, but it doesn't really work, at least not anymore. Feeding people that garbage may maintain the status quo, but it doesn't meet the ambitions of over-achievers, and it hasn't led the national economy to a brighter future.

The axioms of success sounded hollow to me. The school system has gone to pot. Careers hardly ever last a lifetime. Banks rarely pay more than the lowest recent inflation rate in interest even on certified deposits, which of course means that your savings constantly shrink in value. There is no such thing as job security. And now even your house, the most significant investment regular people ever make, may not be worth what you paid for it. If you are fortunate enough to have home equity, then vultures hover ready to give you a reverse mortgage.[1]

---

1. A reverse mortgage is a home loan available to seniors that, whether disbursed as one lump sum or in multiple payments, defers repayment of the loan until the owner dies, the home is sold, or the owner leaves, whereupon the loan is due in full.

No, I was going to find another way. I gave up my earlier goal of pursuing a career in science like my father. Instead of completing an MD-PhD double doctorate, I redirected my training from physics to a degree in medical applications. I worked for a short while in a hospital, but maintained a constant lookout for my first major business venture. I found that the combination of high turnover, 24/7 shifts, vacations, and sick leave makes the entire medical services industry utterly dependent on temporary workers. So I quit my job and started a medical temp service. In short order, I was providing nurses, X-ray techs, and medical assistants to doctors' offices, clinics, and hospitals throughout the mid-Atlantic. I sold out of that business while it was still on the rise.

But I didn't let go of that vine without a firm grip on a new one. Just in time for the PC revolution, I started an IT consulting and training company. It was a natural fit. I had been programming computers since I was ten years old. Remember, my father is a scientist, and there were always computers around the house. In almost no time, I racked up all of the certifications needed to maintain credibility and acquire contracts. This company also grew and flourished until the dot-com crash.

Just before the dot-com crash, the hot thing to do was day trade. A number of online brokerages were bringing the stock market to the masses. Day traders take advantage of online access and cheap fees to rapidly buy and sell publicly traded stocks. I was only too eager to diversify my wealth-building path and join this revolution. For a while, people were making a killing . . . for a while. The dot-com crash affected me on two fronts (both as an investor and as a proprietor of a technology company), and ever since, the market has been anything but a sure thing. All of this made it clear to me and many others that a safer investment vehicle was needed. So, where did I and so many other, far bigger fish turn? It was to real estate.

I played it safer than just real estate. I invested almost exclusively in waterfront property. In fact, I bought waterfront property on the Potomac River in the vicinity of the national capital, Washington, DC. Then I searched for builders to help me develop my land. I was repeatedly disappointed by the offerings of the field. The real estate development industry suffered from an embarrassment of riches. Billion-dollar companies were building cracker boxes and selling them for a fortune because there were no alternatives for homebuyers. Now, don't misunderstand, there was competition, but all of the players were building the same junk. You've no doubt seen it yourself: community after community on vast tracts of land consisting of the same house over and over again, irrespective of the name on the street sign at the corner. Real estate developers only really compete over location, not product. I realized every entrepreneur's dream: I found a vacant niche in a multibillion-dollar business.

It was 2001, and the business of new-home construction was dominated by high-volume, low-quality production developers—as it still is today. The builders had been constantly lowering the expectations and standards of new homebuyers with respect to quality, while increasing the size and superficial amenities of their two or three homogenous designs. Individuality was lost in the home-building business, far from the days of building one unique home at a time. The exception to this ubiquity was principally found among a few ultra-elite design-build firms for the "money is no object" consumer.

The divergence of these two market segments had opened a gap; a class of consumer was being ignored, one that could afford more and wanted more than the cookie-cutter product, but that couldn't afford the custom products currently available. The only companies that were targeting this market segment were just giving them bigger cookie cutters. I was determined to give this market what it really wanted—custom homes at a cookie-cutter price.

On one hand, you can't argue with the simple economic advantage of mass production of a uniform product, but there is always a better way. With my background in information technology, I was certain that technology could be used to normalize the costs of building distinct houses, so I could produce them at a price competitive with the typical cookie-cutter home. I also knew that, given the choice, people would choose individuality. I knew this in my heart, but I had to prove it.

For the next five years, I devoted myself to developing systems and procedures to build entire communities of new homes without ever duplicating the same house design, and to do it at or less than the cost of the competition. Despite being what we call a mature industry, the inefficiencies in even the "best" building businesses were shocking to me. The industry was bloated, paper-oriented, and totally stuck in the systems of the baby-boom era, despite the fact that so much of the work is brainwork that lends itself to automation and efficiency improvements. Not only was my theory going to be proved correct, it would be easier than I'd at first believed. Easier or not, in order to obtain significant expansion capital from private equity investors, I would have to demonstrate five years of financial proof of my concept and impressive growth.

The five-year financial history of my creation began in 2002. If you do the math and you haven't been under a rock with respect to what has happened to the housing and credit market, you already know where this is going. Nevertheless, before the crash, my concept did work, and it worked better with each successive year. We grew at an average annual rate of 317 percent and had gross profit margins exceeding 50 percent. Our banks loved us, our customers loved us, and Wall Street was next.

At the end of 2006, we thought we were moving into the big league. As we were taken on by a reputable investment bank, my company was ramping up to go national. We were holding (actually, trying to sell) about $10 million in real estate, and for the first time, we detected that something was wrong. I had heard rumblings that the hot real estate market was cooling off, so I dropped the prices of the homes I was trying to sell, but the adjustment was too late.

Our cash flow slowly dried up as sales went cold, and I mean stone cold. Months went by and there were no sales—none. Halfway through 2007, a couple other local builders went under. We needed our funding and time was running out. I was covering payroll and other business expenses out of my personal funds. I was overextending myself because I never stopped seeing light at the end of the tunnel. But a sad reality of business is that it is hardest to get financing when you need it the most. The credit was drying up. It was as if we were a microcosmic preview of what the U.S. economy would experience in 2008.

Even so, I still hadn't fully come to grips with reality. Our projected financial reports still looked great, but those were based on sales that weren't happening. We were hemorrhaging all of our cash, but I still believed. I had no choice. Investors and bankers always want to know how much "skin in the game" you have, but I was far beyond skin. Everything I had from all of my previous business pursuits was now tied up in this business. I believed completely in my business plan (frankly, I still do), and so I was "all in," as poker players say.

In the meantime, I was pushing every investment resource that I could. We had passed through due diligence with an investment fund and thought we were just waiting for a check, but when we missed a milestone in our projections because of no sales, they pulled the plug.

We still could have made it, but we needed a sale. Months more went by and still no sales. Fear in business is much the same as fear in the animal kingdom. An animal stricken with fear either runs or attacks—the classic fight-or-flight response. Our vendors and subcontractors were beginning to show this kind of response. Hearing rumors of our financial instability, some stopped showing up to work for us. Material suppliers cut credit lines, and before long, our production operations ground to a halt. It was apparent to all that there was blood in the water. With that, the attacks began.

The only thing that could change our course toward destruction was a sale, but by this point we were solidly in the worst housing crisis to grip the country since the Great Depression. Why was this happening? I had heard of subprime lending, but how did it become so pervasive?

I responded as I'd been trained my whole life to respond. Although I didn't follow my father's footsteps, I was raised to be a scientist. Questions demand analysis. Every action has a cause. I was going to get to the bottom of this, hopefully in time to save my company and my economic life.

I remembered a conversation that I had with a mortgage banker from California. It was years earlier. He was describing to me a variety of loan programs that he wanted to sell my customers. These loan products have since become infamous, including interest-only mortgages, option adjustable-rate mortgages (ARMs), and other creative loans to reduce monthly payments. He explained that homes were so expensive in California that these loans had become very popular. In fact, many higher-priced markets in California were utterly dependant on these loan products. I hadn't given much thought to what he had said until the end of 2007, when these were the very loans blamed for the collapse occurring in the mortgage system.

These mortgages were in play far more than anyone realized. Even some of my customers had used them. From my perspective as a homebuilder, the old adage seemed to apply; I didn't want to look a gift horse in the mouth. To some extent, I wondered how people could afford homes at such rising prices, including the homes I was selling, but hey, if the check is good, the check is good.

Nonetheless, the reality is that the median home prices in most of the major regional markets were and still are two to three times the nationwide median home price, but the same has not been true of income. What if that California banker's statement were true about the broader market? What if a substantial percentage of the housing commerce that had been taking place for those last few years had been based on these loans, now toxic and universally viewed as blight on the economy?

I wondered what metrics are used to track and compare income to home prices. You always hear about Case-Shiller and the sales reports from the National Association of Realtors (NAR) and the National Association of Homebuilders (NAHB), but these don't match consumer buying power to home prices. Analysis of these numbers alone assumes that everything else remains static, but things were no longer static. Approaching the issues of housing supply and forecasting a turnaround without considering the buying power of the market would be futile. Fortunately, when I dug deeper I discovered that there is a much more telling index that gets very little attention. It is the Housing Affordability Index (HAI).

The HAI is the standard established by the NAR to gauge the financial ability of consumers to buy a home. A reading of 100 means a family earning the national median family income (reported by the Census Bureau) can qualify for a mortgage on a typical median-priced, existing, single-family home, assuming a 20 percent down payment. An index above 100 signifies that a family earning the median income more than qualifies, and conversely an index below 100 indicates the inability of the median family to afford the median home.

On Monday, February 11, 2008, after I had analyzed this ratio and its implications, the *Washington Post* published my findings in an op-ed column, which I started this way:

Subprime, subprime, subprime! I am sick of hearing everyone blame the breakdown in the credit and housing markets on subprime loans. The subprime loans were certainly part of the problem, but mainly they are a symptom of a deeper cause. We are not looking at the bursting of a five-year housing bubble. We are looking at the bursting of a forty-year bubble and the failure of a mortgage loan system to meet the need of the marketplace. This is what people don't want to think about, because the deeper problem doesn't have a quick fix. The truth is that the subprime lenders were actually the proverbial "thumb in the dike" for the whole housing market. The real problem is affordability and the incongruity between income and home pricing.

I went on to document and describe the effects of this incongruity and the implications of what was going on to the greater economy. My point was that the housing and credit crisis of the late 2000s has been instructive with respect to the overall pattern of attrition in the national economy. Forty years ago, the median price of a house was about two times the median household income, and in some parts of the country it was closer to one-to-one. Thirty years ago it was about three times the median income. This three-to-one price ratio was fairly stable nationally until the last decade, when we saw the median house price jump to four times the median family's income. In most of the major economic centers of our nation, typical families haven't been able to buy a home for anything near the national median in decades (see Figure I.1). While incomes are higher, they have not come close

Median and Average Sales Price of New Homes of New Homes Sold in United States
1963–2008 Annual Data

Figure I.1

to matching the growth of property values. It's loans that put any home within the reach of normal people.

Take for example the Silicon Valley area, which was the driving force for our economy throughout the nineties. Today the median price of an existing home is $775,000, but the median household income is only $62,020. That means that a home costs almost thirteen times an annual income. The housing affordability index, based on a 5.75 percent loan, is 35.71. Home prices in that market would have to drop nearly 70 percent or income would have to triple, *and* interest rates would have to stay low in that market, in order for the index to rise to a neutral level! And that is not the worst index that I have seen. Similarly low HAIs can be seen in Washington, DC, Boston, New York, San Diego, and all of the other areas hardest hit by the current crisis.

Without mortgage options that provide lower monthly payments than traditional thirty-year mortgages, the whole economy tanked, because the majority of families could not afford homes, either new or existing, in the major population centers of our nation. The economic crisis of 2007–9 was very different from anything prior to it. This time, interest rates were at historical lows, and many other economic indicators were fairly strong. At other times in our history, the housing market was influenced by and therefore an indicator of other parts of the economy. The problem this time was systemic to the housing market itself.

As the foreboding evidence mounted of the actual severity of the housing crisis, there was a consensus of panic between the United States Federal Reserve (the Fed), the global markets, and even our bipartisan government. The fears were not without basis, but they were not understood, nor was there consensus to the remedies required.

As is so often the case, our leaders viewed the problem superficially and sought superficial solutions. The larger problem of America becoming unaffordable for regular Americans still has not been squarely addressed. The housing collapse was merely a rapid acceleration of the slow, consistent pattern of a much longer period, and portended the trajectory of the national economy.

Figure I.2 shows the affordability data for some of the major markets that most clearly illustrate the housing affordability problem at its peak in 2007. To understand these figures, we will take San Diego as an example, and examine the table column by column. The median home price was $601,800; a thirty-year mortgage could be obtained at an interest rate of 5.75 percent, and an adjustable rate mortgage (ARM) could be obtained at 4.88 percent. The median income in the San Diego area was $47,067, but to qualify to purchase a median-priced home using conventional mortgage requirements, a family would need to make $134,859. This gives us an index of 34.9, well below the parity level of 100. Thought of another way, nearly two-thirds of the market is unaffordable using conventional mortgages, even at historically low interest rates. More frightening from an economic perspective is the fact that home prices would have to drop more than 65 percent to reach parity, and more like 75 percent to reach a healthy level. To a prospective homebuyer, this drop doesn't necessarily seem to be that bad, but if you bought a home for $600,000 and its value dropped to $200,000, the effects would be devastating. Consider the effects on the bank that lent 80 percent or more of that $600,000; consider the fact that the builder spent $500,000 to build that $600,000 house; consider how many components to the economy depend on the presumption of value in real estate; and you will begin to understand the depth of the economic crisis.

	Median Existing Price	Fixed Mortgage Rate	ARM Rate	Median Family Income	Income to Qualify	HAI Composite	HAI ARM	Price to Annual Income
San Jose-Sunnyvale-Santa Clara, CA	$775,000	5.75%	4.88%	$62,024	$173,671	35.71	39.36	12.5
San Francisco-Oakland-Fremont, CA	$736,800	5.75%	4.88%	$62,024	$165,111	37.57	41.40	11.9
Anaheim-Santa Ana, CA (Orange Co.)	$709,000	5.75%	4.88%	$45,903	$158,881	28.89	31.84	15.4
Honolulu, HI	$630,000	5.75%	4.88%	$51,914	$141,178	36.77	40.53	12.1
San Diego-Carlsbad-San Marcos, CA	$601,800	5.75%	4.88%	$47,067	$134,859	34.90	38.46	12.8
Los Angeles-Long Beach-Santa Ana, CA	$584,800	5.75%	4.88%	$45,903	$131,049	35.03	38.60	12.7
New York-Wayne-White Plains, NY-NJ	$539,400	5.75%	4.88%	$50,795	$120,875	42.02	46.31	10.6
NY: Nassau-Suffolk, NY	$474,700	5.75%	4.88%	$50,795	$106,376	47.75	52.63	9.3
Bridgeport-Stamford-Norwalk, CT	$473,700	5.75%	4.88%	$49,283	$106,152	46.43	51.17	9.6
New York-Northern New Jersey-Long Island, NY-NJ-P	$469,300	5.75%	4.88%	$50,795	$105,166	48.30	53.23	9.2
Washington-Arlington-Alexandria, DC-VA-MD-WV	$431,000	5.75%	4.88%	$57,291	$96,584	59.32	65.37	7.5
Boston-Cambridge-Quincy, MA-NH**	$402,200	5.75%	4.88%	$52,792	$90,130	58.57	64.55	7.6
Miami-Fort Lauderdale-Miami Beach, FL	$371,200	5.75%	4.88%	$38,632	$83,183	46.44	51.18	9.6

Figure I.2

There certainly wasn't enough space on the opinion page to cover all angles. There is much more to the systemic problems that have brought the world to the brink of economic disaster, and an examination of the unfolding of this crisis is instructive for identifying what the structural problems of our national economy are. Many wrote me or posted comments in response to the article, questioning areas that I didn't have the space to address. While I was interested in even the fiercest criticisms, many simply rehashed the classic partisan viewpoints, which have been shaped by media pundits using the crisis to push their ideological views. It is a sad fact that people always want simple answers to complex problems, and, if someone can match a problem to a political predisposition, it is catnip for the public. This time, though, the stakes are too serious for empty political blather. I am not afraid to address the criticism, because the facts don't lie.

For instance, the easiest response to the housing crisis was to blame the borrowers who "bought homes that they couldn't afford," as so many commentators have repeated. Even respected economists like Bill Wheaton, who runs the MIT Center for Real Estate, made such statements. The fact that I avoided laying blame at the feet of the defaulting borrowers seemed to puzzle some, particularly when you consider the debt accumulation theories of renowned economist Hyman Minsky. There was certainly an epidemic of what Minsky described as "Ponzi borrowers," or those who borrow in the belief that the appreciation of the asset's value will be sufficient to refinance the debt, but who could not otherwise make sufficient payments on either the interest or principal. The term "Ponzi scheme" is a reference to the Charles Ponzi scandal, and is widely used to describe any fraudulent investment operation that pays returns to investors out of the money paid by subsequent investors, rather than from profit.

Now, of course everyone who signs an agreement is responsible for fulfilling the terms of the agreement, and if you can't afford to fulfill an agreement, you shouldn't make it. It is almost pointless to restate something so obvious. Nevertheless, to simply blame the consumers who "recklessly" bought into these loans is shortsighted. Even though I agree that some of these people acted inexcusably, I think that you can't completely blame homebuyers, who were caught up in the same hype that our large institutions were. All the mortgage brokers seemed to have memorized the same line during the run-up years preceding the housing crash: "When the rate goes up, you can just re-fi." In other words, Minsky's "Ponzi borrowing" had become institutionalized! Well, the rates went up, and the mortgage market crashed. You couldn't "just re-fi" and you can't just blame ordinary people for all of this.

Also, the supposition that "these people" should rent instead of buying is undermined by the fact that the differential between owning and renting has recently become negligible in many markets. For example, in 2010, when the median existing-home price was $173,000 and the interest rate for a thirty-year fixed loan was 4.875 percent, covering this whole amount would only require a mortgage payment of about $920 per month. It may not be the case everywhere, but where I live, you would be hard-pressed to find a two-bedroom apartment in a crime-ridden neighborhood for less than that. The rhetoric is empty.

It is also atrocious that the public cares so much about foreclosures and so little about evictions. Eviction is far more shocking and immediate to a family than the months-long process of foreclosure, but banks don't lose money, property values generally don't radically decline, and MBS traders don't lose bets when a family is thrown out of their apartment onto the street at a sheriff's gunpoint after missing one month's rent.

Another "simplistic" response has been to blame the ever-increasing standard size and features of new homes. Robert Lang, codirector of Virginia Tech's Metropolitan Institute, a research organization that focuses on real estate and development, told Reuters, "People had in their head, 'I need a mud room, I need giant columns, I need a media room, and I'm going to do anything to get it.'"[2] At first glance, this seems like a reasonable argument. One person who responded to my article cited the fact that the average size of American homes has increased by 60 percent since 1960. Others drew attention to amenities like granite countertops and hardwood floors that are more common today.

Blaming rising prices on the fact that homes have gotten bigger and tastes more exorbitant is also off base, because, as counterintuitive as it may seem, there is really no significant corollary between the growing average size of homes and price inflation. In fact, many "luxury" amenities are actually cheap to produce. Also, it is simply a fact that Americans seek an ever-improving standard of living. In our economy, we always expect everything to go up, up, up—monthly, annually, and so on. This is a fact of consumerism as well. Right or wrong, it is a fact of life that people expect to have more than their grandparents. When you also consider the pound of flesh that it takes to get a home today, it is only fair to want to feel that you have gotten something out of it. It is only natural for the one selling to try to satisfy the one buying.

More to the point, builders have been building larger homes because it is more profitable to do so. Counter to what common wisdom would suggest, the bigger the houses are, the cheaper they are to build, particularly on a per-square-foot basis. This is because there are many costs that are fixed per unit, but by throwing up a big, cheap box, builders can seemingly "justify" higher prices by offering space. Small, single-family homes are not viable in most major markets. When inexpensive units are needed, the business solution is to build big structures, which are chopped up into townhomes or apartments.

---

2. Andrew Sullivan, "Foreclosures Come to McMansion Country," Reuters, April 7, 2008. http://www.reuters.com/article/idUSN01306132200804074.

Believe it or not, the home-building business is not necessarily as profitable as people may think, partly because of how many hands there are in the pot. Landowners have gotten savvy enough to build development potential into the land prices; gone are the days when farmers sold their land for a pittance. In many cases now, land developers are middlemen that usher raw parcels of land through the legal processes to create "paper" subdivisions so as to sell land at a premium to the builders. This process involves engaging real estate attorneys and civil engineers to create generic subdivisions, further compounding the costs incurred by the builders as they engineer final development and obtain permits. With the increasing influence of so-called NIMBY (Not In My Back Yard) activists, local governments have created more hurdles in the approval process to develop land. Well-meaning or not, this adds to the ultimate costs of new homes, often on a per-unit basis. Add to all of that the escalating costs of material and labor, the cut that goes to lenders, and real estate agents' fees, and you have a situation in which the cost of small homes wouldn't be much lower than what we are seeing for seeming unnecessarily large homes. The truth is that size, granite counters, and other finishes are an excuse to create the illusion of worth in the context of rapidly rising costs.

Furthermore, even if you were to run the numbers based on the costs to the builders, you would still find that homes are unaffordable. You can't decouple the cost of buying homes from the cost of building homes. In addition to the well-known laws of supply and demand, home prices are set by the new-home business. And many of the costs of new-home development continue to rise, even in the face of faltering home values.

It is true, as many economists and commentators point out, that the readily available loans backed by the power of Wall Street (what MSNBC's Dylan Ratigan called a "money party") caused an excessive demand-side run-up in home prices, but with the exception of the 2003–6 run-up, a significant part of home price inflation was the result of natural market inflation. New homes get their prices from costs plus profit margins (sometimes very slim margins). As I mentioned, there are significant costs in the combination of land, material, and labor. To be more specific, there are many market forces at work when it comes to materials and labor. Building materials are international market commodities. Labor costs are tied to the ever-increasing cost of living. There is a floor on how low these costs can go. In fact, there is a danger implicit in allowing market forces to drive existing-home prices too far below the costs of developing new homes. That could mean devastation or perhaps even the end, as we know it, of the largest business in this country, construction, a hundred-billion-dollar-a-year industry. The 2007 housing crisis has already meant the end of certain niches of the construction business.

Of all the comments I have received in response to my *Washington Post* article, the ones that struck me as most significant were the ones that exuded a disdain for the concept of fixing a credit problem with credit. The outspoken congressman Ron Paul stated in a House Financial Services Committee meeting on February 25, 2009, "We have to come to the realization that there is a sea change in what's happening. [That] this is an end of an era and that we can't reinflate the bubble," and many share his sentiments. In fact, so many have echoed Ron Paul's words that it became common wisdom in the wake of the 2007–9 economic crisis. Mr. Paul went on to say, "Capital can't come from the thin air creation by the Federal Reserve System; capital has to come from savings. We have to work hard, produce, live within our means, and what is left over is called capital. This whole idea that we can recapitalize markets by merely turning on the printing presses and increasing credit is a total fallacy, so the sooner we wake up to realize that a new system has to be devised, the better." That also seems to make a lot of sense.

It is to the proponents of these sentiments that I dedicate this work, because I agree with them completely in terms of ideology—even though they are wrong. The right thing to do ideologically is the *wrong* thing to do practically. Even worse, it is utterly fallacious to moralize ideologically along an artificial line. Too many people are focusing on their delusions of what the system *should* be, instead of accepting what it is. The affordability of purchases made possible only through financing is an illusion created by the terms and wording of the financiers. The paradox is that as people wake up to financial reality, as opposed to what they imagine things "should be," they suffer the very crisis of confidence that economists most fear. The frightening thing is that the entire global economy is similarly illusory when you examine credit, leverage, exchange, and even currency. What Congressman Paul says you "can't" do is precisely what has been done in every corner of the global economy over the course of the twentieth century.

People use the term "bubble" as if to designate an aberration in the economy, but frankly, the whole system is a bubble—or rather a bubble bath. Secretly we acknowledge this fact by using terms like "inflation" and "deflation." The Forbes web site Investopedia, defines a bubble as "a situation where the price for an asset exceeds its fundamental value by a large margin. During a bubble, prices for a financial asset or asset class are highly inflated, bearing little relation to the intrinsic value of the asset."[3] By that definition, the price of a can of Pepsi is indicative of a bubble, unless you really believe that sugar water has "intrinsic value" anywhere near what we all pay. How about bottled water, for that matter?

Frankly, the whole monetary system is a bubble. Currency has no intrinsic value beyond that of its paper and ink. Even its implied value is based on abstractions. For instance, who still uses commodity-based currencies, like our old, silver certificates? It's all credit—all bubbles. But what makes all of this so disturbing is that there was no choice. The creation of an inflated system of "bubbles" is what ended the Great Depression. We had to switch away from the gold standard to what some consider "funny money."

The notion that currency-backed by gold is somehow more "real" is attractive to many. Unfortunately, "real money" and the "real economy" could never keep up with the demands of the growing world.

The January 2009 issue of *National Geographic* reported:

> *In all of history, only 161,000 tons of gold have been mined, barely enough to fill two Olympic-size swimming pools. More than half of*

---

3. "5 Steps of a Bubble," Investopedia, 2010, http://www.investopedia.com/articles/stocks/10/5-steps-of-a-bubble.asp.

ICHAEL C. HILL

that has been extracted in the past fifty years. Now the world's richest deposits are fast being depleted, and new discoveries are rare. Gone are the hundred-mile-long gold reefs in South Africa or cherry-size nuggets in California. Most of the gold left to mine exists as traces buried in remote and fragile corners of the globe.

Let's do the math: 161,000 tons is 3.864 billion troy ounces, which, at the crisis-inflated gold price of $1,800 per ounce, amounts to $6.96 trillion. That's less than half of the annual gross domestic product of the United States. Beginning to see the problem? The global GDP (at purchasing power parity) is over $70 trillion. Even if we leveraged all of the gold in the world, and even if the value of gold were inflated to match the global GDP, the price of gold would need to exceed $18,000 per ounce, and would have to rise and fall with global economic activity. This is a gross oversimplification, but it nonetheless makes the point clear. Such gold prices would distort investment; undermine industry, particularly electronics; perhaps render jewelry too dangerous to wear; and to limited degrees damage medicine and scientific research. In addition to those undesirable consequences, the gold standard would still be untenable, because the current distribution of gold would lead to trading that would undoubtedly drop the price, causing worldwide economic turmoil, deflation, and depression. It just wouldn't work. The world runs on funny money.

Really, if you think about money in the absolute, essentially money is a lie that everyone agrees to. It is based on the credibility of the issuing authority and on very broad market conditions. In our country, bills of currency are clearly identified as "notes" signed by the U.S. treasurer and the secretary of the Treasury. The government declares that these notes are "legal tender for all debts, public and private," and we all say, "Fine." Uncomfortable brushes with this tenuous reality cause some to long for the days of gold as currency. Yet even the value of gold is assigned based on sentiment, driven up and down by market trading. At the end of the first decade of the twenty-first century, many economists saw the price of gold as another bubble driven high by panic. In describing the end of the world, the Bible says that people will throw their gold in the streets in recognition of the artificial nature of its value and its inability to save them. Gold as "money" is no more real than our Federal Reserve notes. We can see that the whole system is very fragile if we suspend belief for a minute and look objectively.

Money is supposed to be a means to an end, the end of providing a mechanism to exchange goods and services without direct bartering. The problem is that money has increasingly been seen as an end in itself, to such an extent that the value of currency has been elevated above real assets, goods, and services. Analysts such as business network CNBC's Rick Santelli have lambasted the notion of "debasing the currency" at the very time that the real property values were being debased by policies enacted in the wake of the subprime crash. His perspective is understandable when you consider that he has built his career as a financial expert by focusing on futures, bonds, and currency trading. Frankly, perspective is part of our problem. To those who make money from money, currency is more important. To those who build wealth from *stuff*, stuff is more important. We need a broader view to see beyond these myopic perspectives. Which is really more important: the value of currency, which is ultimately artificial, or the value of land, homes, buildings, labor, and other real things?

This is why the housing crisis is so instructive. It was a smaller version of the global economy of paper wealth and instrument-enabled commerce. By the late twentieth century, real estate was expensive. Building materials were expensive. The skills required to put it all together to produce a modern home were expensive. Middle-class people couldn't afford it, and that was not going to change. The unaffordability of homes had been a reality for decades, but had become even more excessive. A system had to be devised to bring homes within reach of most people. From the beginning of the era of middle-class home ownership, that system has been the mortgage loan. In order to encourage banks to issue mortgages, "mortgage-backed securities" (a bundle of mortgage loans bought from banks that can be traded by investors) were created. Eventually, CDOs (collateralized-debt obligations, a type of structured, asset-backed security in which components are split into different risk classes) and CDSs (credit-default swaps, contracts in which a buyer gets a payoff if a credit instrument, for example a bundled mortgage, goes into default) made trading mortgages in the form of these complex derivatives very profitable. This created a demand for more mortgages to be issued, irrespective of the quality of the loans or creditworthiness of the borrowers. On the ground, this caused a housing boom. The bust occurred when more loans defaulted than expected, the CDSs didn't pay, and investors began to regard all of these securities as toxic.

What really happened? Overvaluing mortgage derivatives drove the market unsustainably high, and excessively undervaluing them caused the whole housing market to collapse. Sentiment drove it all, because ultimately it is all artificial.

To the average Joe, the pain of the housing boom and collapse was very real. When suddenly there was demand for more houses because of the mortgage derivative market, it meant jobs for carpenters, plumbers, electricians, masons, engineers, and architects. Rising home prices meant equity that could be used for everything from consumer activity to investment capital to start businesses. Some thought that their ship had finally come in and trickle-down economics was finally working. To the big derivative traders, though, it was just a game—fun at first, but abandoned when things got tough. In markets where nobody wants to play anymore, the thing traded becomes worthless, burning anyone stuck with it.

Fixing the housing market is no longer enough. Now the whole economic system has revealed its fundamental flaws and is in jeopardy of collapsing in a sustained crisis of confidence, or even worse, unraveling because of idealistic policies that fail to match reality. The revelation of the extent to which the economy is leveraged is now known, and there is a moral drive to deleverage the system. The entire system of commerce is on the verge of collapse because the curtain has been rent and we can now all see the wizard.

My little business went bankrupt like those of so many other builders, but that was nothing compared to the collapse of so many of the great aggregator-distributors of wealth, like Wall Street giants Merrill Lynch, Bear Stearns, Morgan Stanley, Lehman Brothers, and leading mortgage lenders Washington Mutual, Countrywide, IndyMac, and Wachovia. Even the Federal Home Loan Mortgage Corporation (Freddie Mac) and the Federal National Mortgage Association (Fannie Mae), which had no direct connection to subprime loans, as they were required by law to buy only conforming loans, lost billions and ended up under conservatorship. We all now know who Bernie Madoff is. Even Alan Greenspan lost faith in the system.

Why shouldn't we question a system that has brought us to this point?

As dramatic as all of this has been, the one-two punch of the housing and credit crises is not all that is wrong with the economy. We have merely seen symptoms of much deeper problems. The combination of modern communication, the broader practice of democracy, conflicting values and realities, political gridlocks, globalization, and the easy money of arbitrage have perversely combined to catalyze the self-destruction of our economy.

Arbitrage is the simultaneous purchase and sale of an asset in order to profit from a difference in the price and thus profit by exploiting price differences of identical or similar financial instruments, on different markets or in different forms. On one hand, it can be argued that arbitrage provides a mechanism to ensure prices do not deviate substantially from their fair values for long periods of time, but on the other, it can be argued that arbitrage is a product of the inefficiencies of complex markets. The real problem is the scale of these inefficiencies and the opportunities that are created by them. Some of the richest people in the world have amassed tremendous wealth through arbitrage or arbitrage-like trading.

There is a whole class of hedge funds that profits, not by investing in the success of businesses or even by short-selling potential declines from business failures, but by simultaneously taking both long (hoping the share price goes up) and short positions (hoping the share price goes down) in the stocks they trade. Sounds confusing, huh? Not really, though. The whole objective is to profit from volatility.

When the stock price goes up, they liquidate long positions, and when the stock goes down, they cash out the short-sells. They are completely indifferent to the success or failure of the public companies they trade. Such hedge fund managers actually prefer "range-bound" stocks (a stock price oscillates between two points, but neither advances nor declines in a sustained way).

How does profiting from systemic inefficiencies benefit the broader economy? It doesn't—in fact, it may undermine it. This is cannibal capitalism. Investment houses, banks, and the like draw some of the country's best and brightest talents out of the real economy to create new techniques for extracting wealth from the system. People who could have been using their intellect to develop new, tangible commodities that could advance the real economy are instead drawn to the irresistible lure of obscene wealth that can come from making money from money. This sort of thing is making up an ever-increasing chunk of the GDP, and many banks would rather do this than make loans, particularly since the repeal of Glass-Steagall, the law that, in part, separated investment banks from depository banks. We've seen the disaster that results when the scams of these big institutions fail. The paper wealth evaporates, leaving behind only carnage.

Will this economy survive? Can it? If it does, what form will it take? Will there still be a middle class or will the expression "jobless recovery" haunt the foreseeable future? Seeking the answers to these questions is not merely an intellectual exercise, for we all depend on the global economy. Trading in London affects a plumber starting a business in Tupelo. The labor costs in Xinjiang, China, can undermine union negotiations in Detroit. The world has changed, and our system has not changed in concert with it.

In seeking the answers to economic challenges, we always hear from journalists, academics, and Wall Street bigwigs, but in the weeks, months, and years following 2007-9, these experts remained confused by the slow economic recovery, the persistent stagnation of housing and construction, and the failure of tax cuts, zero-percent interest rates, government stimulus, and other public policies to spur job creation. On July 29, 2010, Reuters reported that St. Louis Federal

Reserve Bank president James Bullard said the risk of deflation in the United States had risen, even while many economic and policy leaders were panicking over their inflation fears of loose monetary policy, debt, and deficits. Perhaps the confusion is because the bigwigs all live and breathe in the same echo chamber of narrow views; rich guys sitting around talking to each other about the economic realities of the middle class, which they only understand two-dimensionally. We rarely hear from the little guy or from small businesses.

I am a small business owner, employer, and outsider. I have spent the last twenty years practicing economics in the real world, not studying it in a classroom. I am not part of any political party. I have no agenda other than to relate the truth, because the fundamental flaws in a democratic, free market, capitalist economy are now beginning to take a toll on millions of lives, including yours.

CANNIBAL
CAPITALISM

PART ONE:

WHAT'S WRONG WITH THIS PICTURE?

Economic cycles of bubble and bust have become normal. Political intransigence is normal. And the Great Recession of 2007-9 was indicative of the declining prosperity of America. Instead of finance as a means to enable production, finance has replaced production as the engine of our economy. Cannibal capitalism has become our modus operandi.

CHAPTER ONE

The Face of
Self-Destruction

He must be nuts! There is an obviously troubled man standing with a gun to his head. He profanely screams at some enemy, accusing him of ruining his life. But, curiously, no one else is there. The gun is pressed to his own temple. Then, as if shifting gears, he abruptly changes tone and speaks as if responding to his earlier rant. As he utters the most odiously vitriolic speech, you notice that he is facing a mirror. This man must suffer from some mental illness. Perhaps a multiple personality disorder? His enemy is another part of himself. Will he pull the trigger? Will he actually kill himself in order to dispatch his enemy?

This scene is illustrative of what is going on in America right now. *We* are that disturbed man. Political preferences have hardened into factions. The indivisible nation is the most divided it has been since the Civil War. The leaders of our cannibal country use the time-tested war tactic of "divide and conquer" against their own people to attain and maintain power. As a result, the extreme wings of the political spectrum don't merely disagree, they distrust and seemingly despise their counterparts. Because ideological activists carry so much sway in their respective parties, they restrain their leaders from fully seeking cooperation with political opponents. For that matter, the term "opponent" has become a euphemism for far more severe sentiments; it implies that someone with a different political point of view is a villainous enemy, unworthy of existence. The language of political commentators and activists has become so overheated and hyperbolic that leaders of the opposition must be compared to Hitler, Stalin, Pol Pot, or Mao in order to show dissent.

Liberal commentator Al Franken wrote a book entitled *Lies and the Lying Liars Who Tell Them: A Fair and Balanced Look at the Right*, directed at George W. Bush's administration and political allies. Franken was later elected to the U.S. Senate. Republican insiders Ken Blackwell and Ken Klukowski wrote *The Blueprint: Obama's Plan to Subvert the Constitution and Build an Imperial Presidency*. In 2009, Blackwell was a candidate for chairmanship of the Republican National Committee, who withdrew after the fifth round of voting. These are not exactly fringe characters spewing vitriol.

Fringe elements take matters quite a bit further. They use vulgarity to describe their political opponents, burn effigies, and in the extreme, commit violence. The Southern Poverty Law Center (SPLC) claimed in a 2010 report that the number of antigovernment militias, which it referred to as "extremist," grew from 149 to 512 between 2008 and 2009.[4] Then, as if scripted to validate the SPLC warnings, at the end of March 2010, the nine members of the antigovernment Hutaree militia group were arrested for their plot to kill police officers. Minimizing and dismissing the extremists as harmless would be naive. Lest we forget, Timothy McVeigh, domestic terrorist and murderer of 168 victims in his attack on the Murrah building in Oklahoma City, was a militia-movement sympathizer acting on political motivations.

With sociopolitical chaos as the backdrop, economically we see scheme after scheme by the nation's business leaders to extract more and more wealth from the middle class and from the real economy, further spreading the gap between the haves and the have-nots. The resulting economic malaise feeds people's anger and frustration as they

---

4. Mark Potok, "Rage on the Right," *Intelligence Report*, no. 137 (Spring 2010), http://www.splcenter.org/get-informed/intelligence-report/browse-all-issues/2010/spring/rage-on-the-right.

look for someone to blame. The blame game causes a deepening of ideological rifts, undermining efforts for political accommodation. Then, the apparent incompetence of the political structure undermines confidence in the economy, further hastening the extraction of wealth as investors flee to "safe haven" financial instruments. This in turn increases the sociopolitical chaos, as the downward spiral of cannibalization continues.

Where will this go? Will we actually kill ourselves?

We already are. Slowly but surely, this country is eating away at all of the things that built it up. This slow destruction comes not from without, but from within. It is as if we were a nation of cannibals feeding on one another, with no regard for the self-defeating nature of such conduct.

The Systemic Flaw: Catabolism

Catabolism is defined by *Random House Dictionary* as a "destructive metabolism; the breaking down in living organisms of more complex substances into simpler ones, with the release of energy." If you think of the nation as an organism, we have seen a destructive breakdown of the means of production and a release of "energy" (wealth) to the rest of the world. At the core of government and economics, there are mortal defects.

The disease *kwashiorkor* is a form of catabolism (the human body eating itself) that occurs when a person is getting what would seem to be adequate caloric intake, but little or no protein. You're getting calories, but they are empty calories. To get "meat," your body eats itself. Analogously, the economic system, feeding off itself, has aped the operation of healthy markets while not actually sustaining healthy growth. The system has suffered from the worst kind of malnutrition.

There are eight principal factors that make this a sort of "cannibalism":

1. Selfishness. This is the fundamental human flaw behind all that is evil in the world. Overcoming it is an individual struggle, a war we must each wage within our own hearts. There is nothing we can do about that, but, to the extent that selfishness is the

core ethic of our institutions and economy, its effects have far-reaching consequences that are ultimately self-defeating.

2. **Suicide-Enabling.** With selfishness as a core ethic, short-term profits are always chosen over long-term benefits. Whether you are considering broad-based issues such as energy, arbitrage finance, and international trade, or personal matters of tobacco use, diet, or consumerism, both macro- and micro-level destructive habits are enabled, whether intentionally or not, for fiscal advantage.

3. **Money Politics.** There is a perverse relationship between politics and economics. Whether or not intended, politics creates opportunity for wealth. Also, our democratic process requires expensive elections, and so it only makes sense that those seeking to benefit from the opportunities afforded by public policy would seek to shape politics, thus forming a corrupt circle of dependencies.

4. **Selective Morality.** There is no honest debate when there is no consistent standard of truth. The practice of ignoring or obfuscating inconvenient facts is all too common in all ideological corners. Oversimplification of the contrast between capitalism and socialism, liberal and conservative, and right and left overheats rhetoric and stunts potential progress. When an ideology becomes a pejorative, those holding to it cease to exist as your fellows and become something foreign, immoral, even evil.

5. **Superpower Coasting.** America has been a significant international power for a century, a superpower since World War II, and the only superpower for a generation. It has been resting on those laurels for quite a while. There has been a lack of internal investments to maintain healthy growth. Some of the apparent growth has come by exploiting this attrition.

6. **Easy Money.** Instead of healthy growth, economic advancement has often been related to the "empty calories" of arbitrage

wealth creation, thus creating bubbles and subsequent busts. The lure of easy money has redirected talent and capital away from the real economy to the world of finance.

7. Monopoly Madness. The solution to difficult market situations is far too often business consolidation, which creates monster companies that can become "too big to fail" enterprises that can threaten the national or even global economy. Also, as such companies grow larger, barriers to competition become so high that new business is undermined.

8. School (out to) Lunch. Society undervalues education, as evidenced by the deterioration of public education. American students are scoring below the youth of many other nations in core educational metrics. Whether it is because these other nations are advancing or this one is falling behind, for all intents and purposes the public school system has become little more than national day care. Anti-intellectualism is viewed as a virtue in far too many circles, and erroneously linked to the attractive personal quality of humility. What was once anti-elitism has become a visceral aversion to well-reasoned, logical dialogue in nearly any form. It is considered better to follow your gut than to think a subject through. Snap judgments are viewed as a sign of strength, while careful deliberation is seen as a sign of weakness. Even children are indoctrinated against intellectual development, dreading the label of "nerd." This growing anti-intellectual culture breeds an utter disinterest in the matters that matter most. Many would rather follow the minutia in the lives of celebrities than engage in the things that shape their world. Few take the time to examine history, economics, sociology, and anthropology, and yet still vote, charting the path of future history, only doing so in ignorance.

This is certainly not an exhaustive list, but it gets to the catabolic systemic flaws of our republic. Not mentioned here are the destructive divisions and waste of resources within the nation caused by racial and cultural animosities; a criminal justice system that turns petty delinquents into hardened career criminals; the military-industrial complex; or other societal ills that are far too many to enumerate.

A House Divided

The focus here has to be the catabolic, systemic flaws of the republic that affect the broadest swath of human civilization—economics and the sociopolitical mechanisms that catalyze the hastening of self-destruction. We can neither wish these away nor ignore them. Ignoring them, as we do now, perpetuates catabolism. The selfish nature of human beings may be immutable, but some of these flaws are *possible* to correct. Most of these problems are artificially created by public policy, and could be redesigned if confronted boldly.

Take, for example, the issue of money politics. Financial interests bankroll the campaigns of politicians, thus ostensibly obligating these public officials to vote for their "benefactors'" preferences. Critics view the government as bought and paid for by the corporations. However cynical it may seem, this is a reasonable conclusion. True or not, it seems rare for a politician to ever violate the interests of his or her benefactors, even when those interests are not aligned with those of the broader public. Politicians need contributors' cash to keep their jobs. It is in their self-interest to play this game, irrespective of the public good. Do wealthy elites thus really control a nation supposedly ruled by the people?

Throughout all human history, mankind has experimented with every conceivable form of government and economics. None has ever worked completely. There are really only three fundamental types of government: rule by one, rule by some, or rule by all. The variances in specific instances are tied up in the who's, how's, and why's. Whether autocratic, oligarchic, or democratic, the attempts to correct one system's flaws have consistently created systemic flaws in the next.

The root problem of all forms of government is human selfishness. The thought of entrusting a selfish individual with ultimate power is what makes the prospect of an autocracy horrifying to all others. Oligarchies may dilute and distribute power, but the result of a group pursuing its self-interests has consistently been the creation of disparate classes, inequity, and even oppression. Pure democracy is chaos—anarchy incapable of producing efficient governance. So for all practical purposes, countries that don't want totalitarian rule have to live with some variation of democratic republicanism, which wobbles between classism and ineffectiveness. As bad as this may be, history has proved the alternatives to democracy have been far worse.

Nonetheless, democracies like ours can be "rule by mob." More often, power is conferred based on quips exchanged in juvenile popularity contests. Whoever can better shape opinion wins. Logic is rarely given a hearing among the puerile syndicates of party power that behave as sophomorically as high school cliques. The media follow suit as if they were kids chanting *"Fight!"* in the schoolyard. While the adults in the general public are disgusted by such useless adolescent behavior, most are too busy to really engage. Life is stressful enough without reacting to this schoolyard behavior; paying attention to it would only result in insufferable anxiety.

"High school" politics can efficiently confer wealth and opportunity upon cronies but is utterly impotent to confront the great crises of the day or match the strategic positioning of international competitors with more unified governments. Even leaders with great rhetorical skill can be immobilized by the fickle whims of a pessimistic public inclined to consider optimism as the most naive credulity. To compound matters even further, there are financial interests backing every possible position on every conceivable issue, many of which hold no fidelity to the truth. The result is indecipherable noise with no meaningful progress coming of it. The public is left only with vague, general impressions that are more cliché than reality—party of this or party of that.

There are also endemic flaws in the concept of career politicians. The very fact that political office is a "job" creates a dependency on those who get politicians elected. For the sake of job security, politicians need financial backers to fund their campaigns year after year, leaving them beholden to their backers—and vulnerable to corruption. This is mainly because they cannot rely on regular citizens to get elected every time. There may be times of heightened interest every now and then when issues awaken the general masses, but in the end it is the perennial special interests that are the consistent base of support for most politicians.

Who do we mean by "special interests"? We mean influencers—people, groups, or organizations—that levy financial power in attempts to influence leaders in favor of one particular interest or issue. They have money, are always there, and don't forget. Regular people may or may not have enough money, are only there when passions are aroused, and quickly forget. So, why would a sane politician who wishes to keep his or her job ever really challenge the special interests? They may rail against special interests in the abstract or specifically attack groups that have no influence among their constituencies, but that is about as far as it ever goes.

On the other side, you can't really blame the corporations and other groups for using their money to protect their interests. It is a systemic flaw that makes their money the indispensable support of the electoral process. As unpalatable as the concept of "career politician" may be, what choice is there, really? The alternative of only electing the independently wealthy who need no financial support could create a neo-aristocracy.

Ideology makes matters even worse, because ideology insists on purity in politics, as oxymoronic as that is. Add together C-SPAN, talk radio, Internet blogs, and cable news, and politicians have no room or reason to negotiate. Whenever a politician negotiates, he looks like a "politician," and people hate "politicians." Politicians would rather be known as "public servants" and will only threaten that elevated status with good reason. As ugly as this truth may be, in Congress, compromise has more often than not been based on "pork"—a Washington term for an appropriation of government spending for localized projects secured solely or primarily to bring money to a representative's district or state. To negotiate a compromise, both parties to the negotiation must want something, and "pork" creates a reason to negotiate and, ultimately, the political will to pass legislation. Those elected may claim to act in the best interest of the country, and a few may even mean it, but the congressional record belies most claims of eschewing "pork" projects. Take away the pork, and all you may be left with is ideology. Why would any politician accept a compromise to his ideals and those of his constituents in exchange for nothing? The problem is that compromise requires *compromise*, which is dangerous territory in ideological terms. If all one side wants is for the other side to not get what it wants, you can only succeed at reaching an agreement by giving that side something it wants more. But, in an environment where such deal making is abhorrent and pork is poison, even that "functional" dysfunction fails.

This circle of dysfunction is completed not at the top, but at the grassroots level. This is, after all, a democracy. Regular people have to go to the polls and pull the lever. Money does not actually elect anyone. What makes us a cannibal country is not only the greedy exploitation by the powerful of the weak, but also the laziness, self-ishness, and stupidity of the public. A person may be smart, but collectively people are stupid. It is the aggregate thinking of the voting public that not only permits or enables one bad decision after another to be made, but which is directly responsible for them.

Aggregate thinking can be leveraged by politicians, who appeal to idealists who are unwilling to see things as they are and insist on approaching the world as it should be. Groups organize around ide-alistic principles. These groups in turn confer power to those who can personify their ideals. Once elected, their commitment to ideology, irre-spective of its applicability to circumstances, adds a level of rigidity to the process of governing. A system that depends on consensus is immo-bilized when there is ideological gridlock. You can blame the elected person of being a rigid ideologue, but the real problem is that many voters are idealistic, too. Constituents of an ideologue can be fiercely loyal, giving him or her absolutely no incentive to ever compromise.

Even if a given leader's nature is to be pragmatic in matters of importance, he will find that there is a severe price to be paid for any-thing that could be construed as a compromise, and that it's considered best to follow opinion polls about what's "right" or "wrong." There are twenty-four-hour networks and media personalities that hold to particular persuasions and that perceive any dissenters as traitors worthy only of evisceration. When there are greater risks involved in doing something than in opposing everything, progress is immobilized.

It is possible to correct this self-defeating pattern—but the question is, for whom. A democracy is made up of individuals. The "public" is not a voter. No one represents the whole public interest. Each individual pursues his or her self-interest, and individuals with common interests form coalitions. The largest coalitions win. You can only hope that either the broad interest will be served or that it will not be harmed too severely.

Populism may be in vogue, and railing against the "powers that be" may be a resonant political tactic, but it is the populace that bears the blame. Whether people are duped by misleading campaigns, motivated by specific interests or priorities while ignoring others, disengaged from the political process except for the act of voting (which is then done on a last-minute whim), each voter bears the responsibility for the official he or she elects. The leaders reflect their followers.

The danger of aggregate thinking is that it consistently results in bad decisions. This is the real invisible hand: the stupidity of the masses. It is the pursuit of instant gratification at the cost of ultimate success. It is the unwillingness to confront long-term issues. It is the inability or refusal to comprehend complex situations and logical solutions. It is the loathsome attitude that right and wrong must be subjective, unknowable, or relative, except for what I, the individual, believe. While groups may understand certain matters clearly and hold certain sentiments deeply, their inability to effectively convey their thoughts and feelings to reach consensus with other groups leaves a net effect of electoral stupidity. Aggregate thinking is confused, conflicted, distracted, and given to errant reductionism.

Yet that is our system. That is yet another reason why this is a cannibal country. We eat each other because, among other reasons, we are too stupid to realize it's not chicken.

Opinion polls are considered indicative of the correct position, even when the majority opinion is ludicrous when viewed objectively. Is it intelligent to say that we should not have prevented the collapse of the largest banks in the world, thereby staving off another Great Depression? Following the onset of the financial crisis of 2007-8, opinion polls consistently indicated just that; that the bailouts should not have been done. This was the will of the people? It is stupid to vehemently suggest that the "too big to fail" institutions should have been allowed to fail just because they caused the crisis. It is stupid to complain as these now-largely-government-owned institutions begin to turn profits. If you own it, you should want it to make a lot of money. The government paid $3.25 per share for its stake in Citigroup during the notorious bank bailout of 2008. The taxpayers should want the stock to double, or even better, return to its precrisis price of $20 per share. Imagine that! What if the taxpayers got back six times their money?

That would be smart, but that is not what we get. By the way, starting in 2010, the Treasury did sell Citigroup shares for a profit, but little attention was given to that. Positive outcomes of politically unpopular actions by the government were not, and rarely ever are, part of the media narrative. By late 2009, a majority of the public was irate about the quick rebound of financial giants and the subsequent bonuses paid to the employees responsible for the business decisions that led the recovery. What do they want? That the financial sector remain in a disabled state, teetering on the brink of collapse?

It can be argued that this sort of anger represents transference of the troubles in the broader economy, but anger in politics is dangerous. Anger of any kind takes over the political dialogue and stifles any continuity of purpose or direction. Politicians are far too fearful to oppose public anger, irrespective of how incoherent or self-defeating it may be.

Instead of focusing on the fundamental flaws in our economic system, it is politically expedient to pick a boogeyman and appear to be in line with the people. Instead of being true to reality, the ideology of what the system "should be" takes the floor. Break up the banks, audit the Federal Reserve, return to the gold standard, throw the bums out, cut spending, cut taxes, create jobs-jobs-jobs, tax the rich, fix health care, stop all greenhouse gas emissions, fight terrorism but get someone else to pay for it, and get it all done right now. The truth is that some of that intentionally won't be done, some of that can't be done, some of that shouldn't be done, and none of that can be done immediately in a free market democratic system.

"Indeed," as Winston Churchill said, in part to the House of Commons in 1947, "democracy is the worst form of government except all those other forms that have been tried from time to time." It is a sad truth that what is popular is not necessarily right or good, but in democracy you are stuck with it all the same. Worse still, because public opinion can be shaped by money, lies, distortions, and appeals to prejudice, there is no guarantee what public opinion will ever be, even in matters where one would expect the right thing to be obvious. Ads, slogans, sound bites, and imagery win elections and public debate.

The system is not only broken, it is destroying itself. As people suffer, they focus their ire on the "villains" they are convinced are to blame, instead of on the devil who is truly behind their pain. They train their sights on their fellow citizens, particularly those who can easily be labeled as the "other," and as a result get nothing except more pain. It is as insane as putting a gun to your head to kill your alter ego.

"Every kingdom divided against itself is brought to desolation; and every city or house divided against itself shall not stand."
—Jesus, Matthew 12:25, King James Version

There are very serious issues facing the country. Empires rise and fall, and this one isn't exactly rising right now. It is involved in international wars without conceivable ends, the economy has been increasingly showing signs of systemic flaws, deficits have been rising, the dollar has been falling, there is a looming energy crisis, an entitlement crisis, various moral crises, and our standing in the world is falling on a variety of scales, including business, education, and health—and the list goes on.

CHAPTER TWO

Putting the Cannibalism
in Capitalism

Why does a baby cry? It usually does so because it wants
something. Nothing else matters beyond the immediate
desires of the young child to have its demands met. The needs of
others are irrelevant. Our nature from infancy is utterly selfish. Even
the most superficial consideration of others is a quality that must
be learned. Unfortunately, many never learn more than negligible
consideration of others, and altruism has become a lost quality in a
world of superficiality.

Did You Say Ponzi?

While decorum and civility restrain bad behavior on a personal
level for most people, this is not maintained on organizational
levels. The institutions of high finance have been revealed to have
been caught effectively gambling in a shadow market of derivatives,
taking extraordinary risks with overleveraged resources and bringing
the global economy to the brink of a global depression. Financial
collapse caused the public to revile big business, big banks, and
big government, while most of the puppet masters of these entities
remain safely anonymous. The fact that these banks were regarded as

"too big to fail" created circumstances in which their potential failure threatened and still threatens life as we know it. The big banks and big business cried like babies, until the big government was left with no choice but to rescue them, so that whether these guys win or lose, they win. Thus, some would call the whole process of risk taking by big banks a giant Ponzi scheme in which the taxpayer is the victim.

"The whole thing was a fraud and it gets back to the accountants valuing the assets incorrectly," said Howard Davidowitz of Davidowitz & Associates, a retail consulting and investment banking firm, while complaining that the government's attempts to better regulate Wall Street were completely off target. "It was a massive fraud. . . . The assets were completely valueless. . . . All the profits didn't exist. . . . When we say there's a problem with leverage. . . . They couldn't have gotten the leverage . . . [but] everybody said it was great . . . all the audit firms signed off . . . that it was fine and it was a gigantic Ponzi scheme, a lie and a fraud," he exclaimed in a July 2010 interview with *Yahoo! Finance* reporter Aaron Task. His ultimate argument was that more regulation wasn't needed, but merely better enforcement of basic laws like those targeting fraud.

While many Ponzi references are hyperbolic, there are real Ponzi schemes out there, too. The biggest of these was perpetrated by a billionaire—Bernard Lawrence "Bernie" Madoff. What is the difference between a mugger and Madoff? Prestige, perhaps. The mugger exists at the bottom echelon of our society, while Bernard Madoff luxuriated at the very top. The mugger is reviled, is likely a drug addict, is perhaps the child of poverty and a broken home, if ever there was one to break. Madoff was revered before he was revealed and later reviled, though he too was an addict of sorts. Pimps, prostitutes, drug dealers, and gang bangers are all so easy to loathe, to fear, to pity, and to prosecute. However, the Bernie Madoffs of the world confuse and perplex. We've seen documentaries and countless hours of talking heads pondering why a man with so much would do what he did.

This man was a Wall Street institution, the once-head of NASD (National Association of Securities Dealers), and cofounder of NAS-DAQ. Despite all of that, in March 2009, Madoff pleaded guilty to eleven felonies and admitted to turning his wealth management business into a massive Ponzi scheme that defrauded thousands of investors out of billions of dollars. In fact, prosecutors estimated the size of the fraud to be $64.8 billion. This man, who had been one of the most powerful men on Wall Street for decades, did this. Wasn't he rich enough? He didn't exactly *need* the money.

It would be simple enough to write off Madoff as just a psychopath, an aberration. But this is not about Bernie Madoff. Think bigger. What does it say about the whole system when this guy, the perpetrator of perhaps the most egregious financial crime in history, was considered a "close personal friend" of the head of the government agency charged with preventing such fraud?

People are similarly confused as to why American International Group (AIG) and Wall Street bankers took risks that threaten the viability of the national—no, global—economy. The richest and most powerful people and institutions drove the global economy off the proverbial cliff. While Lehman Brothers was allowed to disintegrate, the rest were only rescued by the "socialist" bailouts of governments around the world. Former Federal Reserve chairman Alan Greenspan, a man who perhaps would have seen it all coming if not for the fact that he was a true believer himself, was shocked by their temerity.

Sanitized, Institutionalized Selfishness

The society in which we live suffers from the delusion that there exists a form of moral selfishness. Greed and selfishness at their crudest levels are condemned, but when these same principles are institutionalized, sanitized, and connected to a high standard of living, they become not only accepted, but aspired to. Worse still, our whole system is based on the principle of self-interest. Some would even say that it is the cornerstone of free market capitalism.

Bernard Madoff was the reification of the unbridled, unregulated pursuit of self-interest. The rub—which true believers will dismiss as proof that he was an aberration—lay in that he clearly and unequivocally lied to his clients about everything. As for the peddlers of complex derivatives, their lies were not so clear, and there was a great deal of equivocation. Yet what was a triple-A rating on a bundle of mortgage-backed securities laden with subprime loans in an over-heated real estate market during a period of rising interest rates, if not a lie? How was collecting billions off the top of the unsustainable houses of cards that were the mortgage-backed security, collateralized-debt obligation, and credit-default swap markets anything less than a Ponzi scheme?

Some idealistic free marketers would argue that these events were a perversion of our system, the result of greed run amok. They would contend that the pace of innovation was not equaled by the regulations crafted in a bygone era (some of which were repealed, arguably setting the scene for the crash). We need new regulations for a twenty-first-century global economy, they argue. Their point is that greed must be checked, guided, and harnessed to drive our free market to better days. Unfettered free market capitalism is still the solution to the ills of economic malaise.

Irrespective of the damaging side effects of capitalism, generally American capitalism is perceived as *good*. It creates opportunity, drives innovation, and arguably is responsible for the rising standard of living that we have enjoyed. Nevertheless, capitalism is often tantamount to institutionalized greed, or, at least, it could be said that greed is the engine of capitalism. Greed is *bad*, isn't it?

In our system, it is not enough to win; the goal is to keep winning. It is understood and accepted that there have to be winners and losers in a capitalist system, even if the winners win, not by outcompeting, but by killing the losers through other means. Sadly, more often than you would think, "losers" with fresh ideas, good people, and superior products but less financial heft are killed through the "winners'" anti-competitive behavior. How does that benefit the broader interests?

We have to ask, can a system of institutionalized greed really be good? Is it really enough to accept that greed is a powerful force for good, provided that it is managed and moderated?

To be clear, when I say greed, I am not talking about inequity. Human beings are not equal in the absolute sense. Some are tall, some are short, some are skinny, some are fat, and while it is not politically correct to say so, some are smart and some are stupid. A person with great talent in one area may be utterly inept in another. It is hardly surprising that some excel beyond others, make more money, amass more wealth, and achieve more in life. Unfortunately, some completely *undeservedly* make more money, amass more wealth, and obtain "more" in life. The ideal of capitalism may be meritorious, but the reality is that success is often circumstantial. Nevertheless, the pursuit and the achievement of excellence is not in and of itself greed.

Greed is the pursuit of "more" (generally money), specifically through the losses of others. Put a different way, it is utter disregard for the damaging effects on others caused by the pursuit of one's self-interest. It is not the reasonable give-and-take illustrated by economic patriarch Adam Smith's "butcher, brewer, and baker," but rather the all-out exploitation by the slave trader in the same era, who kidnapped and trafficked human beings. That is not to say, however, that conduct must reach levels as extreme as slave trading in order to be considered greedy. It can come in far milder forms, and yet still reflect that ultimate spirit.

Such greed can be advantageous for the individual, but we must consider its implications in the broader context. Is it really a win when the success of an individual robs the greater majority of prosperity?

When Capitalism Becomes Cannibalistic

Capitalism encourages individual achievement in the hope that the proverbial rising tide lifts all boats. Yet that is only the case with industries in which there is a significant amount of mutuality. Sometimes individual achievement only benefits the individual, and, worse still, overburdens everyone else.

Take for example those who made millions selling subprime mortgages before the subprime crisis. Did they give the money back? Individual bank executives made colossal bonuses playing mortgage-backed securities and collateralized-debt obligations, before the credit crunch that collapsed some of the same banks. Did they transfer their ill-gotten gains to the Troubled Asset Relief Program (TARP) fund?[5] The financial wing of AIG raked in the profits selling credit-default swaps, before AIG went bust because of the very same. Did they make reparations?

In these cases, unfettered capitalism failed the greater number. Frankly, that is the point: self-interest does not meet the needs of the many. For that reason, pure capitalism is ultimately self-defeating, even for the individual who sees initial benefits.

That is not to say that communism or socialism are any better. In fact, in practice they are worse, for they follow the opposite extreme. The interest of the group takes precedence over the interest of the individual. In fact, throughout the Soviet era, self-sacrifice was deemed a duty to the state. Individual achievement was nullified, if not effectively punished, for the greater national interest, and in the end even that interest was not served. There was no motivation for innovation. It was as if everyone settled for being poor together, though no one was actually happy about it. Centralized planning, as it was practiced in the Eastern Bloc, fails to chart the best course and fails to give the individual any incentive to develop solutions to needs that arise.

Too often people confuse communism with socialism. Socialism is when the government owns and controls the means of production and distribution, of capital, land, and the output of their national product. Also, the words "socialism" and "socialistic" are far too often conflated, even though not everything that is "socialistic" rises to the level of full state ownership and control. The Soviet Union and other so-called communist regimes were actually socialistic dictatorships. The same is true in Cuba. Communism in its purest form eliminates the existence of government in favor of the governing principle "from those who can to those who need." There has never been a pure communistic nation, other than small tribal societies, because theoretical communism would require a selfless population. This is the fundamental problem with communism: people *are* selfish. An effective economy must struggle to find balance between these extremes, to attempt mitigation of this failure of the human condition.

---

5. TARP was a 2008 government program to purchase assets and equity from financial institutions to strengthen the financial sector in the throes of the credit crisis.

Taken formulaically, communism equates success with the group interest, while capitalism defines success through individual achievement. Perhaps neither extreme is correct, but it *is* the case that the formula needs a Boolean "and" to really work. In other words, success can only really be achieved when both the needs of the individual and the group are served simultaneously. It is not enough to benefit the group while sacrificing the individual, nor is it appropriate to benefit the individual at the expense of the group. As with so many things, the extremes in both directions are wrong, and moderation is needed.

Perhaps the most bitter fruit (economically speaking) of the Cold War has been our subsequent, ubiquitous aversion to socialism—an aversion that prevents us from recognizing the areas in which socialism is appropriate or even in the best interest of the free market. Markets, driven by profit, cannot afford to do everything that the broader community needs, particularly when the benefit horizon is so far into the future that the investment risk is substantial. Quite simply, there are times when centralization is needed.

The Socialism We Forget We Like

There are many socialistic programs that most Americans enjoy, appreciate, and certainly don't want eliminated, like public schools, public libraries, Social Security, Medicare, garbage collection, and other municipal services. And there are other programs that have done far more to drive the economy than these entitlement services. The free market did *not* create the national highway system, microcomputing, or the Internet. The free market leveraged, advanced, and improved all three of these, but it would not and could not have produced any of them as we now have them.

While the national interstate highway system has led to great profit, where was the profit in producing it? In inflation-adjusted numbers, the 160,000-mile system cost about a half trillion dollars, with no direct return on investment. Even now, this mostly toll-free transportation infrastructure, which serves nearly all of our major cities, enables trillions of dollars of commerce. At some point or another, the distribution of virtually all goods and services involves interstate highways.

There has also been a tremendous impact on living standards and the way we live and work when you consider the role that urban interstates play for commuter travel. Many urban and suburban workers use these highways to travel to their places of work. The vast majority of long-distance travel, whether for vacation or business, uses the national road network created by the Federal Aid Highway Act of 1956 and championed by President Dwight D. Eisenhower. It is hard to find a strong position against this government project, even among those who adamantly believe in "small" government.

"Microcomputing" is now an archaic term, but its development led to what we today call computers. Thomas Watson, chairman of IBM in 1943, famously and shortsightedly said, "I think there is a world market for maybe five computers." While we now consider that one of the dumbest public statements in history, it is actually quite true given the definition of "computer" in that era. At that time, computers cost a fortune and occupied the space of entire buildings. Surprisingly enough, such things still exist. Many think of massive mainframe computers as obsolete, but that is far from the truth. In fact, such computers need to exist, but there is a very limited market for them. Actually, the mainframe supercomputer market of today is much as Thomas Watson described. Most organizations do fine with blade PC servers that approximate the power of centralized computing. Only a handful of governments and research institutions need mainframe supercomputers, the modern equivalent of Watson's "computer."

What we today call "computers," then, were only conjured in the imagination of science fiction writers when Mr. Watson made his ignominious quote. If you carry an iPhone, you are carrying more computer power in the palm of your hand than the supercomputers of a couple generations ago. What drove these advances and the redefinition of computing? The free market, right? Uh, no.

It was the government, particularly NASA—or, more precisely, the space program, which included what would become the National

Aeronautics and Space Administration. You see, you couldn't fit what was then thought of as a "computer" on a plane, much less on a spacecraft, so they had to develop something a bit more small and sophisticated to get themselves into space. Add to that the development of the transistor, and we have an information revolution. Now, the transistor was primarily the development of a private sector entity, AT&T's Bell Labs, with some valuable work done by other private organizations, like Texas Instruments, but even considering that, it can't be ignored that this work of private enterprise was related to government contracts. It was government spending that brought us into the information age.

Despite the revisionist history commonly told by free marketers regarding government intervention in business, the U.S. federal government (and therefore the U.S. taxpayer) did the heavy lifting and funding to give us everything from PCs to smartphones. Private entrepreneurs may have pieced together the fragments of government-funded research and development to give us the PC (personal computer) revolution, but the government created the framework and was the engine that initially drove the train.

This is especially true of the Internet. The Internet began as a government project. The U.S. Department of Defense laid the foundation of the Internet when, in 1957, the Advanced Research Projects Agency (ARPA) was formed, which led to ARPANET, the network that served as the incubator for the technologies of today's net. Entities without a profit motive developed these technologies before things were turned over to the free market, which of course ran with it.

Another government agency moved the ball forward when, in 1985, the U.S. National Science Foundation (NSF) commissioned the construction of the NSFNET, which would later become the backbone of the Internet. The general public didn't use the Internet much until after the development of hypertext transfer protocol (HTTP) in the early 1990s.

In 1989, after NSFNET had been tied to commercial e-mail networks, three commercial Internet service providers (ISPs) were created: UUNET, PSINet, and CERFNET. Various other commercial and educational networks, such as Usenet, BITNET, Telenet, Tymnet, CompuServe, and JANET were interconnected with the growing Internet. Telenet (later called Sprintnet) was a large, privately funded, national computer network with free dial-up access in cities throughout the U.S. that had been in operation since the 1970s. This network was eventually interconnected with the others in the 1980s as the TCP/IP protocol became increasingly popular (TCP/IP being the communications protocol that the Internet is based upon). The ability of TCP/IP to work over virtually any preexisting communication networks allowed for greater ease of growth. That said, the rapid growth of the Internet was due primarily to the availability of commercial routers from companies such as Cisco Systems, Proteon, and Juniper; the availability of commercial ethernet equipment for local-area networking; and the widespread implementation of TCP/IP on the UNIX and later Windows operating systems.

Even the commercial use of the Internet grew from a nonprofit, government-developed core. Before the business community had the slightest inkling of this growing network of networks, the National Science Foundation (NSF) was putting together the information superhighway. In the early days, to become a major player on the Internet, a business would have to physically connect to the NSF network. For that reason, the real estate around the NSF facilities in Northern Virginia became the East Coast's answer to Silicon Valley. Perhaps you wondered why AOL and other Internet giants' corporate headquarters were located outside of Washington, DC. It was not a coincidence. They had to be physically close to the NSF.

The most powerful, multinational telecommunication companies entered the network as peers, equals. I guess that makes the Internet communistic. I say that facetiously, but some sincerely argue that point. Many of the larger network providers would like to toll all usage, and content providers would like to collect subscription fees, thus seeking ways to monetize the Internet—both in terms of access and content. Most, though, agree that the "free" Internet has driven economic growth in the global economy like nothing else in history.

It is understood that the free nature of the Internet creates so much economic activity that it is in the common interest to minimize the cost of its use, even if it means little or no profit for some players, some of the time.

Imagine for a moment, however, that the Internet had been the for-profit project of one company. What is the likelihood that Internet users would have ever seen unlimited access for less than ten bucks a month? What if every click on the web cost you money? Would it have cost the same to access a web site on the other side of the planet as to access one around the corner? Would the Internet have grown so quickly? Would there even have been such a thing as a web site? Really, would Tim Berners-Lee, the inventor of web-site technology, have selected a for-profit, limited network as his platform to meet his purpose of free information sharing between scientists? Would the world have ever seen Google, Yahoo!, eBay, Amazon, Facebook, or any of the rest?

Nope, no way, forget about it.

If Eisenhower hadn't pushed for a national highway system, if Kennedy hadn't set the sights on getting to the moon, and if Al Gore hadn't pushed for the expansion of NSFNET, the world would be a very different place—a lesser place.

To create the best results for the market system, government has to do the things that the broader community needs or could benefit from, but for which there is no viable profit initially or for which there shouldn't be a profit motive. Call it infrastructure, call it framework, or call it direction, but the greatest achievements of this nation have been the results of public/private collaboration, not *all* free market or *all* government.

Enter Reaganomics

Unfortunately, thirty years ago the country bought the line "government is not the solution to our problem; government is the problem." When President Ronald Reagan said this in his first inaugural address, he crystallized an economic philosophy that was heavily slanted toward privatization and pure capitalism. From there he embarked on a series of policy changes, colloquially referred to as Reaganomics.

Previously, the balance may have tipped toward the left more than was healthy, with the social programs of the New Deal and Great Society and the massive defense department coming out of World War II. Reagan headed in the opposite direction. Greatly influenced by his economic advisor, Nobel prize-winning economist Milton Friedman, Reagan relentlessly pursued an agenda that focused on cutting domestic spending, reducing taxes, deregulation, and control of the money supply. While critics would deride this as "trickle-down economics," these policies sought to stimulate the business and investor sectors. Proponents of these policies claimed (and still do) that if the top income earners invested more in the business infrastructure and equity markets, it would in turn lead to more goods at lower prices, and create more jobs for middle- and lower-class individuals—simple supply-side economic theory. Defense was the only area that was not targeted for ratcheted-back spending under Reaganomics; quite to the contrary.

From this we have the basic Republican platform in a nutshell: lower taxes, smaller government, and a strong national defense. Politically, this has worked very well for them over the last thirty years. It's clear and concise, easy to make into a bumper sticker. The question is whether or not it has actually worked.

The growing disparity between rich and poor, explosive growth in the prison population, the cycles of boom and bust, the erosion of wages, the decline in manufacturing jobs, the weakening of the dollar, the growth of the budget and trade deficits, and the falling standing of the U.S. education system in the world all seem to indicate that it hasn't.

Nevertheless, by buying into Reaganomics, we embraced what George H. W. Bush had called at the outset "voodoo economics." For a while, it seemed to work. By the end of Reagan's first term, the economy was stronger and the rich started getting richer. But was it solid or was it a bubble? Could it be that the economic successes of the early '80s were overly credited to Reagan and the supply-siders?

Could it be that, while appropriate when applied to a 70 percent top-tax bracket, double-digit inflation, and 13 percent interest rates, the Reagan agenda is not sound fiscal policy generally? Perhaps Bush's "voodoo economics" descriptor was right after all.

The money has been spinning upward ever since, with no significant trickling down. In 1982, when *Forbes* magazine began its annual list of richest Americans, the richest man was Daniel K. Ludwig. One of thirteen billionaires, his net worth was $2 billion. By 2000, there were nearly three hundred billionaires, and a year earlier in 1999, the perennial richest man, Bill Gates, peaked at a net worth of $85 billion. In 2010, they published an international list of 1,011 billionaires, 40 percent of whom were United States citizens, even as the downward trend of America's share continued.

That's only the top half of the story. The Working Poor Families Project reports that 29 percent of working families in America are low income. In October of 2009, according to the U.S. Bureau of Labor Statistics, the number of unemployed persons increased by 558,000 to 15.7 million. The unemployment rate rose by 0.4 percentage points to 10.2 percent, crossing the psychological milestone of 10 percent. It was the highest rate since April 1983. The median household income has little more than doubled in this period (from $20,000 in 1982 to $41,000 in 2000), while the net worth of the holder of the top spot on the *Forbes* list rose by more than forty-two times.

Contrary to some politi-speak, it isn't so much that income hasn't kept up with inflation on the average. Buying power is about what it was in those terms. (We will talk about how misleading the national averages actually are later. Also, it shouldn't be overlooked that today the "all-important" data point, household income, is more often the aggregate of multiple salaries from multiple breadwinners.) Yet the explosive growth of wealth at the top has increased the masses' sense of dissatisfaction and the feeling of being left behind. The standard of living they demand is not the standard they can afford. Furthermore, the cost of living in metropolitan areas has so dramatically increased that a median household income seems little higher than the poverty level.

China and the World Gaining

While here there is complacency, political infighting, and economic hanky-panky, the rest of the world is strategically positioning for the future. This is most notably the case with respect to Europe and China.

In the first year of the administration of William Jefferson Clinton, which was the beginning of the intense political rancor that now dominates the national dialogue, the nations of Europe signed the Treaty of Maastricht (November 1, 1993), forming the European Union (EU) to match the political and economic power of the United States. In fact, "match" may be an understatement, since, as an international organization operating through a hybrid system of supranationalism and intergovernmentalism, the EU now controls nearly a third of the global economy, with a GDP of $18 trillion. Given Europe's history of colonialism, the EU has ties to developing countries with rich natural resources and is leveraging that international power to position itself strategically. In a short span of time, its currency, the euro (nonexistent a couple of decades ago) grew from a value of little more than half a U.S. dollar to nearly a dollar and a half. Even New York lost its rank as the financial capital of the world to a European city, London (though England is not part of the EU). On October 8, 2009, the *Telegraph* reported, "The ranking, compiled by the World Economic Forum (WEF), places the UK at the top of a leader board of 55 of the world's largest financially-focussed countries."[6] Yet Europe's advances on America are nothing compared to those of China.

In November of President Obama's first year, his tour of Asia included Japan, Singapore, and South Korea, but he reserved the most time for China. There, Obama stated that the bilateral relationship between the U.S. and China would define the course of the twenty-first century. There is little doubt that he was right, and it seems that the story will be one of the transfer of wealth, power, and international dominance.

---

6. James Quinn, "Britain Overtakes US as Top Financial Centre," *Telegraph*, October 8, 2009, http://www.telegraph.co.uk/finance/newsbysector/banksandfinance/6272639/Britain-overtakes-US-as-top-financial-centre.html.

China, a nation that is not merely socialist, but supposedly communist, is outpacing the economic growth of capitalist nations. In 2007, it saw a growth rate of 11.4 percent, the highest in thirteen years. Since 1991, the lowest annual growth number China reported was 7.1 percent (1999), and the average over that period has been about 10 percent. Technically, it is still a developing nation, but what development! Its official 2009 GDP hit about $4.3 trillion, and its GDP at purchasing power parity is about twice that, $8 trillion. If it maintains this pace of growth, it will surpass us within two decades. It could possibly do it in one.

China already outpaces the U.S. in a number of sectors, including auto manufacturing. Of the top four banks in the world, three are Chinese. It has the world's largest population, with a labor force of 807.3 million, and it has leveraged that labor force to become the world's leading manufacturing complex. Nearly half of China's GDP is industrial, compared to 19 percent here; we are an 80 percent service economy. Now, as surprising as it may seem, we are still number one in manufacturing, but China outpaces us on total exports (a difference of $158 billion).

Perhaps the most telling statistics are the national account balances of China versus the U.S. The *CIA World Factbook*, which is available online, defines this as "a country's net trade in goods and services, plus net earnings from rents, interest, profits, and dividends, and net transfer payments (such as pension funds and worker remittances) to and from the rest of the world during the period specified. These figures are calculated on an exchange rate basis, i.e., not in purchasing power parity (PPP) terms."[7] On that list, according to 2008 estimates, China was number one and the United States was dead last. The numbers were $426.1 billion for China and –$706.1 billion for the U.S., or a spread of $1.1 trillion. The gap closed a bit in 2009, but we were still on opposite ends of the list. Behind China, the top ten of this list included notable nations like Germany, Japan, Saudi Arabia, Russia, and the whole EU.

---

7. Central Intelligence Agency, *World Factbook* (Washington DC: GPD, 2010), https://www.cia.gov/library/publications/the-world-factbook/docs/notesanddefs.html.

To me, though, what really matters is the control of natural resources. Once upon a time, wealth was not a matter of manipulating currency, trading pieces of paper, and clever accounting. It was all about tangible commodities, like fuel, food, precious metals, and materials needed to make stuff. In the final analysis, such things will again determine wealth and power, and it seems that China gets that while we don't. Early in 2009, there were reports that Beijing had begun aggressively trying to extricate itself from dollar dependency. Nobu Su, head of Taiwan's TMT group, which ships commodities to China, said, "China has woken up. The West is a black hole with all this money being printed. The Chinese are buying raw materials because it is a much better way to use their $1.9 trillion of reserves. They get ten times the impact, and can cover their infrastructure for 50 years."[8] They have been strategically positioning themselves around the planet. They have been aggressively investing in the parts of the world that are rich with natural resources, most notably in Africa.

In 2009, they entered into a multibillion-dollar deal with Guinea to build desperately needed infrastructure in exchange for access to the impoverished nation's vast reserves of bauxite and iron ore. Earlier in 2007, China announced a $9 billion deal with the Democratic Republic of Congo for access to its giant trove of copper, cobalt, tin, and gold in exchange for developing the roads, schools, dams, and railways needed to rebuild a country roughly the size of Western Europe and shattered by more than a decade of war. In large oil-exporting countries like Angola and Nigeria, China has been building or fixing railroads, and in Congo and Guinea it's been landing giant exploration contracts. China takes things even further, signing long-term deals for rights to natural resources that allow countries otherwise unworthy of credit to repay their debt in oil or mineral output. How's that for strategic thinking! It sure ain't philanthropy.

Many found the opening ceremonies of the Beijing Olympics as frightening as they were impressive, considering all of the foregoing.

---

8. Ambrose Evans-Pritchard, "A 'Copper Standard' for the World's Currency System?" *Telegraph*, April 15, 2009, http://www.telegraph.co.uk/finance/comment/ambrose-evans_pritchard/5160120/A-Copper-Standard-for-the-worlds-currency-system.html.

They might find it even more frightening to consider the facts that China's manpower fit for military service is larger than the entire U.S. population and that in 2009 they increased military spending by nearly 15 percent. (To avoid confusion, let me clarify that their actual standing military forces are about seven million, but, according to the CIA, China has 314 million men and 297 million women ages sixteen to forty-nine fit to be conscripted into military service.) It boggles the mind to think that a nation of 1.3 billion is rising to a middle-class lifestyle and what that could mean for global consumption, waste, and the distributions of commodities. Where is this thing going?

We can complain all day about how China is not a free country and that its government controls everything, but in this economic contest, centralized management has an advantage that the West has no way to match. Moreover, any attempt in America to consolidate management or set the direction for the economy is utterly distasteful, would be tagged as socialistic, and would therefore be a nonstarter politically. China is making moves with brutal efficiency; the nations of Europe are increasingly subordinating their respective economic sovereignties to the EU so as to act almost autocratically in economic matters; and America, America is eating itself to death—figuratively and literally. While we are following celebrity Twitter feeds, fighting over minutia, and are immobilized by one political stalemate after another, these autocratic capitalists are positioning themselves like chess masters about to declare checkmate.

On November 12, 2009, *Time* magazine ran the feature article "Five Things the U.S. Can Learn from China." After acknowledging how politically incorrect it is to present advice modeled on a repressive country, they listed the need for America to (1) be ambitious, (2) improve education, (3) look after the elderly, (4) save more, and (5) look over the horizon. The theme of the article was fundamentally that there are clear reasons for the success of the world's fastest growing economy. Some of the things that they are doing are worth noting, if not imitating.

One of the most interesting and disturbing (from an American nationalist perspective) quotes from the article is the following:

Tam, a graduate of MIT and the University of California, Berkeley, says he does deals in Beijing rather than Silicon Valley these days "because I believe this is where these new industries will really take shape. China's got the energy, the drive, and the market to do it."

Isn't that the sort of thing venture capitalists used to say about the U.S.?

That was the recurring theme. This repressive, communist country is outdoing America in those areas that made America the supposed "bastion of freedom and opportunity." They have a "can do," optimistic spirit, manifest in projects throughout their country. For instance, their investment in education has already given China a higher literacy rate than the U.S.

America, on the other hand, has become a country of cannibals where the overriding ethic is "I got mine." American capitalism is not practiced as a team sport. Individualism has been taken to such an extreme that many now find it difficult to see common interests, let alone find common ground. The unemployed are viewed as dead weight. Social programs are viewed as burdensome. Government is viewed as a problem. Our economic superstars are showboats with no concept of passing the ball.

China, on the other hand, is operating as a unit, and even Europe is aggressively pursuing a team effort. Even when weighed down by the bad debt and economic shortfalls of member nations like the so-called PIIGS (Portugal, Ireland, Italy, Greece and Spain), the EU has maintained a unity of purpose that is surprising given Europe's history. How can we counter the growing dominance of China or the EU with the "I got mine" viewpoint?

As I mentioned before, it takes a government to do the big stuff to increase national capacity, but there is no political will to do it. Political refrains like "No new taxes," "we can't afford this," or "government is getting too big" are all that is needed to kill any strategic, national economic agenda. In fact, government engagement in the realm of business is anathema to many. Right or wrong, that is what the international competitors are doing, and doing with efficiency.

Worse still, we have to deal with numerous species of vulture that prey on the rest of us. Bernie Madoff typifies this cannibalism in our country. His victims were largely from his own community, people he met at synagogue or through personal connections. While Madoff was an overt cannibal capitalist, there are many more subtle forms of this cannibalism.

For instance, many of the nations against which America competes have very clear competitive advantages with respect to health care. Health care in America, on the other hand, does not enhance international competitiveness. Frankly, you could say that this nation is being swindled.

According to some surveys and studies, the U.S. health care system ranks the lowest among developed nations. In 2000, the World Health Organization (WHO) ranked the U.S. health care system thirty-seventh in overall performance, right next to Slovenia, and seventy-second in overall level of health (among 191 member nations studied). The majority of personal bankruptcies in America are related to medical expenses. The U.S. pays twice as much in such measures as infant mortality and life expectancy, yet lags well behind other wealthy nations. Health insurance costs even pervert or restrain the hiring decisions of countless businesses, thus undermining job creation and full employment. Insurance companies rake in billions of health care dollars in profit without directly providing medical services. They hoard money (collected premiums) from a pool of the insured, while paying for as few services as possible or even denying medical care. They drain resources from every other industry without adding value to the system. What do we get for the money?

In addition to a neglected health system, the educational system is suffering similar inequities. Much as the American health care system has some of the best doctors and medical institutions in the world but a subpar overall average because of the limited access and affordability of care, the school system is a dichotomy of outstanding and awful. In much of the country, education is underfunded, mismanaged, and unequal to the task of producing a twenty-first-century, globally competitive workforce. Schools are often first in line for budget cuts and the last in line for increases.

Cannibal capitalism has rarely been better portrayed than by a piece by NBC-affiliate WRC, which was about the grand opening of the Hollywood Casino at Charles Town Races in West Virginia's Eastern Panhandle. Jefferson County voters, in an effort to cover budgetary shortfalls, passed a referendum to expand gambling in November 2009. Their budgetary woes were not unlike those of many communities across the country, but that is not the part of the story that makes the point. What struck the note of cannibal capitalism was an interview with a laid-off teacher who was starting a job as a card dealer. This woman had a master's degree in education, but was reduced to tending tables in a casino. What does that say about us?

The health of the people and the education of the nation's children are being undermined. What is more fundamental to economic potential than the health and education of a people? Is this some foreign plot to weaken America? No. The villains are not foreign, but Americans.

Villainy and Waste

What about the villains of the worst economic crisis the nation had seen since the Great Depression? AIG, Lehman Brothers, Bear Stearns, and the rest were American companies. The same is true for the peddlers of subprime loans and their derivatives, who were so focused on short-term gains that they couldn't have cared less about the toxic assets they were pumping into the broader economy. These were our fellow citizens. When it came time to bail out the economy, though, it was these same Americans who were all for it. Their cannibal nature can be seen in their support of the socialization of their debt and the privatization of their profit.

Some want to blame the North American Free Trade Agreement, others free trade practices, outsourcing, illegal immigrants, or some other external threat, but the truth is that we have been doing it to ourselves. We have developed a culture of self-interest, self-gratification, self-aggrandizement, and utter selfishness. We have institutionalized and disseminated these values as never before in human history.

The further we go down this road, the worse the prognosis may be. We are eating ourselves to death, while squandering the greatest opportunity in history, the opportunity created in the space following World War II.

World War II was not fought on American soil. The cities in this nation were not firebombed, leaving its economic capabilities decimated. The Eisenhower recession was tied to the overcapacity of American manufacturing. But the opposite was the case in Europe and Japan.

In the years leading up to the war, the brain trust of Europe fled from fascist pogroms to America, thus building up the intellectual heft of the U.S., while the war itself pumped up its industrial capacity. Our advances in science and technology can be directly tied to these circumstances. Read the lists of names of the scientists who worked on the Manhattan Project, guided the early space program, and taught the subsequent generation of scientists in our universities. You will see a disproportionate number of European names, starting with Einstein himself.

After the war, in many respects, no one had the capacity to compete with America's economic output. Both the Allied and Axis powers alike had to rebuild nearly from scratch. This country had such an embarrassment of riches with respect to industrial capacity that it would have been a shame not to emerge as the powerhouse that it did after the war.

It may feel good to believe in American exceptionalism, but, while belief may be an inspirational starting point, believing alone rarely causes things to come true. Though we have been taught to believe that America leads the world economically because of its intrinsic qualities as a free country, being the only game in town for decades after World War II has been a significant factor in our economic growth. What if that were actually the principal reason?

Complacently, we have come to simply expect we'll maintain the dominant role in the world. Worse, in addition to complacency, we have shifted to a consumer-driven service economy, which feeds on the consumerism of a shrinking middle class and which gives us less and less to export to the developing world. Worst of all, America faces competition as never before. I would even go so far to say that this is the first time in the modern era that America has faced economic challengers who are capable of dispatching this country from its position of dominance. Frighteningly, some of these competitors can move their entire economies strategically because of centralized management.

While here we see socioeconomic cannibalism, other parts of the world are educating their children, caring for their sick, luring in global business, developing infrastructure, and securing natural resources. This country is not leveraging its current position to develop a stronger future position. Instead, it finds new ways to fake growth and feed on itself while waiting for salvation by an invisible hand.

Can this trend be reversed? Will it be?

Rather than forever surrendering to the fantasy of a moral selfishness, it is possible, if not probable, for us to turn this around—but it will take broad-based teamwork and some of what I will outline in this book. First, let's get a sense of what we are dealing with by taking a close look at the housing and credit crises of 2007, which culminated in what some call the Great Recession. Perhaps more than any other economic reversal, this crash speaks to the core of why cannibal capitalism undermines even the good that is possible in a free market system, robs the nation of its potential, and concentrates too much wealth in the hands of far too few, leaving far too many with a future of declining prosperity.

CHAPTER THREE

Suicide-Enabling Case Study:
Crash of 2007–9

Because the U.S. economy had suffered a series of collapses in each of the major sectors, the crash of 2008 is particularly historic, as it was a failure of what many viewed as the last equity-safe havens: real estate and financials. The most recent of the preceding crashes was the dot-com crash, followed quickly by the 9/11 attacks at the physical heart of our financial system. Investors, banks, insurance companies, hedge funds, and entrepreneurs like me all flocked to the seemingly safe haven of real estate. Responding to this demand, in addition to traditional MBS (mortgage-backed securities), CDOs (collateralized-debt obligations) became a popular way of playing real estate assets. In 2001, David X. Li, a quantitative analyst and an actuary, pioneered the use of Gaussian copula models, which allowed for the rapid pricing of CDOs. His approach became the tool du jour for financial institutions to correlate associations between multiple securities and price a wide range of investments that were previously too complex to price, namely these CDOs. The result? Thomson Reuters, Deutsche Bank, Celent, and many others heralded 2006 as "a banner year for the global collateralized-debt obligation (CDO) market." Some estimated this market at nearly $2 trillion by the end of that year. With this much capital pouring in, a housing boom was certain to occur.

Fannie Mae was created in the wake of the Great Depression in order to facilitate liquidity within the mortgage market and thereby enable home ownership. To sustain liquidity, long-term tradable instruments were created to facilitate the exchange sale and resale of mortgages as securities. Both rates of home ownership and home values have steadily risen ever since. Fannie Mae was privatized in 1968, and two years later Freddie Mac was created. Both of these GSEs demonstrated long-term, stable histories of success. It only makes sense that other investment institutions would find ways to get in on the action. That is exactly what they did.

Beyond simply buying and selling MBS, investors came to prefer CDOs—including mutual fund companies, unit trusts, investment trusts, commercial banks, investment banks, pension fund managers, insurance companies, and private banking organizations. Essentially, a CDO is a corporate entity constructed to hold assets as collateral and to sell packages of cash flows to investors.

An investment in a CDO is an investment in the cash flows of the assets and the promises and mathematical models of this intermediary, rather than a direct investment in the underlying collateral. This differentiates a CDO from a mortgage or an MBS, but also means that, effectively, pools of mortgages are sliced and diced, with the underlying real estate rights decoupled from the income streams received as loans are serviced. This is further complicated by the fact that CDOs are divided by the issuer into different tranches (one of many influxes of cash that is part of a single round of investment): senior tranches (rated AAA), mezzanine tranches (AA to BB), and equity tranches (unrated). Losses are applied in reverse order of seniority, and so junior tranches offer higher coupons (interest rates) to compensate for the added default risk. This being the case, an investor can "own" the subordinate rights to a portion of the interest collected on a group of unrelated mortgages with no way of knowing what, how, or where the real estate fits into the picture.

CDOs provided a way for a number of players to profit from mortgages beyond the normal cash flows. For instance, the issuer of the CDO, typically an investment bank, earns a commission at time of issue and earns management fees during the life of the CDO. Rating agencies are needed to rate the tranches, and then there are the credit-default swaps (CDS), which were provided to give investors a false sense of security—but that is another story.

The various players were making so much money with these mortgage derivatives that there was overwhelming demand to issue new mortgages. Although this synthetic securities market was not fully monitored or regulated, at least one study estimated the size of the CDO global market was close to $2 trillion by the end of 2006.[9] Virtually everyone owned a piece of these mortgages, even if it was only a derivative of a derivative valued with a complex formula that no one understood. MBS, CDOs, CDS, and other mortgage derivatives had bored deep into the global economy and touched nearly everything. Their failure was certain to have far-reaching effects.

The acceleration in the housing market was evident in the upward acceleration of the Case-Shiller Home Price Values Index between 2001 and its peak in 2006 (see Figure 3.1). As money was pushed disproportionately from the finance sector to the real estate sector, demand

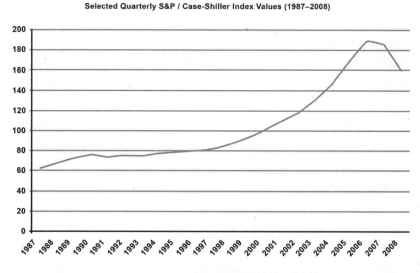

Selected Quarterly S&P / Case-Shiller Index Values (1987–2008)

Figure 3.1

9. Celent, *Collateralized Debt Obligations Market*, press release, October 31, 2005, http://reports.celent.com/PressReleases/20051031/CDOMarket.htm.

grew at a rate that exceeded the capacity for new development as well as existing resale inventory. The bottom line was that prices rose at an unhealthy rate.

The collapse, which began in 2007, demonstrated systemic flaws in our economy that run far deeper than a five-year market correction. Frankly, the collapse was precipitated by the Federal Reserve's series of increases to the federal funds target rate, which started in 2004. By mid-2006, interest rates were at the levels the Fed used to pop the dot-com bubble. Whether or not the Fed meant to pop the housing bubble, the higher interest rates meant that home owners who had kept their homes by periodically refinancing as their rates adjusted—in other words, Minsky's "Ponzi borrowers"— could no longer obtain mortgages. Millions of families were now facing the prospect of losing their homes as the rates on their loans were now dramatically adjusting upward, whether the loans were typical ARMs or the more exotic reverse-amortization, minimum-payment loans. Individually, these loans were ticking time bombs, but the rapid rise in interest rates detonated them all at once. The problem is that there were millions and millions of loans that fit into this category, far more than the number of textbook subprime loans. The major financial institutions that were playing this market via CDOs and other derivatives saw their values implode as default rates exceeded expectations. It all unraveled. As all of these institutions were dumping these securities while others were "shorting" them (which means selling securities you don't own but will buy later in order to profit from a decline), the trillion-dollar derivatives market collapsed, and the nonfinance world expanded its vernacular with the phrase "toxic asset."

Let's take it step by step from the beginning, not from the run-up, which had all the bliss of irrational exuberance, but from the slow crash of 2008, which actually started at the beginning of '07. By understanding what toxic assets are, how they proliferated, and, most importantly, why, we can grasp the nature of our national economic catabolism.

The Crash Timeline: 2007

On January 3, 2007, Ownit Mortgage Solutions filed for Chapter 11. Ownit Mortgage was well known in the industry for providing 100 percent financing on new purchases, hence the name of the company. This type of loan, irrespective of the credit of the borrowers, had become the archetypal subprime loan. As more and more investors got the picture about the implications of buying these loans, they had to steeply discount their packages to such an extent that they went bankrupt. Records show that Ownit Mortgage Solutions owed Merrill Lynch, which had a 20 percent stake in Ownit, around $93 million at the time of filing. That may not seem like much to a company with nearly $300 billion in assets at the time, but with their leverage ratio exaggerating such losses and the forthcoming collapse of the stock market, this was the first milestone on the road to September of the following year, when Merrill would be no more.

The next month, on February 5, 2007, another company, Mortgage Lenders Network USA, the country's fifteenth-largest subprime lender, with $3.3 billion in loans funded in the third quarter of 2006, filed for Chapter 11 bankruptcy. Unlike Ownit Mortgage Solutions, which was tied principally to Merrill Lynch, the collapse of this subprime lender spread panic throughout the industry. Over the next couple of months, the entire subprime industry collapsed. Several major subprime lenders declared bankruptcy, announced significant losses, or put themselves up for sale, including Accredited Home Lenders Holding, New Century Financial, DR Horton, and the behemoth Countrywide Financial.

Once word got out that the good times were over, all of the dominoes were doomed to fall. By the end of 2006, subprime loans represented 20 percent of all mortgages issued. If that 20 percent alone had collapsed, it would have been devastating enough, but the risk had spread far beyond that point. The thing about a bubble is that, when it's on the rise, everyone wants to get in on it before they miss the boat, even the largest institutions. Subprime loans had been bundled together with traditional loans and sold as mortgage-backed securities. Despite the name "subprime," these loans performed well for years while real estate values were steadily climbing and the players involved were making out like the bandits they were. When a security performs well, it gets rated highly, even rated with a triple A. It seems that virtually everyone owned them, and why not? Everything—*everything*—else was already in the toilet.

When it all hit the fan in March 2007, U.S. subprime mortgages were valued at an estimated $1.3 trillion, but the broader MBS market was around $7 trillion. As lenders and banks began to tumble, fear led to panic, and before long, all mortgage-backed securities were viewed as toxic. As the G20 summed it up in its "Declaration of the Summit on Financial Markets and the World Economy" on November 15, 2008:

> *During a period of strong global growth, growing capital flows, and prolonged stability earlier this decade, market participants sought higher yields without an adequate appreciation of the risks and failed to exercise proper due diligence. At the same time, weak underwriting standards, unsound risk management practices, increasingly complex and opaque financial products, and consequent excessive leverage combined to create vulnerabilities in the system. Policy makers, regulators and supervisors, in some advanced countries, did not adequately appreciate and address the risks building up in financial markets, keep pace with financial innovation, or take into account the systemic ramifications of domestic regulatory actions.*

In short, after two years of deterioration of the global economy, the world leaders effectively said, "Oops, our bad. We were more concerned about reward than risk."

Nevertheless, on March 6, 2007, in a speech before the Independent Community Bankers of America's (ICBA) annual convention in Honolulu, Hawaii, Ben Bernanke, quoting Alan Greenspan, warned that the government-sponsored enterprises (GSEs) Freddie Mac and Fannie Mae were a source of "systemic risk" and suggested legislation to head off a possible crisis. The conclusion to his comments is as follows:

Legislation to strengthen the regulation and supervision of GSEs is highly desirable, both to ensure that these companies pose fewer risks to the financial system and to direct them toward activities that provide important social benefits. Financial safety and soundness can be enhanced by giving the GSE regulator capital powers comparable to those of bank supervisors and by creating a clear and credible receivership process that leads debt holders to recognize that they would suffer financial losses should a GSE fail. Finally, the Federal Reserve Board believes that the GSEs' investment portfolios should be firmly anchored to a measurable public purpose, such as the promotion of affordable housing. I believe that this approach provides a reasonable balance of social costs and benefits for the GSE portfolios. In particular, this approach would refocus the GSEs on the affordable housing objectives given to them by the Congress.[10]

Bernanke and the other Federal Reserve governors recognized the risk in the market, but they didn't yet understand it. They were worried about the GSEs trying to get into the subprime game instead of focusing on the pervasiveness of adjustable rate mortgages in trillions of dollars of mortgage-backed securities held by major institutions throughout the world. Wall Street had dwarfed the investments of the GSEs. Greenspan, Bernanke, and the rest still thought of the "subprime" thing as a little, aberrant bubble that just needed to be popped.

By the summer, there were many more bank failures, particularly in the subprime sector, and yet the greater crisis was still rumbling below the surface. Most "experts" saw only a localized problem and had no idea of the pending threat. The Federal Reserve had held rates at the recent peak for over a year, and the defaults were racking up as borrowers couldn't meet their higher payments and couldn't refinance into new loans. It's easy to blame the borrowers for their recklessness and lack of foresight, but just because something is possible doesn't mean that most of these people were expecting their mortgage payments to suddenly reset to levels two to three times higher with no ability to sell or refinance. These may have been bad loans, but there were millions of them,

---

10. In this section, footnotes for widely publicized, well-known quotes will not be provided.

and they were now deeply embedded in Wall Street. These defaulting mortgages would have far-reaching implications.

The first signs of the depths of the impending crisis were slowly being revealed. On June 7, 2007, Bear Stearns sent a letter to inform the investors in two of its funds, the High-Grade Structured Credit Strategies Enhanced Leverage Fund and the High-Grade Structured Credit Fund, that it was halting redemptions, which are the returns of investors' principals in securities. In April, one of these hedge funds had posted an 18.97 percent decline, with 6.5 percent lost just in April. Two weeks after the letter, on June 20, Merrill Lynch seized $800 million in assets from the two Bear Stearns hedge funds—and this was still just the beginning of their problems.

Bear Stearns wasn't the only big investment firm with a hedge fund that ran into trouble making bets on the subprime market. In May, UBS, the Swiss-based banking giant, announced it was shutting down its Dillon Read Capital Management hedge fund after incurring a $123 million loss because of its exposure to the U.S. subprime market. The hedge fund's woes helped drag down the 2007 first-quarter profit at UBS.

On June 25, 2007, Federal Deposit Insurance Corporation (FDIC) chair Sheila Bair cautioned, "There are strong reasons for believing that banks left to their own devices would maintain less capital—not more—than would be prudent. The fact is, banks do benefit from implicit and explicit government safety nets . . . In short, regulators can't leave capital decisions totally to the banks." She was very concerned about the more flexible risk management standards of the Basel II international accord and lowering bank capital requirements. Basel II (as the name suggests) is the second of the Basel accords, which are recommendations on banking laws and regulations issued by the Basel Committee on Banking Supervision. The purpose of Basel II, which was initially published in June 2004, is to create an international standard that banking regulators can use when creating regulations about how much capital banks need to put aside to guard against the types of financial and operational risks banks face.

Despite the clearly foreboding tremors and warnings, the stock market was still in a period of exuberance, with the Dow Jones Industrial Average closing above 14,000 for the first time in its history on July 19, 2007. Happy was anyone retiring and liquidating his portfolio on that day, because it all went downhill from there. The worldwide "credit crunch" then began in earnest, as subprime mortgage-backed securities were discovered in portfolios of banks and hedge funds around the world, from BNP Paribas to the Bank of China. Many lenders stopped offering home equity loans and stated-income loans. Detecting the situation, in August the Federal Reserve injected about $100 billion into the money supply for banks to borrow at a low rate, but it was too little, too late.

On August 6, 2007, American Home Mortgage Investment Corporation (AHMI) filed Chapter 11 bankruptcy. The company expected to see up to a $60 million loss for the first quarter 2007. Two days later, on August 8, 2007, Mortgage Guaranty Insurance Corporation (MGIC) of Milwaukee, Wisconsin, announced that it would discontinue its purchase of Radian Group after suffering a billion-dollar loss of its investment in the New York-based company Credit-Based Asset Servicing and Securitization. The next day, August 9, 2007, French investment bank BNP Paribas suspended three funds that invested in subprime mortgage debt, due to a "complete evaporation of liquidity" in the market. The bank's announcement was the first of many credit-loss and write-down announcements by banks, mortgage lenders, and other institutional investors, as subprime assets went bad, due to defaults by subprime mortgage payers. This announcement compelled the intervention of the European Central Bank, which pumped €95 billion into the European banking market.

The worldwide scope of this crisis was made apparent on August 10, 2007, when central banks coordinated efforts to increase liquidity for the first time since the aftermath of the September 11, 2001 terrorist attacks. The United States Federal Reserve injected a combined $43 billion, the European Central Bank infused €156 billion ($ 214.6 billion U.S.), and the Bank of Japan injected one trillion yen ($ 8.4 billion U.S.). Smaller amounts came from the central banks of Australia and Canada.

On August 14, 2007, Sentinel Management Group, a cash management firm based in Illinois that invested for clients such as managed futures funds, high-net-worth individuals, and hedge funds, suspended redemptions for investors and sold off $312 million worth of assets; three days later, Sentinel filed for Chapter 11 bankruptcy protection. As important as this fund was to its investors, this was small potatoes. The next day, on August 15, 2007, the stock of Countrywide Financial, which was the largest mortgage lender in the United States, fell around 13 percent on the New York Stock Exchange after Countrywide announced foreclosures and mortgage delinquencies had risen to their highest levels since early 2002. The next day, they narrowly avoided bankruptcy by taking out an emergency loan of $11 billion from a group of banks.

As the collapse was gaining momentum, the next day (August 17, 2007), the Federal Reserve cut the discount rate by half a percent, from 6.25 to 5.75 percent, while leaving the federal funds rate unchanged, in an attempt to stabilize financial markets. The last day of a disturbing August, President Bush announced a limited bailout of U.S. homeowners unable to pay the rising costs of their debts. Nonetheless, on the same day, Ameriquest, once the largest subprime lender in the U.S., went out of business.

Matters would not improve in September. On the first three days of the month, the Federal Reserve convened its annual economic symposium in Jackson Hole, Wyoming, to address the housing recession. It was little more than an aimless blame game. Several critics argued that the Federal Reserve should use regulation and interest rates to prevent asset-price bubbles, some blamed former Fed chairman Alan Greenspan's low interest-rate policies for stoking the U.S. housing boom and subsequent bust, and Yale University economist Robert Shiller warned of possible home price declines of 50 percent. No effective solutions held sway.

Worse still, on the next day, September 4, 2007, the London Interbank Offered Rate (LIBOR) rose to 6.7975 percent, its highest level since December 1998 and above the Bank of England's 6.75 percent base rate. LIBOR-based, adjustable rate mortgages had been "all the rage" for years, but now, with this peak in LIBOR, millions of homeowners would see their payments jump dramatically, and, due to the collapse of the credit market, most would be unable to refinance into more manageable loans. This collision of crises would create the epicenter of the coming foreclosure tsunami that would collapse so much of the world economy. As if this "perfect storm," as so many have labeled it, were not enough, three days later on September 7, the U.S. Labor Department announced that nonfarm payrolls fell by four thousand in August 2007, the first month of negative job growth since August 2003.

Scrambling to respond to the warning of former Fed chairman Alan Greenspan, who said that "we had a bubble in housing" and that "large double digit declines . . . larger than most people expect" were impending, on September 18, the Federal Reserve lowered interest rates by half a point (0.5 percent). It was an attempt to limit damage to the economy from the mounting housing and credit crises. Such efforts were lost on most experts, including television finance personality Jim Cramer, who warned Americans on the *Today Show* on September 28, "Don't you dare buy a home—you'll lose money," causing a furor among realtors.

Sadly, time would prove his warning to be well-founded. On September 30, affected by the spiraling mortgage and credit crises, Internet-banking pioneer NetBank went bankrupt, and the Swiss bank UBS announced that it had lost $690 million in the third quarter. Less than a week later, on October 5, Merrill Lynch announced a $5.5 billion loss as a consequence of the subprime crisis, which was revised to $8.4 billion on October 24—a sum that credit rating firm Standard & Poor's called "startling."

In an attempt to curtail the spreading disaster, the HOPE NOW Alliance was created by the U.S. government and private industry on October 10, 2007, to help some subprime borrowers. Between October 15 and 17, a consortium of U.S. banks backed by the U.S. government announced a "super fund" of $100 billion to purchase mortgage-backed securities whose mark-to-market value had plummeted in the subprime collapse. Both Federal Reserve chairman Ben

Bernanke and Treasury secretary Hank Paulson expressed alarm about the dangers posed by the bursting housing bubble. Paulson said, "The housing decline is still unfolding and I view it as the most significant risk to our economy . . . The longer housing prices remain stagnant or fall, the greater the penalty to our future economic growth."

On October 31, the Federal Reserve again lowered the federal funds rate by 25 basis points to 4.5 percent. The next day, the Federal Reserve injected $41 billion into the money supply for banks to borrow at a low rate, which was the largest single expansion since it had injected $50.35 billion on September 19, 2001.

After a whole month with no improvement, on December 6, 2007, President Bush announced a plan to voluntarily and temporarily freeze the mortgages of a limited number of mortgage debtors holding adjustable rate mortgages. He also asked members of Congress to (1) pass legislation to modernize the Federal Housing Administration (FHA), (2) temporarily reform the tax code to help homeowners refinance during this time of housing market stress, (3) pass funding to support mortgage counseling, and (4) pass legislation to reform GSEs like Freddie Mac and Fannie Mae. Nevertheless, the year ended on a sour note when, on Christmas Eve, the consortium of banks officially abandoned the U.S. government-supported "super-SIV" mortgage crisis bailout plan announced in mid-October. They cited the lack of demand for the risky mortgage products on which the plan was based and the widespread criticism that, other complaints aside, the plan would be difficult to execute.

Rock Bottom in 2008

The New Year marked the beginning of the major downturn in the stock market, as effects of the worsening economy spread. On January 4, a Labor Department report was released showing U.S. employment growth slowing markedly in December, the job market's worst performance since 2003. The unemployment rate hit 5 percent, a two-year high, indicating a weak finish for the U.S. economy in 2007. Retailers posted weak December sales figures due to a sluggish Christmas season. Retail store Target reported a 5 percent decrease in same-store sales, while rival Walmart posted a meager 2.4 percent gain, excluding fuel. Department stores, including Macy's, JCPenney, and Kohl's all posted declines. Macy's sales fell 7.9 percent, worse than expected, and Kohl's reported an 11 percent decline and lowered its earnings outlook. The latest *Wall Street Journal* survey of economic forecasters saw 42 percent odds of a U.S. recession for the year along with mounting inflationary pressures, an uncomfortable mix, to be sure. The average of the fifty-four forecasts saw the economy growing at slower than a 2 percent annual rate for the first and second quarters of the year.

On January 11, the fate of Countrywide Financial, a company that had been teetering on the edge of bankruptcy for months, was determined when Bank of America agreed to acquire Countrywide for about $4 billion. Many hoped the move could build a bulwark against the mortgage default crisis by protecting one of its biggest casualties from collapse. The deal came just months after Bank of America plugged $2 billion into Countrywide during the height of the summer's global credit crunch. The market value of Countrywide had plunged to about $3 billion amid a continuing surge in defaults and foreclosures afflicting the Calabasas, California, company. This company, which had been the largest lender in the residential mortgage business with assets totaling $211 billion and annual revenue over $6 billion, was now gone.

On January 17, a report was released that home construction plunged in December to the slowest pace since 1991, and permit figures showed future groundbreakings had also dropped sharply. Builders had been pulling back because sales for new homes had plunged, while the supply of unsold homes hovered at a high level. Along the same line, a week later the National Association of Realtors (NAR) announced that 2007 was witness to the largest drop in existing-home sales in twenty-five years, and "the first price decline in many, many years and possibly going back to the Great Depression."

More and more writers (myself included), economists, and politicians began making references to the Great Depression in February. The January economic data reported that U.S. employment tumbled in January for the first time in more than four years, fueling worries for the U.S. economy. According to the Labor Department, nonfarm payrolls fell by seventeen thousand in January, the first drop since August 2003, when payrolls slid by forty-two thousand. Retailers reported weak January sales figures, further fanning fears about the U.S. economy. Walmart stores posted same-store sales below its forecast, while Nordstrom, Macy's, JCPenney, and Gap posted significant same-store sales declines. The inflation data indicated that the U.S. consumer price index rose 0.4 percent in January, matching December's rise, while the "core" CPI, which excludes volatile food and energy prices, was reported by the Labor Department to advance by 0.3 percent. The numbers, which slightly exceeded Wall Street forecasts, presented a challenge for Federal Reserve officials, who had to balance a sharp slowdown in economic activity with stubbornly elevated price pressures. Separately, the Department of Commerce reported that home construction rose a slight 0.8 percent in January, but an indicator of future groundbreakings fell to the lowest point in sixteen years, suggesting more pain ahead for the housing sector. At the same time, existing-home values continued to decline. Federal Reserve policy makers said downside risks to the economy remained even in the wake of recent interest-rate cuts, according to the minutes of their January 29–30 meeting. In their quarterly economic summary, central bank officials lowered the forecast for gross domestic product for the year from 2 percent to 1.3 percent. In addition, the central tendency for core inflation was revised up, with officials now expecting core inflation in 2008 to range between 2 percent and 2.2 percent. The officials said inflation could tick higher if energy and commodity prices were to weigh on consumers more heavily than expected. The severity of the housing downturn, tightening in the credit markets, and high oil prices were factors leading to the cloudier outlook, the officials said.

What a time for the chairman of the Federal Reserve Bank to make his semiannual report to Congress! On February 27, 2008, chairman Ben Bernanke delivered an economic forecast fraught with risks from housing, labor, and credit markets, suggesting policy makers remain on track to lower interest rates further the next month.

"It is important to recognize that downside risks to growth remain," Bernanke told members of the House Financial Services Committee in his prepared testimony on the state of the economy and monetary policy on February 14. Fed officials "will need to judge whether the policy actions taken thus far are having their intended effects," Bernanke went on to say, adding that the central bank "will act in a timely manner as needed" to keep the economy on track.

At times like this, fear and frustration give way to anger and blame. Between March 1 and June 18, 406 people were arrested for mortgage fraud in an FBI sting across the U.S., including buyers, sellers, and others across the wide-ranging mortgage industry. On June 19, ex-Bear Stearns fund managers were arrested by the FBI for their allegedly fraudulent role in the subprime mortgage collapse. The managers purportedly misrepresented the fiscal health of their funds to investors publicly, while privately withdrawing their own money. Alas, while these sorts of arrests feel good, they do very little to correct the broader problem.

The pain was still in its early stages. On March 10, the Dow Jones Industrial Average fell to its lowest level since October 2006, a drop that was more than 20 percent lower than its peak just five months earlier. Bear Stearns led the market decline as its shares plummeted. By October 16, Bear Stearns would be acquired for $2 a share by JPMorgan Chase in a fire sale to avoid bankruptcy. Founded in 1923, Bear Stearns had been one of the largest global investment banks and securities trading and brokerage firms. At its recent peak, Bear was worth nearly $16 billion, but the $2 share price amounted to only $236 million. Further, the deal was backed by the Federal Reserve, which provided up to $30 billion to cover possible Bear Stearns losses. The backing was not entirely surprising, considering the leverage ratio of 35.5 to 1 revealed by their 2007 financials. A few months later, in response to fervent protests by shareholders, the sale price was adjusted to $10 per share for a total of just over $1 billion. Nevertheless, another mighty giant had fallen.

On June 18, 2008, the Senate Banking Committee proposed a housing bailout to the Senate floor that would assist troubled subprime mortgage lenders such as Countrywide Financial. During the session, the chairman, Connecticut's Christopher Dodd, admitted that he had received special treatment, perks, and campaign donations from Countrywide, who regarded Dodd as a "special" customer and a "friend of Angelo" (Countrywide CEO Angelo R. Mozilo). Specifically, Dodd received a $75,000 reduction in mortgage payments from Countrywide. The chairman of the Senate Finance Committee, Kent Conrad, and the head of Fannie Mae, Jim Johnson, also received mortgages on favorable terms due to their association with the Countrywide CEO.

Just when everyone thought that the loss of Bear Stearns and Countrywide was the worst of it, on July 11, IndyMac Bank, a subsidiary of Independent National Mortgage Corporation (IndyMac), was placed into the receivership of the FDIC by the Office of Thrift Supervision. It was the fourth-largest bank failure in United States history, and the second-largest failure of a regulated thrift. Before its failure, IndyMac Bank was the largest savings and loan association in the Los Angeles area and the seventh-largest mortgage originator in the United States. Indicating the pain to come, major banks and financial institutions that had borrowed and invested heavily in mortgage-backed securities reported losses of approximately $435 billion as of July 17, 2008.

However hopeless, you can't blame them for trying. On July 30, President Bush signed into law the Housing and Economic Recovery Act of 2008, which authorized the Federal Housing Administration to guarantee up to $300 billion in new thirty-year, fixed-rate mortgages for subprime borrowers if lenders would write-down principal loan balances to 90 percent of current appraisal value. A little over a month later, on September 7, the federal government took over Fannie Mae and Freddie Mac, which at that point owned or guaranteed about half of the U.S.'s $12 trillion mortgage market.

This effective nationalization of these institutions caused a panic, because almost every home mortgage lender and Wall Street bank relied on Fannie and Freddie to facilitate the mortgage market, and investors worldwide owned $5.2 trillion of debt securities backed by the two enterprises. No one could fully grasp what it would mean for the engines of the mortgage industry to be nationalized.

Monday, September 15, marked another terrifying moment in the decline, as Merrill Lynch was dissolved and its assets sold to Bank of America amid fears of a liquidity crisis and the imminent collapse of Lehman Brothers. The same day, Lehman Brothers filed bankruptcy, which would spell the end of the 158-year-old firm. The shock waves felt by the demise of Lehman have extended to such a degree that many have questioned the thinking of the Treasury and the Federal Reserve in allowing it to fail. A week of terrible news continued on the next day, when both Moody's and Standard & Poor's downgraded their ratings of AIG's credit over concerns about continuing losses to mortgage-backed securities. Given the preceding events, the company's apparent insolvency sent panic across the market. AIG was then effectively seized by the federal government, and on the following day the Federal Reserve loaned $85 billion to AIG to avoid bankruptcy. On Friday 19, the secretary of the Treasury, Hank Paulson, unveiled his financial rescue plan and ending a volatile week in stock and debt markets on a moderately hopeful note.

The next week, the FBI revealed that it was looking into the possibility of fraud by mortgage financing companies Fannie Mae and Freddie Mac, Lehman Brothers, and insurer AIG, bringing the number of corporate lenders under investigation to twenty-six. On September 25, Washington Mutual was seized by the FDIC, and its banking assets were sold to JPMorgan Chase for $1.9 billion. The following Monday, after the Emergency Economic Stabilization Act was defeated 228 to 205 in the United States House of Representatives, the FDIC announced that Citigroup would acquire the banking operations of Wachovia. Later, using tax law changes made September 30, Wells Fargo made a higher offer for Wachovia, scooping it from Citigroup.

With the apparent failure of yet another major bank, on Tuesday, September 30, the Treasury changed tax policy to allow a bank acquiring another to write off all of the acquired bank's losses. Incidentally, when it was revealed in 2010 that this policy would lead to a $1.4 billion tax refund for JPMorgan Chase for the losses of Washington Mutual, despite the fact that JPMorgan Chase had paid only $1.9

billion in 2008 for the distressed banking operations, outraged policy makers looked for ways to reverse matters.

On Wednesday, October 1, the U.S. Senate passed HR 1424, the $700 billion bailout bill. Then on Friday, October 3, President George W. Bush signed into law the Emergency Economic Stabilization Act, creating a $700 billion Troubled Assets Relief Program (TARP) to purchase failing bank assets. The new law included provisions allowing for an easing of the accounting rules that forced companies to collapse because of the existence of toxic mortgage-related investments. Also key to winning GOP support was a decision by the Securities and Exchange Commission (SEC) to ease mark-to-market accounting rules that require financial institutions to show the deflated value of assets on their balance sheets.

Despite the intervention by the Federal Reserve, the Treasury, the SEC, FDIC, the president, Congress, and central banks all around the world, the next week, October 6–10, would be the worst week for the stock market in seventy-five years. The Dow Jones lost 22.1 percent, its worst week on record, down 40.3 percent since reaching a record high of 14,164.53 on October 9, 2007. Standard & Poor's 500 index lost 18.2 percent, its worst week since 1933, down 42.5 percent in value since its own high-water mark on October 9, 2007.

Even as this was happening, on Monday, October 6, the Fed announced that it would provide $900 billion in short-term cash loans to banks. On Tuesday, October 7, it made an emergency move to lend about $1.3 trillion directly to companies outside the financial sector. Also on Tuesday, the IRS relaxed rules on U.S. corporations repatriating money held overseas in an attempt to inject liquidity into the U.S. financial market. The new ruling would allow the companies to receive loans from their foreign subsidiaries for longer periods and more times a year, without triggering the 35 percent corporate income tax. On Wednesday, October 8, central banks in the United States, Great Britain, China, Canada, Sweden, and Switzerland, as well as the European Central Bank, cut rates in a coordinated effort to aid the world economy. Also, the Federal Reserve reduced its emergency lending rate to banks by half a percentage point, to 1.75 percent.

Yet none of this could stem the Dow Jones Industrial Average's worst week ever, which included the highest-volatility day ever recorded in its 112-year history. Paper losses on U.S. stocks now totaled $8.4 trillion from the market highs of a year earlier.

On Saturday, October 11, the G7, or rather a group of central bankers and finance ministers from the Group of Seven leading economies, met in Washington and agreed to pursue urgent, exceptional, and coordinated action to prevent the credit crisis from throwing the world into depression. This proved to be little more than empty rhetoric, as the G7 did not actually agree on a concrete plan as had been hoped.

The next week, the government began to tap into the $700 billion available from the Emergency Economic Stabilization Act and announced the injection of $250 billion of public money into the U.S. banking system. The rescue was to include the U.S. government taking an equity position in banks that chose to participate in the program in exchange for certain restrictions, such as limits on executive compensation. Nine banks agreed to participate in the program and received half of the total funds: (1) Bank of America, (2) JPMorgan Chase, (3) Wells Fargo, (4) Citigroup, (5) Merrill Lynch, (6) Goldman Sachs, (7) Morgan Stanley, (8) BNY Mellon, and (9) State Street. Other U.S. financial institutions eligible for the plan would have until November 14 to agree to the terms.

On October 21, the U.S. Federal Reserve announced that it would spend $540 billion to purchase short-term debt from money market mutual funds. The large amount of redemption requests during the credit crisis caused the money market funds to scale back lending to banks, contributing to the credit freeze on interbank lending markets. They could only hope that the injection would help unfreeze the credit markets by making it easier for businesses and banks to obtain loans. Yet, by November 12, Treasury Secretary Paulson abandoned plans to buy toxic assets under the $700 billion TARP. Mr. Paulson said the remaining $410 billion in the fund would be better spent on recapitalizing financial companies. Many in Congress took this as the worst kind of bait-and-switch scam.

If at first you don't succeed, try, try again. This time the Group of Twenty (G20), which consists of the world's largest economies, met November 15 in Washington, DC, instead of only the G7. They released a statement of the meeting, but again, no detailed plans were agreed upon. The meeting focused on implementing policies consistent with five principles: strengthening transparency and accountability, improving regulation, promoting market integrity, reinforcing cooperation, and reforming international institutions.

Two days later, the Treasury gave out $33.6 billion to twenty-one banks in the second round of disbursements from the $700 billion bailout fund. This payout brought the total to $158.56 billion, without any clear sign that it was working. A week later, on November 24, the U.S. government agreed to rescue Citigroup after an attack by investors caused the stock price to plummet 60 percent over the week. This detailed rescue plan included injecting another $20 billion of capital into Citigroup, bringing the total infusion to $45 billion. The next day, the U.S. Federal Reserve pledged $800 billion more to help revive the financial system. Six hundred billion dollars would be used to buy mortgage bonds issued or guaranteed by Fannie Mae, Freddie Mac, the Government National Mortgage Association (Ginnie Mae), and the Federal Home Loan Banks. The week ended (November 28) with the Bank for International Settlements (BIS), the global organization behind the Basel Accords, issuing a consultative paper providing supervisory guidance on the valuation of assets. The paper provided ten principles that should be used by banks to value assets at fair market value.

December began with Federal Reserve Chairman Bernanke saying that further interest-rate cuts were "certainly feasible," but he warned there are limits to how much such action would revive an economy likely to stay weak well into the next year. Mr. Bernanke also said the Federal Reserve's powers wouldn't end with the federal funds rate, and its ability to inject liquidity into markets through its balance sheets "remains effective." Two days later, on December 3, the Federal Reserve's Beige Book survey showed that, with few sectors spared from the deepening downturn, nearly every area of the U.S. reported sales declines, drops in manufacturing activity, weakening real estate markets, tighter lending, and deteriorating labor markets. Even the sectors that had been bright spots until recently—such as agriculture and energy—also softened as commodity prices declined.

Evidence of the far reaches of the economic meltdown was particularly notable on December 8, when Tribune, a major player in the newspaper industry, filed for bankruptcy-court protection. Tribune had been on wobbly footing for a year, since real-estate mogul Samuel Zell led a debt-backed deal to take the company private. Tribune owned eight major daily newspapers, including the *Los Angeles Times*, *Chicago Tribune*, and *Baltimore Sun*, plus a string of local TV stations.

The American automobile industry was also teetering on the edge of collapse. Three days later, a frantic, last-ditch attempt to forge an emergency-relief package for the Big Three automakers collapsed in the U.S. Senate, amid a sharp partisan dispute over the wages paid to workers at the troubled manufacturing giants.

Adding insult to injury, on the same day, December 11, details emerged of the worldwide pyramid scheme run by a prominent U.S. financier, Bernard Madoff. The market collapse had dried up the flow of new investors into his Ponzi scheme, and with existing investors looking to cash out, Madoff was exposed. Over the weekend, European banks, including Spain's Grupo Santander and France's BNP Paribas, said their clients and shareholders faced billions in losses on investments with Bernard Madoff, underscoring the global reach of the alleged Ponzi scheme run by the veteran New York money manager.

The line between what was a criminal scheme and what was merely imprudent fund management was becoming increasingly blurred. Only one major investment bank was still standing, Goldman Sachs. Later in 2010, we would find out how Goldman was able to weather the crisis, when the SEC filed a fraud lawsuit against it, and its executives were brought before the Senate for a tongue-lashing that extended late into the night. Nevertheless, on December 16, Goldman posted its first quarterly loss since it went public in 1999, losing $2.12 billion, or $4.97 a share, during its fiscal fourth quarter. Net revenue was a negative $1.58 billion.

The same day, the U.S. Federal Reserve board slashed official interest rates to a historic low range to combat the deepening recession. Further, they signaled that they would keep rates "exceptionally low" for some time, amid rapidly waning price pressures. The Federal Open Market Committee voted unanimously to reduce the target Federal Reserve funds rate for interbank lending from 1 percent to a range of zero to 0.25 percent, the lowest since the Federal Reserve started publishing the funds target in 1990. The market-determined effective Federal Reserve funds rate had already hit record lows. The Federal Reserve signaled in minutes from its meeting that the recession could drag well into the New Year, with economic output contracting for 2009 as a whole and inflation possibly "uncomfortably low." The new fear was not of inflation, but of a more devastating threat, deflation.

Three days later, on December 19, the Bank of Japan lowered interest rates to support an economy increasingly feeling the pain of a global slump, becoming the next central bank to cut rates to rock-bottom levels. Japan's central bank also announced new steps to provide liquidity to capital markets, aiming to make it easier for cash-starved firms to raise funds.

The same day, after failing to get the vote for a bailout through Congress, the White House announced a $17.4 billion rescue package for the troubled Detroit automakers to avoid bankruptcy. Allowing the Big Three to fail, President Bush said, was "not a responsible course" in the midst of a recession. The deal extended $13.4 billion in loans to General Motors and Chrysler in December and January, with another $4 billion likely available in February. The deal was contingent on the companies showing that they were financially viable by March.

The end-of-the-year financial data told the tale of how horrible 2008 had been. Retail sales tumbled by 2.7 percent in December, marking the sixth consecutive decline, the Commerce Department reported. The deep, broad drop indicated that worried consumers were adding to savings instead of spending at the height of the holiday season. Nonfarm payrolls tumbled by 524,000 in December, the twelfth straight decline, following a revised drop of 584,000 in November. In all, in 2008 the economy lost 2.6 million jobs, the most since the end of World War II. The unemployment rate jumped to 7.2 percent, the highest since January 1993, but it was a number that would later be dwarfed. U.S. consumer prices rose for the year by their slowest pace in over a half century. Much of the reversal was due to a roughly 75 percent decline in oil prices from their July peak.

For December, the consumer price index dropped 0.7 percent on a seasonally adjusted basis from the previous month, according to the Labor Department. Economists had expected a 0.8 percent decline. The core Consumer Price Index (CPI), which excludes food and energy, was unchanged. For the full year, consumer prices rose just 0.1 percent, the lowest increase since 1954, and well below the Federal Reserve's 1.5 percent to 2 percent reference over the long run. The core CPI, however, was up 1.8 percent for the year, suggesting the U.S. didn't yet face economy-wide deflation. The median home price was $175,400 in December, down 15.3 percent from $207,000 in December 2007, according to the National Association of Realtors. The median price in November 2008 was $180,300. Home resales rose to a 4.74 million annual rate, but of all sales in December, about 45 percent were distress sales at discounted prices. New-home sales fell 14.7 percent in December to 331,000. The drop capped the worst year for sales since 1982.

That was not the only thing that was the worst since 1982. Gross domestic product decreased at a seasonally adjusted 6.2 percent annual rate October through December, the Commerce Department reported. In its original estimate, issued a month before, the government had reported that the fourth-quarter 2008 GDP fell 3.8 percent. They had earlier estimated a rate of 3.8 percent, before sharply lowering the number in a revision that reflected downward adjustments in inventory investment, exports, and consumer spending. The 6.2 percent decline meant the worst GDP quarterly showing since a 6.4 percent decrease in the first-quarter 1982 GDP.

Making Sense of It

By all accounts, 2008 was a year from hell financially. The World Economic Forum estimated that, by 2009, the crisis had destroyed

40 percent of the world's wealth. In America, the Labor Department reported 2.6 million jobs lost in 2008 alone, and, according to the Federal Reserve, the nation's households lost $14 trillion in net worth from their peak in 2007.

The country and the world were changed. More than that, our self-image had changed. Looking at the history of what happened is informative, but it is still easy to miss the cause, as so many have. The superficial explanations that we have heard over and over again are radically wrong this time, perhaps because the wrong answer seems obviously right. Ideologues have the mic, and there is a major clash between ideals and reality right now. The right wing and the left wing are saying what they always say, but they are shockingly clueless, blinded by their ideological lenses. Both the general sentiment, based on overly simplistic reporting, and the positions taken by the "best" economic minds reveal fundamental misunderstandings of what is wrong or what is needed.

If there is anything that I know well from years in business, it is that financial pain doesn't exactly make people smarter. More often than not, such pain leads to utterly idiotic behavior and decision making that worsens the worst problems. Leaders have argued and will argue back and forth rancorously and continue to pass legislation that won't even come close to adapting to the needs of the new global economy or our role in it, just as the many efforts detailed above have fallen flat. Even the premise of "let's prevent that from ever happening again," which was so common in the wake of the crash, betrays a lack of understanding of what happened.

The entire bubble and bust was the result of investors *believing* they had a formula to make a fortune without risk and selling the world on that illusion, followed by a slow awakening to the axiom that there is always risk. Once these players stopped *believing*, they stopped playing, and the game fell apart. Modern economics is often based more on sentiment and emotion than anything else. Nevertheless, the game pushed hundreds of billions of dollars into the real economy, and we all used it. We built, bought, and sold millions of homes, bought all of the latest gadgets, and lived like this money in the economy was a new reality. We all believed it was *real*. After all, what is the difference between money from a casino and money from hard work? Lots and nothing.

Of greater note in the crisis is the revelation of the need for better capital flows *into* the real economy. There was and is a clear need for more affordable mortgage products. The presence of cheaper mortgages created millions of jobs and stimulated the middle class as never before. The manner in which and the reason that capital flowed into the real economy were the problems. That it stopped so abruptly became a greater problem. Worst of all was the problem that, at the end, there was very little appetite to even return to the capital flow levels prior to 2001. Despite the pain of the crash, we need to take a lesson from the temporary good that was accomplished by capital derivative trading, namely, the capital flow to regular people through their home equity and the demand for housing.

The truth is that we must embrace the reality of how our system works and then make it work for the general good. You can't create and expand a system of fiat currency and credit, and then complain that the real economy uses or even depends on our system of fiat currency and credit. Most people don't even know what fiat currency is, and worse, if they did they wouldn't like it. But that is the system we have and need. (We'll talk about fiat currency and monetary policy later.) My goal is to put a little reality out there from the perspective of the small guy who is not an observer, but a participant in the real economy.

PART TWO:

HOW DID WE GET HERE?

The Founding Fathers had hoped to "form a more perfect union," but no system can fully mitigate the human condition. Smith, Keynes, and Friedman, all brilliant men, could not devise a perfect system of commerce and national economics. We have seen devolution of their ideals in the face of immutable human realities. Where did they or we go wrong?

CHAPTER FOUR

The Evolution of
Cannibal Capitalism

The slow crash of 2008 will live in infamy. The safest of "safe" havens, real estate, collapsed. What was myopically viewed as a subprime crisis was soon revealed to be a broad-based failure of the global financial system. Freddie Mac and Fannie Mae, the giant GSEs chartered to provide liquidity to the housing market by buying conforming loans (loans meant to be conservative), were brought down, along with everyone else, by the crisis of confidence over the pandemic defaults of nonconforming loans. Default-rate and home-foreclosure records were broken as values steadily collapsed. Overleveraged mortgage-backed securities collapsed, as panic spread through the public and private markets, leading all of the major investment banks to either fail or to become commercial banks. Even by the end of 2008, early efforts to assist troubled homeowners with modified mortgage loans seemed hollow, as redefault rates exceeded 50 percent. Tremendous wealth has evaporated all across the global economy. The losses have amounted to tens of trillions of dollars! Millions of jobs have been lost. And the last vestige of the old U.S. manufacturing base, the auto industry, has teetered on the edge of oblivion.

We often hear the questions: How did we get here? Is this just a natural cycle, or are the so-called cycles of the past fifty years also symptoms of a deeper problem?

What Is Normal?

The fact is that we were doomed to end up here because of structural flaws in the entire economic system. As Shakespeare's Cassius said in *Julius Caesar*, "The fault, dear Brutus, is not in our stars, but in ourselves." It is not the mysterious forces of the market. It is not the work of a secret society pulling the strings behind the scenes. It is not as simple as political demagogues who point fingers at two-dimensional villains would like to characterize it. The problem that has come and is yet still emerging is fundamental and systemic. Perhaps former Federal Reserve chairman Alan Greenspan put it best when he was before Congress in October 2008: he said that the economic crises that had begun to grip the world revealed "a flaw in the model that [he] perceived is the critical functioning structure that defines how the world works."

Many free marketers were deeply offended by Greenspan's statements, and some accused him of deepening the problem, but I believe that he is exactly right—perhaps far more than even he intended, if you distinguish between the words "work" and "function." The implication of how the world "works" carries a greater implication than merely the "function" of markets.

A self-destructive system can certainly "function," but only for so long. How long can you use your foundation as a quarry before your home collapses? How long can you eat your young before you become extinct? How long can America feed off the shrinking middle class before the great democracy of recent memory dies a painful death? This was not the first recession, and it won't be the last. Whether bullish, bearish, or erratically both, the markets do function, but do they really "work" for the best interests of everyone with a stake in the system?

Even though recessions cause us to pause for a moment and rethink many aspects of the way our society works, most of the time, because the numbers seem to indicate steady growth, we feel fine. When things are good, we are less than inclined to acknowledge any deep-seated problems with the system. After all, the gross domestic product (the market value of all the output produced in a nation in one year) for the U.S. was estimated in excess of $14 trillion for 2008, nearly a quarter of the world total. And this was the worst contraction of the GDP since 1982.

We have generally seen our economy grow year after year, and, even when things are bad, it seems that there is someone who is doing well. In 2008, Amazon saw its profits rise 9 percent, and ExxonMobil broke its own record for the highest earnings of any U.S. company ever, making $45.2 billion in profit. Recessions are often viewed as healthy exhalations necessary to purge excesses from the economy. Even in the area of manufacturing, many would be surprised to know that, according to the BEA (Bureau of Economic Analysis), U.S. manufacturing output has continued to rise even during the last twenty years of free trade and offshoring. All of this lends plausibility to the argument that the ebbs and flows of the economy are natural and healthy.

Just as if we suffered from kwashiorkor, we've been getting the calories to simulate growth, but they have not been healthy calories. How much of the GDP is connected to bizarre derivatives and amorphous financial instruments? On Sunday, April 25, 2010, Senator Sherrod Brown of Ohio told Jake Tapper of *ABC News,* "Fifteen years ago, the assets of the six largest banks in this country totaled 17 percent of GDP. The assets of the six largest banks in the United States today total 63 percent of GDP." His statement was confirmed by Pulitzer-award-winning PolitiFact.com. That reflects kwashiorkor-like attrition, not healthy growth (see Figure 4.1).

More importantly, how many are sharing in the wealth of the economy? How many of the employed are actually underemployed, failing to earn a living wage? In 2010, Gallup reported an under-employment rate of more than 20 percent, but even that number fails to account for millions of Americans who are off of the radar. There is where we see the malnourishing effect of the way our economy is now operating. While manufacturing output has risen and company profits have risen more often than not, manufacturing jobs have steadily declined. Even when you completely factor out China, which became a global manufacturing behemoth upon its entry into the World Trade Organization (WTO), the means by which most Americans benefit from American prosperity, jobs, have been drying up (see Figure 4.2).

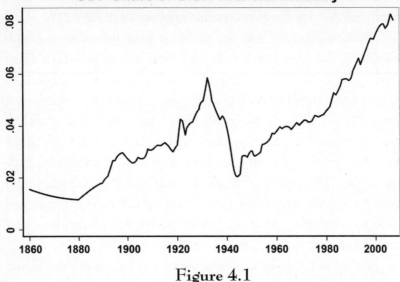

Figure 4.1

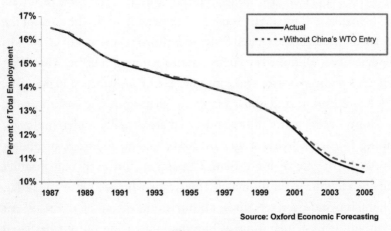

Figure 4.2

The nature of the economic ills facing the nation is most evident in the "muscle" of our economy—the middle class. The middle class must get in on the action. The fact that the wealth and buying power of the middle class has been shrinking with each successive decade since the modern economy was developed in the mid-twentieth century is proof that there is a systemic problem facing the nation. When you examine the causative factors driving the attrition of the middle class, it is not hard to realize that the villain comes not from without, but within.

Dependencies versus Ideologies

When the Big Three automakers came before Congress to plead for a bailout, many were aggressively pushing the idea of bankruptcy reorganization as the "best" solution to Detroit's shortfalls. You may remember they had to come to DC twice, because the first time the CEOs were so politically tone-deaf as to fly to Washington in private jets. For a while, it seemed that one or two of the auto giants weren't going to survive the winter. But they came back, and the second time they drove hybrids. They came arm in arm with the head of the United Auto Workers union and a dealers-association representative. By this point, matters seemed more urgent, and the price tag went up. Still, prospects for the economy appeared bleak, because it seemed that the political will to save the American auto industry was lacking.

The ideological gridlock was as intransigent as ever. Laissez-faire ideologues loathe all bailouts and readily label them as socialism, so the request of the Big Three U.S. automakers amped up the ire of the anti-bailout crowd. Across the board, most agreed that the collapse of the automakers could be catastrophic, costing up to three million jobs and perhaps even accelerating the recession downward into a depression. So the lines in the sand were drawn, not between bailout and no bailout, but between bailout and some sort of "prepackaged" Chapter 11 bankruptcy or conservatorship.

During the media and lobbying battle that ensued, the devil was, as always, in the details. The bankruptcy camp used the obfuscation of clever wordsmiths to bury the truth behind terms like "legacy costs" and "out-of-date business models." With what seemed to be unimpeachable reasonableness, the economists and pundits would say, "These companies are weighed down by legacy costs and their costs structures are not even competitive with the Japanese carmakers that build in America!"

In the first hearing, sitting next to the Big Three CEOs who were testifying to Congress was the bow-tie-wearing Peter Morici, a business professor at the University of Maryland and self-described macroeconomist. A media darling, he regularly appears as a guest commentator on several news programs. In all of his testimony, he was pushing bankruptcy reorganization as the "only" means to really fix what's wrong in Detroit. To the committee, he detailed what the "legacy costs" were and described how, through Chapter 11, automakers could shed labor contracts, severance costs, and pensioners' health care costs. The economist on the panel during the second hearing was not so certain, but "feared" that bankruptcy would be inevitable without intervention.

A troubling reality is that from a certain perspective, Professor Morici was right. It's just that that perspective is one of heartless, cannibal capitalism. In the strict terms of cold business economics, bankruptcy may have been a more efficient way to streamline the American car companies, and not doing so when these companies were on the brink of collapse was a missed opportunity. Yet doesn't that miss the point? Will the labor expenses of experienced, middle-class, American union workers ever be truly competitive with those of workers in the developing world? Of course not! For that matter, the whole country is carrying "legacy costs," so to speak. According to cold business logic, the U.S., with its bloated middle class, has an out-of-date business model and should give up, letting the invisible hand confer a leading position on a fast-growing country in Asia.

It's also not fair to compare average salaries in a ten-year-old factory owned by a Japanese car company to average salaries across the board at a hundred-year-old American company. It is neither fair nor in our best interest to permit market forces to shift our wealth overseas. In any case, the real question remains: is the idea of chopping jobs, benefits, and pay of Americans a good thing, particularly in times of economic stress?

Bankruptcy could have been a shortcut to a more streamlined auto industry. However, that path would be carved across the backs of thousands, perhaps millions of Americans. Cannibal capitalism is never compassionate conservatism.

My fears during that debate were never that consumers would fail to buy cars from a company in reorganization. I correctly believed that, with a well-executed media blitz, they could have convinced the public that there was enough government backing to mitigate risks, particularly given a public that is often uninterested in these sorts of matters. No, what I feared was that bankruptcy provisions would actually allow companies to completely reorganize. As a businessman, even I have to admit that if I were given the chance to completely reshape the American car companies and had no concerns other than profit-oriented business strategy, I'd go far beyond just burying legacy costs: I would shut down nearly all U.S. manufacturing, cut between 70 and 80 percent of the U.S. workforce, and realign to target emerging consumer markets. See, the dangers didn't lie solely in allowing the auto giants to fail; they also lay in allowing them to leave.

The message of the bankruptcy solution proponents was that high-paying jobs, health care for retired career workers, and taking care of the workers in an inactive plant until production could be ramped back up are all things that should be eliminated from the balance sheet by any means necessary. If Big Three autoworkers effectively cost $70 per hour and Toyota workers only cost $40 an hour, the Big Three should fire all their workers, hire them back at the lower wage, and use the bankruptcy court to sanitize this immorality. Indeed, they wanted to take such measures as making workers pay for their own health care through their union dues. That would make business sense, and bankruptcy would have given them the cover to do it, but what's the morality of that? Is it in the best interest of the nation? What the bankruptcy camp failed to acknowledge is the cold reality that there would be little reason to keep more than a token domestic business after Chapter 11 reorganization.

Some of the more determined opponents of the Chapter 11 option, like Senator Richard Shelby of Alabama, pointed to the success of foreign automakers operating in the United States and promoted the notion that there would still be a viable American auto industry even with the loss of the Big Three American companies. "Who cares who owns the company?" some said. How shortsighted! Had they all forgotten why these foreign companies manufacture here? Don't you remember?

Foreign car companies operating in the U.S., now called transplants, were forced to create American jobs to be allowed to grow their American market share. The climate was that buying a foreign car was unpatriotic *until* those companies set up substantial U.S. operations. It is critical to recognize that the pressure created by a domestic auto industry is ultimately why Toyota and the rest are here. Their U.S. operations are the least efficient for these companies. What would prevent these foreign companies from shutting down U.S. operations if the domestic industry collapsed? Any threat of a lost market share would ring hollow, as there would be no alternative. We could actually lose them all!

If you must, use the situation to force innovation down the throats of execs in Detroit, because, frankly, the only way to save the highest-paying jobs in the industry is for these companies to start building the best cars in the world. Fortunately, the bailouts seemed to work, and by the middle of 2010 there was excitement surrounding the rebound of Ford and GM. Some, though, stuck in their ideology, still bemoaned the bailouts and the avoidance of bankruptcy for the car companies. They still don't get it. Killing these high-paying jobs, whether through bankruptcy or not, would always be a bad idea, because all bulwarks against cannibal capitalism would be removed. People need to reflect on the passionate rebuke from chairman Christopher Dodd in the first hearing with the Big Three automakers: "Taking care of people isn't a bad thing!" The common view that taking care of people is socialism is part of how we have become a cannibal country.

A combination of governmental incompetence, corporate greed, unchecked market forces, trade imbalances, immigration patterns, consumerism, globalization, and declining standards of education have all factored in, and yet these are all problems caused by or contributed to by our own American institutions.

In other words, we have been slowly killing ourselves. Like junk food, which may send signals to the "happy" centers of the brain that all is well, bighead-sanctioned economic data sends signals of strength, when the country is in fact weak. Days before we found out that the nation has been in recession for a year, we heard reports that the fundamentals of the economy were strong. Corporate financials cannot be the only guiding line that defines success.

This could be the end of the golden age of America, after which this country could fall in line with the status quo of much of the rest of the world, where the gap between rich and poor is immense and the middle class is virtually nonexistent. How did we get here, and how can we get out?

New World Economics

America was to be the New World, the "great experiment," and mankind's best hope for independence, liberty, and opportunity. There would be no peasants here; rather, "that all men are created equal" was held as self-evident truth. As the grandchild of sharecroppers, I cannot ignore the fact that this has been an unrealized ideal. The history of slavery and the genocide of indigenous people discredit any notion that "created equal" means "treated equal." Nevertheless, in all fairness, an examination of world history elevates the United States of America above every other form of government tried—albeit the monarchies and republics of the past set a rather low bar. Even looking around the globe today, we can scarcely find an equivalent middle class. Yet the system that created this middle class is now at risk.

The problem is systemic, and can be found in our fundamental national economic philosophies and our practice of capitalism. Certainly, we must consider the history of the economy to understand our economic woes and to chart a better course.

Not only was 1776 the year that this nation declared its independence, it was also the year that Adam Smith published his magnum opus, *An Inquiry into the Nature and Causes of the Wealth of Nations*. Although Adam Smith, an eighteenth-century British subject from

Scotland, is often credited as the father of modern economics for the entire world, he could also be credited as the absent founding father of the U.S. economy. His theories and descriptions of wealth and commerce greatly influenced the architects of our economy, including Alexander Hamilton, our first secretary of the Treasury and an actual Founding Father. More notably, Smithian dogma is at the core of every aspect of the way modern economics is practiced.

Now, Hamilton certainly would not have considered himself to be a disciple of Smith; quite the contrary. For one thing, he vehemently opposed free trade as promoted by Smith. Nonetheless, it cannot be doubted that this new republic was shaped by Smith; he was rising into the pantheon just as this nation was being birthed. The core principles in *Wealth of Nations*, particularly the concept of meritocracy and the invisible hand of self-governing markets, are cornerstones of the U.S. economic system today. While other nations would have to institute reforms to incorporate Smith's theories and free-trade policies, the fledging republic was a blank slate.

Over successive generations, and especially as America's fledgling economy developed more durable industries, Hamilton's protectionist approach, which favored government intervention to protect businesses, came to predominate. Hamilton's approach was modeled on that of Jean-Baptiste Colbert, the French minister of finance under King Louis XIV, who achieved his reputation by improving the state of French manufacturing and bringing the economy back from the brink of bankruptcy. But in time, protectionism gave way to the invisible hand of Smithian free market economics. By the Roaring Twenties, Smith's theory was the modus operandi of the entire U.S. economy.

That is not to say that economists are all of one mind. Not even close! Just as the political right and left war over a variety of social theories, there are equally partisan economic theories. In fact, most of the partisan political battles are rooted in opposing economic theories. Karl Marx castigated the capitalist system he saw around him, which he thought was exploitative and alienating, ultimately leading him to the conclusion that the world needed stateless, classless societies. Communism in theory isn't so bad, but most would agree that the practice has been deeply destructive and debilitating to normal economic and social progress. Closely related to communism is socialism. Marx viewed socialism as a stepping-stone to true communism. True communism is functionally impossible and has never existed in the real world, since true communism requires that there be no state, no government, and no central authority. Socialism has been applied in a variety of forms and to various degrees. Socialism is, at least theoretically, a system in which the state owns and administers the means of production and distribution of goods, and society is characterized by equal opportunities for all individuals with a fair or egalitarian method of compensation.

With that, we have our extremes on the spectrum of economic theory. On the one extreme, we have the laissez-faire free market, and on the other extreme we have socialism where the government fully controls the economy. As with most things, the extremes at both ends are bad. Opposing pundits often take advantage of this obvious fact in order to insult each other; each accuses the other of being at the extreme of his end of the spectrum. A free marketer is quick to call his more liberal counterpart a socialist, which in the wake of the Cold War carries a powerful sting, but when the liberal calls him a capitalist, he takes it as more of a compliment than insult. Ironically, both communists and libertarians believe in the same end, the elimination of the state, although for opposing ideological reasons. Fortunately, American economic debate is not at the extremes, despite the excessive rhetoric.

At the end of the laissez-faire Roaring Twenties, the market collapsed and we entered the Great Depression. That period brought forth the great economist John Maynard Keynes. Keynes established the now widely held view that there are times when the economy simply cannot be left to Smith's "invisible hand" theory.

According to Keynesian economics, the state should stimulate economic growth and improve stability in the private sector through, for example, adjusting interest rates and taxation and funding public projects. In Keynes's theory, certain microlevel actions of individuals and firms can lead to aggregate macroeconomic outcomes in which the economy operates below its potential output and growth. Many classical economists had believed in Say's law, which states that supply creates its own demand, so that a "general glut" would therefore be impossible. Keynes contended that aggregate demand for goods might be insufficient during economic downturns, leading to unnecessarily high unemployment and losses of potential output. Keynes argued that government policies could be used to increase aggregate demand, thus increasing economic activity and reducing high unemployment and deflation. Keynes argued that the solution to a depression was to stimulate the economy ("inducement to invest") through some combination of a reduction in interest rates and government investment in infrastructure. He allegedly said that in periods of economic woe, it would be beneficial for a government to employ people to dig holes in the ground and fill them up again.

A central conclusion of Keynesian economics is that in some situations, no strong, automatic mechanism moves output and employment toward full employment levels. This conclusion conflicts with economic approaches that assume a general tendency toward equilibrium. Keynes's theory led to a realignment of classical economic theory, and what emerged is now generally called neoclassical economics. To fully recognize why Keynesian economics became standard, we must consider the environment that led to its acceptance.

Genesis of Irrational Exuberance

Following World War I, the country entered a time of peace and great prosperity fueled by increased industrialization and new technologies, such as the radio, the automobile, and air transportation. During the Roaring Twenties, the Dow Jones Industrial Average soared. Most economists viewed the stock market as extremely safe, leading a plethora of investors to purchase stock on margin (using a loan). Just as companies in the 2008 crisis exacerbated matters through leveraging, margin users in the '20s worsened matters by borrowing $9 worth of stock for every dollar they invested. (It is notable that this was ten-to-one leveraging. Mortgage-backed securities involved in the recent collapse were leveraged by major financial institutions by as much as forty to one.) As is the case with all leveraging, margin users saw an exaggeration of not only minor gains, but also minor losses. As you can imagine, if an investment dropped too much, margin holders could lose all of their money and then some.

Millionaires were created instantly as the Dow Jones rocketed from 60 to 400 from 1921 to 1929. Stock market trading became America's favorite pastime, as exuberant investors, intoxicated by the thought of possible gains, mortgaged their homes and foolishly invested their life savings in not only the hottest stocks, such as Ford and RCA, but also in almost any stocks. Viewing stocks as a sure thing, few actually studied the fundamentals of the companies they invested in. Worse still, many companies were formed for the sole purpose of defrauding unsavvy investors overeager to get in on the action. Most investors, even the more experienced, never imagined a crash.

Doesn't this all sound rather familiar? They say hindsight is 20/20, despite the utter failure of the market to ever actually learn from hindsight. So many so-called experts rarely demonstrate wisdom to match their education and experience. Many of these bigheads have built their careers around the lessons supposedly learned from the crash of '29 and the Great Depression, and yet always seem to be dumbfounded when history repeats itself.

It's not actually that no lessons were learned. There hasn't been a repeat of the bank runs that actually caused the Great Depression. The most devastating effect of the 1929 market crash was the chaos in the banking system, triggered as banks tried to collect margin calls of investors whose holdings were now worthless.

As we've seen again and again since then, the banks themselves want in on the action during a boom, so they've invested depositors' money in the market. Inevitably, word spread that banks' assets contained huge, uncollectable loans and almost worthless stock certificates, leading to a broad-based panic. Depositors rushed to withdraw their savings, and banks began failing by the hundreds in 1932 and 1933.

By early 1933, the U.S. banking system, as well as those of much of the rest of the world, had effectively ceased to function, plunging the world into the Great Depression.

Thankfully we now have depositors insurance backed by the government. The Federal Deposit Insurance Corporation (FDIC) would prevent another epidemic of bank runs, especially now with the increased limits, but nothing has corrected the systemic flaws that allow real wealth to be exchanged for synthetic wealth, rapidly expanding the economy only to reverse it on an emotional whim. These flaws have caused recession after recession and the slow, painful destruction of the middle class. The banks still share in the irrational exuberance, participating in and exacerbating every bubble.

The former chairman of the Federal Reserve Board, Alan Greenspan, once said in testimony to Congress, "While bubbles that burst are scarcely benign, the consequences need not be catastrophic for the economy." This statement was meant to build confidence in the ability of the Federal Reserve and other policy makers to prevent errors similar to those that caused the Great Depression. Yet in 2008, Greenspan had to return to Congress to essentially apologize for his failure to see the subprime crisis coming. It's not that surprising that these bigheads are always blindsided when you consider that they still cannot agree on the correlation between the 1929 crash and the Great Depression. There are economic theories to support every conceivable political and philosophical position. Perhaps this is why so many would prefer to trust an invisible hand rather than their colleagues.

Nevertheless, the bigheads have at least given us terminology to describe the events that they can never prevent, manage, or correct. For instance, today we call it a "bubble" when the money supply extends beyond what genuine capital investment supports and expanded credit taking the place of an expanded pool of investors. The suspension of disbelief, the expectation of large profits, and ever-rising (and unsustainable) prices in an open market are all now recognized as classic characteristics of the prelude to a crash. Yet the preoccupation with self-interest (and yes, selfish greed) causes markets to repeat the same mistakes over and over again, to the point that both experts and novices consider expansion and recession to be natural cycles of the economy.

So, is this an indictment of Adam Smith? Not exactly. But the interpretation and application of his theories have led to the mess we have seen since. Despite the fact that the words "economy" and "capitalism" were not used in Smith's day, his descriptions persist as the fundamentals of capitalist economics. His main theme was that of an invisible hand that leads to the best results, because opposing self-interests lead to equilibrium. This is best expressed in the most-quoted passage in *Wealth of Nations*: "It is not from the benevolence of the butcher, the brewer, or the baker that we expect our dinner, but from their regard to their own interest. We address ourselves, not to their humanity, but to their self-love, and never talk to them of our own necessities but of their advantages."[11] The clear rhetoric with which he describes bargaining ("Give that which I want and you shall have this which you want," and "It is this manner that we obtain from one another the far greater part of those good offices which we stand in need of") has proven hard to resist.

Depression and Recessions

The blind acceptance of this dogma as divine wisdom has led to each and every one of the market crashes and recessions, and to the attrition of the middle class. Just look at the circumstances around each of the major recessions of the last century. We begin with the Great Depression, which is generally viewed as a benchmark for the worst that can happen. It lasted for about 120 months, from roughly 1929 to 1939, though, as a worldwide economic downturn, it ended at different times, in the 1930s or early 1940s for different countries. The usual consensus is that it began with Black Tuesday, the first day of the crash of 1929, and ended with the onset of the war economy of World War II, beginning around 1939.

While some ideologues hold the line for Smith dogma at all times, Herbert Hoover, president from 1929 to 1933, proved to many that a government failing to intervene in an economic crisis was almost

---

11. Adam Smith, *An Inquiry into the Nature and Causes of the Wealth of Nations*, 5th edition (London: Hanlins Press, 2007), 122.

as bad as a government causing the crisis. Hoover feared that too much intervention or coercion by the government would destroy individuality and self-reliance, which he considered to be important American values.

It is not that Herbert Hoover did nothing while the world economy eroded. President Hoover made attempts to stop the downward spiral of the Great Depression. Rather, it's that his policies had little or no effect. As the economy quickly deteriorated in the early years of the Great Depression, Hoover declined to pursue legislative relief, believing that it would make people dependent on the federal government. His ideology, though perhaps not completely laissez-faire, prevented him from really getting ahead of and thereby shortening the Great Depression.

Even though the New Deal under Franklin D. Roosevelt was on the right track, it wasn't until the nation suspended the gold standard and leveraged itself with bonds to build a war machine that enough liquidity entered the economy to truly end the Great Depression.

After the war, the gold standard was never really restored. The Bretton Woods system of monetary management was established to shift from a representative currency system to fiat money, which would in time allow the Federal Reserve to print money without restraint. (We'll talk more about this later, because monetary policy is also at the heart of the catabolism of our country.)

The next major decline was the recession of 1947. This was perhaps the most honest recession of the nation's history; the market just got too hot. Coming out of the war, there was a combination of euphoria, industrial overproduction, and too much money in the pipelines that led to rapid inflation. More significantly, this was the beginning of a shift away from the New Deal. President Truman had been nominated to be vice president in 1944 under the powerful influence of party bosses who were opposed to the notion of the incumbent vice president, Henry Wallace, becoming president. They viewed Wallace as too liberal. Truman was the beginning of a sea change.

Though Truman was a Democrat and voiced support for New Deal policies, he also didn't view Smith dogma as mutually exclusive with the New Deal. He strongly supported laissez-faire-like policies and had even denounced market controls as marks of a police state, but by the end of 1947, he had reversed himself. This was in many ways the beginning of the inflationary economy that we know so well. Also, one of the most significant lessons of this recession was that the U.S. could not isolate its economy from the world. The year 1947 marked the birth of the global economy in ways that even the Great Depression did not.

Not learning from our mistakes, we effectively repeated the 1947 recession in 1953, when, as after a post–Korean War inflationary period, more funds were transferred into national security. The Federal Reserve also contributed to matters by making monetary policy more restrictive in 1952 due to fears of further inflation. Economists agree that this was a demand-driven recession due to poor government policies and high interest rates. It was also the first of three recessions for Smith disciple President Dwight Eisenhower, the most of any president. The Eisenhower years marked the beginning of total domination of Smith dogma in economic thought. These years also illustrated the new political reality that would shape the country for the foreseeable future: voters ignore the economy when there is no boogeyman to fear.

Ike's next recession ran, arguably, from July 1957 through April 1958, and was global in impact. Monetary policy was tightened during the two years preceding 1957, followed by an easing of policy at the end of 1957. There was a contraction in the purchases of both agricultural and mineral raw materials, which hit economically disadvantaged countries the hardest. Unemployment rose across the board, but in Detroit it stood at a high of 20 percent. Auto sales dropped 31 percent throughout 1957, making 1958 the worst auto year since World War II.

It is typical for prices to fall during recessions, but this time they went up, not including raw materials. In the U.S., consumer prices rose 2.7 percent from 1957 to 1958, and after a pause they continued to push up until November 1959. Wholesale prices rose 1.6 percent from 1957 to 1959. The continued upward creep of prices became a cause of concern among economists. The budget surplus of 0.8 percent of GDP in 1957 gave way to a budget deficit of 0.6 percent of GDP in 1958, and then to a widening deficit of 2.6 percent of GDP in 1959.

A recession from 1960–61 was the mildest of Eisenhower's three recessions. Economists often scratch their heads at this one, because it lacked some of the indicators of other recessions. With Ike finally out of power, the country entered a period of prosperity under Kennedy and Johnson. Their economic policies harkened back to the New Deal, with initiatives christened as the New Frontier and then the Great Society. Even though these were turbulent times socially, there would not be another recession until Ike's vice president came to power.

On January 20, 1969, Richard Milhous Nixon took the oath of office, and the economic expansion came to a halt in the United States by autumn. Ever the ideologue, Nixon acted on his conservative philosophy of "gradualism" and moved to cut the budget. This, together with an environment of higher interest rates, caused the 1969 recession and a bear market until May 1970. This recession was less severe than the two-year recession that marred Nixon's second term nearly as much as did Watergate. Nevertheless, Nixon continued destructive economic policies. In 1971, the Nixon administration unilaterally canceled the Bretton Woods system and stopped the direct convertibility of the U.S. dollar to gold. Meeting in December 1971 at the Smithsonian Institution, representatives of the Group of Ten (G10) nations signed the Smithsonian Agreement, thereby agreeing to appreciate their currencies against the U.S. dollar. Although the Smithsonian Agreement was hailed by President Nixon as a fundamental reorganization of international monetary affairs, it led to devaluation of the dollar.

To be fair, this was inevitable. By the early 1970s, as the Vietnam War accelerated inflation, the United States was running not just a balance of payments deficit, but also a trade deficit for the first time in the twentieth century. The crucial turning point was 1970, which saw U.S. gold coverage of the paper dollar deteriorate from 55 percent to 22 percent. This theoretically represented the point at which holders of the dollar had lost faith in the U.S.'s ability to cut its budget and trade deficits. In 1971, more and more dollars were printed and then sent overseas, to pay for the nation's military expenditures and private investments. In the first six months of 1971, $22 billion in assets fled the United States.

Relaxed monetary policy, however, could not prevent the recession of 1973, the worst since the Great Depression to that point. Double-digit inflation and unemployment characterized this textbook recession, which ran from April of 1973 until the spring of 1975. On October 6, 1973, Syria and Egypt launched a military attack on Israel, starting the Yom Kippur War. When the members of OAPEC (Organization of Arab Petroleum Exporting Countries, consisting of the Arab members of OPEC plus Egypt and Syria) proclaimed an oil embargo "in response to the U.S. decision to resupply the Israeli military during the Yom Kippur War," the effect on the U.S. economy was severe. Worsening this oil crisis, OPEC realized its power over the global economy when OPEC members agreed to use their leverage over the world price-setting mechanism for oil in order to stabilize their real incomes by raising world oil prices. Ultimately, oil prices quadrupled. This period also saw a crash of all the major stock markets in the world, particularly the London Stock Exchange in the United Kingdom. The New York Stock Exchange's Dow Jones Industrial Average benchmark lost over 45 percent of its value. In fact, Pierre Perron of Princeton University argued that the 1973 "oil price shock," along with the 1973–74 stock market crash, combined as the first event since the Great Depression to have a persistent economic effect.

The Iranian Revolution sharply increased the price of oil around the world in 1979, causing the 1979 energy crisis. This was caused by the new regime in power in Iran, which exported oil at inconsistent intervals and at a lower volume, forcing prices to go up. Tight monetary policy in the United States to control inflation led to another recession. The changes were made largely because of inflation that was carried over from the previous decade due to the 1973 oil crisis and the 1979 energy crisis.

There was a brief period of relief and positive sentiment during the second Reagan presidential campaign, but it is arguable whether there was actually a reprieve from the oil shock and the recession of the early 1980s. The '79 recession lasted until the end of 1982. Unemployment floated around 7.5 percent before peaking at 10.8 percent at the end of this recession, and the inflation rate peaked at 13.5 percent. Before the crisis of 2007–10, this was regarded as the worst recession since the Great Depression. In the wake of the 1973 oil crisis and the 1979 energy crisis, "stagflation" began to afflict the economy of the United States. Stagflation is an economic situation in which inflation and economic stagnation occur simultaneously and remain unchecked for a period of time. The concept is notable partly because, in postwar macroeconomic theory, inflation and recession were regarded as mutually exclusive, and also because stagflation has generally proven to be difficult and costly to eradicate once it gets started. Several key industries—including housing, steel manufacturing, and automobile production—experienced a severe downturn, and many of the economic sectors that supplied these basic industries were also hard-hit.

Determined to wring inflation out of the economy, Federal Reserve chairman Paul Volcker slowed the rate of growth of the money supply and raised interest rates. The federal funds rate, which was about 11 percent in 1979, rose to 20 percent by June 1981. The prime interest rate, at the time a highly important economic measure, eventually reached 21.5 percent in June 1982. It is generally agreed that the contradictory monetary policy established by the Federal Reserve was a primary cause of this recession. This is particularly disturbing when you consider that the 2008 crisis came amid low inflation and interest rates in the low-to-middle single digits. Volcker's determination to "wring" inflation out of the system produced the sort of collateral damage that in hindsight seems inevitable. In contrast, in the recent collapse, the monetary policy was the sort that would "normally" cause the economy to overheat.

Even the recession of the early 1990s could be directly tied to the rapid decrease of industrial production and manufacturing-trade sales in early 1991. There was a drop in demand caused by a debt buildup in the 1980s by individuals, businesses, and the federal government. Apprehension caused by high structural unemployment of both blue- and white-collar workers slowed the recovery. Some even considered this recession to be a delayed reaction to the Black Monday crash of October 1987, in which the Dow Jones Industrial Average suffered an unprecedented loss of 22 percent. The collapse (larger than that of 1929) initially seemed to have been handled well by the economy and the stock market, but it soon turned out that the quick recovery was illusory, and by 1990 economic malaise had returned with the beginning of the Gulf War and the resulting 1990 spike in the price of oil. For the next several years, high unemployment, massive government budgetary deficits, and slow GDP growth affected the United States economy.

The failure of traditional industry was soon muted by a revolution: the PC revolution. By the middle of the 1990s, millions of personal computers had been sold and a previously little-known government project (the Internet) became the worldwide information superhighway. Nevertheless, too much of a good thing is never a good thing, and the idea that the Internet changed everything was overhyped, which eventually gave way to the collapse of the dot-com bubble. Adding insult to injury, the September 11 attacks and accounting scandals of the Enrons and Arthur Andersens of the world contributed to a relatively mild contraction in the North American economy.

After the collapse of the so-called "new" Internet economy, we were left where we'd been after the 1987 stock market crash. With each of the crashes and recessions since World War II, the country has subsisted off the ingestion of one after another of its industries. Each recession has left us weaker than we were before it. We have fed like cannibals off mergers and acquisitions, as real productivity has been replaced with accounting tricks.

When Smith and Keynes Break Down

We should question why residential housing became the linchpin of the global economy. We have to consider the systemic problems. Can we really thrive as a 99 percent service economy? Will the economic model of the Bahamas carry the last remaining superpower? The answer is obvious.

Pure free markets can achieve equilibrium in certain circles but cannot achieve broad-based progress. Each of the recessions detailed above demonstrates a breakdown in both the philosophies of Smith and Keynes.

The free market would not and could not have created the Internet, for the fundamental reason that it would not have been profitable to create. Its development would have been cost prohibitive for any one company, and, without the benefit of our hindsight, it would have seemed like a highly speculative investment that the shareholders of any major corporation would not have stood for. Interests other than the bottom line created the Internet.

Also, we now know that Volcker's 20 percent interest rates were destructive. Lowering interest rates and raising interest rates do not have balanced, alternate effects, perhaps mostly because there is a limit of zero to lowering rates, but there is no limit to how high rates can go.

Despite Keynesian theory, the best role of governments in economics is not to substitute for market interests, but to provide the infrastructure, environment, and regulation for market interests to thrive. That is not to say the government should have as little a role as libertarians would suggest. As with the Internet, the government and not-for-profit organizations must do the heavy lifting of creating a platform for commerce, allowing the private sector to come behind and create the businesses and innovations to drive continual growth. Smith takes for granted that the platform for commerce is already in place.

Further, one has to ask if Smith dogma really encompasses the scope of a global, Internet-based, jet-set economy, in which stakeholders sit in the far-flung corners of the world and not necessarily at the bargaining table. Twentieth-century economic history strongly suggests that when large, systemically important entities act purely in their own self-interests, there are damaging effects felt, most often by regular people. In bilateral, arms-length transactions, mutually opposing self-interests may create a fair exchange that is further improved by competition. The problem is that there are many, many more ways in which business takes place. Today, the participation of banks, governments, corporations, labor unions, investment funds, and exchanges has elevated the complexity of economic behavior and transactions. The depths of complexity have given cover to those whose self-interest has led them to commit fraud, distort valuations, pervert markets, and cash out of bubble after bubble.

We must look at the underlying morality of the whole system that promotes and encourages the concept that pursuing self-interest is a good thing. Defenders of Smith emphasize that Smith was not advocating a social policy (that people *should* act in their own self-interest), but rather was describing an observed economic reality (that people *do* act in their own interest). It may be true that he did not argue that self-interest is always good, but rather that self-interest is not necessarily bad.

The problem, though, is not whether self-interest works when it works, but rather whether it excludes—or worse yet, suppresses. Many capitalists believe that without unfettered markets, innovation starves, prosperity weakens, and societies stagnate, and therefore the selfish pursuit of money is good, even moral. While there is some truth to that, is it *entirely* true? Are the best technologies the most frequent winners? Do the largest companies generally allow competing innovations from small, unknown sources?

The fact is that, more often than not, the "real world" application of Smith is to squelch competition to such a degree that even so-called venture capitalists are terrified to back new companies that intend to go head-to-head against entrenched companies. The thing about the butcher, the brewer, and the baker is that they are on relatively even ground, occupying complementary roles. In the modern economy, there are corporations with greater wealth than entire nations. According to an Institute for Policy Studies report, "Top 200: The Rise of Corporate Global Power," by Sarah Anderson and John Cavanagh, released December 4, 2000, a majority of the world's largest economic entities are corporations: fifty-one are corporations, while forty-nine are countries in the top one hundred. Some would argue that a number of these corporations actually *control* some nations. Private enterprises with this much power devote great resources to maintaining the status quo and bolstering barriers to competition from up-and-coming busi-nesses, all with the "justification" of self-interest.

In the highly competitive realm of small businesses, Smith works out fine, but let's take a look at a few examples of what has happened to innovative technologies that were not backed by major corporations and that could actually have threatened the business of large, multinational corporations:

- The ultrasonic washing machine (U.S. Patent 4727734): Created as an alternative to traditional washers that use agita-tion and chemicals to wash textile products, the machine, for which the inventor received his patent on March 1, 1988, has no moving parts, can be cheaply mass-produced, needs no chemicals, and most importantly, works arguably better than anything now on the market. Clothes are placed in a basin of water and an ultrasonic wave generator at the base of the machine creates millions of tiny air bubbles to help loosen grime and grit on clothes in a purely mechanical action. The benefits of this invention are too plentiful to enumerate here. Any textile that could be placed in cold water could be cleaned. With no moving parts, maintenance would be negligible, and the reduced use of detergent chemicals would minimize environmental impact. The device could easily be mass-produced, making it cost-competitive with existing machines. So, why has this obviously superior technology been sitting on the shelf for over twenty years? The answer is that the inventor was contacted by several major corpora-tions representing various entrenched interests, each seeking an angle by which they could profit from his invention. Yet lacking any intrinsic obsolescence or external dependencies, they could find none. Did they pay him off to bury it? Who can say . . . or rather, who *would* say? Assuming that no crimi-nality was involved, and even that they may have achieved an equitable agreement, how was the public good served by the withholding of this technology?

- Electrolytic hydrogen combustion engine (U.S. Patent 7273044): This hydrogen fuel system for an internal combustion engine is one of dozens of patented technologies to run a car on water. You read correctly! This is one of dozens of patented technologies to run an internal combustion engine on water. Water is, after all, two parts hydrogen and one part oxygen. Hydrogen is ultimately what we "burn" in gasoline, natural gas, or any other hydrocarbon. An engine that splits and combines water to produce all the power (maybe more) of a gasoline- or diesel-powered engine is not just theoretically possible; it is a very real technology that is here now. The patent cited above was issued on September 25, 2004, but the existence of this technology is virtually unknown. There are other "hydrogen-on-demand" vehicles that have been produced that use a chemical reaction to produce hydrogen as needed to run the car or truck. Either way, the idea of engines that don't pollute, don't require gas stations, and that can power the same cars (everything from compacts to SUVs) we have today, without depending on some phantom, future technology that is always in the offing, should be a no-brainer.

Yet it is the self-interest of entrenched powers that preclude the development and distribution of these technologies. More than 97 percent of the world's petroleum is used for transportation. Some of the richest nations in the world are rich only because of their oil exports. ExxonMobil made over $45 billion in profit in 2008. Many agree that petroleum commerce is the cornerstone of the global economy. Even governments that are compromised by their nation's dependence on foreign oil fear the ramifications of a wholesale shift away from it. It is in the self-interest of all of these powers to suppress or destroy any real competition to fossil fuels. It may also be in their self-interest to give lip service to alternatives by promoting untenable energy sources, but not to endorse real alternatives.

Short of the dramatic instances above, history has proven time and again that the best innovations are often squelched by more powerful competition. No one who really knows software believes that Microsoft writes the best computer programs, particularly in terms of power, stability, and security. Anyone who knows videography knows that Betamax was superior to VHS. No doubt there are many other examples buried in the files at the U.S. Patent Office.

I experienced this reality personally as a callow young investor. More times than I can recall in my early days trading stocks, I lost money investing in companies with remarkable, innovative technologies that were more advanced than the competition. My technical knowledge was my Achilles heel. One such company in which I bought stock was Paradigm Technology, a company that was known in its day by the computer engineering community to produce the most sophisticated SRAM (memory) chips for computers at the time. No reputable source that I can recall or find denied that fact. But the more powerful interests in the industry, companies like Micron and Samsung, instead pushed DRAM memory-chip technology, which everyone in the business knows is functionally inferior to SRAM. I could elaborate on why, but that is not the point. The whole industry followed the big business interests of companies like Micron (still a king of the memory-chip business) instead of delivering the best actual product to the masses. To this day, most computers use the inferior DRAM, and Paradigm has been out of business for years.

Some would suggest that history is replete with David and Goliath success stories of business started in garages, like Dell or Microsoft, but a closer examination of this history show almost without exception that the successful upstart always targets an aspect of business that entrenched companies either neglected or hadn't conceived of. Microsoft targeted a market that IBM had little interest in at the time. In fact, IBM helped them get up and going because they saw the PC market as trivial. Dell pioneered the negative cash-conversion accounting model and a cutting-edge product-delivery system. Much harder to find are examples of small startups that succeeded at going head-to-head against behemoths without such radical innovations. Simply a better product at a better price is not enough for success in a cannibal capitalist system.

All of this suggests that the Smith doctrine, when allowed to grow dramatically beyond the scale of the butcher, the brewer, and the baker, breaks down and fails to provide the greatest benefit to the greatest number. On the other hand, Keynesian practices can also go too far and create conditions for unsustainable dependencies. Without clearly charting a course between competing theories and ideologies, we have drifted into cannibal capitalism, a system in which innovation is starved, prosperity has declined, and a stagnant economy subsists on recycled debt financing.

A financier from whom I once sought project financing summed it up. After acknowledging that I had a great project that should be very profitable, he asked me, "Why would I tie my money up in a project for a year or more when I can get the same return with a leveraged financial instrument in a couple months?" This is the sort of cannibal capitalist thinking that has devolved the economy from one that makes stuff to one that just grows debt. The word "finance" should more often be a verb, a means to an end, but the reality is that it is more often a noun, an end in itself. Instead of a mechanism to drive the real economy, it is solely a mechanism to make money by draining the real economy of its wealth.

CHAPTER FIVE

Devolution of the Real Economy through Cannibal Capitalism

Born into an impoverished family later broken by the Great Depression, he dared not dream for too much in life. He survived combat in World War II and was witness to hopelessness and death, but survived it all and returned home, victorious and determined to make his life count.

His sweetheart had fearfully yet patiently waited to become his wife and to raise a family. She too shared his positive view of the future: their life would be better. His name is not important, because you could likely substitute any name I provide with a member of your own family.

Ten years later, they had a home in one of those planned communities later described as suburbia, six children, a dog, a new car, and he had a good job earning $4,600 a year, slightly higher than the national median in 1955. The home cost $9,000 with a mortgage payment of about $50 a month. A gallon of milk cost 92¢, a loaf of bread was 18¢, a dozen eggs cost 61¢, and a five-pound pot roast could be bought for $2. With a modest income, he could support his family by himself, build their savings, and set a course for a better future for his children.

Fifty-one years later, in 2006, the median salary of a single income family was $45,757. If you lived near a major city, the median cost of a single family home was over $550,000, which at a 6.5 percent interest rate on a thirty-year fixed mortgage would cost about $3,500 a month, not counting escrows for taxes and insurance. With a biweekly take-home pay of $1,400, owning the median home was a pipe dream. A gallon of milk cost $3.75, a loaf of bread was $3, a dozen eggs cost $2, and a five-pound pot roast at $5.99 a pound was nearly $30! While income rose by multiples of ten, the cost of a loaf of bread rose to 16.6 times what it was, and the cost of a home rose sixty-fold.

Visible Decline of the Middle Class

Any way you slice it, it is simply not possible to reproduce the lifestyle of our parents in today's economy without earning an income that is substantially higher than the median. Once upon a time in America, a man could support his family working as a door-to-door vacuum salesman. There were "good jobs," such as milkman or elevator operator, that only required a minimal education. Today, a "good job" is computer programmer, architect, or engineer, all of which require extensive education, though less than that of a doctor or lawyer. Yet even these "good jobs" aren't good enough.

According to Salary.com, at the time of this book's publication, a moderately experienced computer programmer makes about $60,000 per year, a fully licensed architect makes about $70,000, and a mechanical engineer can make $80,000. What you may find utterly shocking is that, by some measures, the buying power of a mechanical engineer today is less than that of a milkman in the fifties. A mechanical engineer making $80,000 cannot afford a median-priced single-family home in most of the major metropolitan suburbs, where an engineer is most likely to command that kind of income. In these places, an $80,000 income can mean living paycheck to paycheck. I know that, where I live, at that income you are either living in an apartment, a rough neighborhood, or commuting three hours a day. At best, with a spouse that is just as well paid, you can squeak by with a double income.

How the *heck* did that happen?

Think about this. You do all the right things. Get good grades, go to college, develop a reputable skill, even pursue a graduate-level degree, and still barely make ends meet. If that is the case for those who are exceptional, what hope is there for the average folk?

This is the destruction of the middle class, and we are complicit in this villainy. Our system has cannibalized our people. The wealth of millions is being devoured to such a degree that even the best are doomed to little more than corporate serfdom.

Corporate serfdom? Isn't that an extreme characterization? I don't think so. Serfdom was the enforced labor of serfs (members of a servile feudal class) on the fields of landowners, in return for protection and the right to work a little for themselves on their leased fields. Serfdom involved not only work in fields, but also various other activities, like forestry, mining, transportation (both land- and river-based), and crafts. Manors formed the basic unit of society during this period, and the lord and his serfs were bound together legally, economically, and socially. Serfs were laborers who were bound to the land; they formed the lowest social class of the feudal society. The serf worked harder than the others and was the worst fed and paid, but at least he had his place and, unlike the slave, he enjoyed the illusion of his own land and property (although it could always be taken away). Serfdom bound not only an individual, but also all of his future heirs. His status and that of his family remained the same or worsened as he enriched the life of his lord.

Sound at all familiar?

Today, instead of land, working people are attached to the abstract economic system and are indentured to corporations. Corporations are the barons of our day. Corporation employees are now the core economic engine of our society. "Protection" is conferred through salary, benefits, and credit. Your home is actually "owned" by another corporation. In fact, all major personal property is acquired through financial schemes to enrich corporations. Most people are utterly dependent on the corporation. Despite the illusion of independence and self-determination, if one's employing corporation suffers losses, there is a risk of losing everything. People may struggle and save to build better lives for their children, and yet they raise their children to live the same way, as serfs to corporations.

It's a cliché but true that the more things change, the more they stay the same. The big difference is that the quality of life of the modern corporate serfs is astronomically better than the serfs of the past. For most of the last fifty to sixty years, technology has given rise to an ever-improving standard of living, and people are relatively content despite the subtly felt reality of their decreasing share of the nation's wealth. The almost imperceptible degradation of the middle class, though shrouded by pacifying distractions, has been constant since its broad-based creation at the end of World War II.

One must first recognize that the concept of a middle class is relatively new and is very fragile. Frankly, it is a product of the twentieth century. The combination of industrialization, unionization, early globalization, education, financial ventures, and government programs and subsidies transformed post–World War II America, creating the world's largest middle class. Since then, changes in each of these contributing forces have threatened to rip us apart.

Historically, the modern middle class is an anomaly. Even today, most of the world consists of rich and poor, elites and peasants, as has been the case for millennia. Considering that it has been that way for centuries, we must fear that, without intervention, natural economic forces will continue to drive the economic status of Americans into those extremes. Many agree that income disparity is at an all-time high. Yet because the drift has been moving incrementally, almost imperceptibly, no one but those on the extreme left are outraged. Most take for granted that the middle class will always exist and falsely believe that it always has. Something that has been a certain way for fifty years cannot be assumed to "always" be the same. Frankly, the free market is ambivalent about maintaining and developing the middle class.

The invisible hand of the free market seeks a balance between buyer and seller, supply and demand, producer and consumer. Cost is a critical component to commerce, and labor is a component of cost. From a dispassionate, market-centric view, full employment is a terrible thing because it forces employers to compete with others for human resources, thereby raising labor costs and upsetting market balances. Ideally, from that point of view, for every job, there should be multiple, qualified applicants effectively competing to do the job for the least money.

Regular workers rarely recognize that. That is why unions are such a force; unions accomplish labor-price fixing through collective bargaining. When various, equally qualified individuals apply for the same job, the employer will generally pick the one who will do the job for the least pay. As an employer, I loved to see high unemployment rates among people with skill sets that I needed. You run an ad, get more applicants than you can handle, and get to have your pick. But is that good for the broader society? I think not.

A very tough reality to come to grips with is that the large middle class that was needed in the recent past is not needed anymore. Globalization, automation, and the maturity of the country's infrastructure and marketplace have all contributed to a lessening of the demand for an unspecialized workforce, historically a large component of the middle class. The transition to a service economy has created jobs, but only in parity with losses, and, generally, these new service jobs pay less than lost industry jobs. Even when the numbers look innocuous or even positive, the reality is often dire for regular people. While economists focus on the means, modes, and medians, the numbers do not reveal the problem. Upper incomes skyrocket and lower incomes crash, but the macroeconomic numbers seem just fine. However, when you divide the population into wealth groups as shown in Figures 5.1 and 5.2, you begin to see the seriousness of the actual disparities.

Nevertheless, it's not all bad news. We have seen growth in technology in recent decades, which then drives job creation in supporting industries. It is for this reason that we haven't seen constant declines, but rather cyclical contractions. Yet with the declines in other areas of the job market, new grads find themselves in a more competitive environment that also suppresses wage growth. The net effect is stagnation. In fact, more recently, the net effect got so bad that mainstream economists finally started to notice.

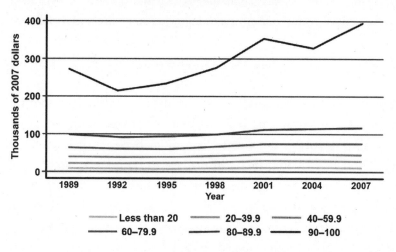

Figure 5.1

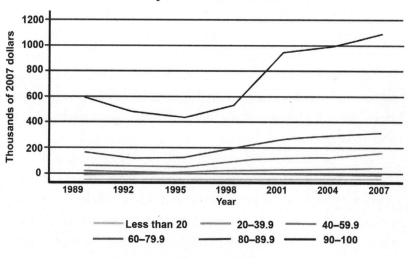

Figure 5.2

This is all simple supply and demand. We don't need many factory workers. The best price to market involves outsourcing to India and China. The market is seeking equilibrium. If we mess with the natural market flows, it's socialism! We're not socialists!

Thus, we have the conundrum: what is the proper balance between (1) leaving the free market alone, unchecked, and (2) direct government involvement or even economic planning, what some decry as socialism?

New Deal Gone Wrong

Franklin Delano Roosevelt was called a socialist, communist, and fascist, all because he believed that the government had to do something to correct the Great Depression. Between the New Deal and World War II, Roosevelt did manage to lead the country out of the Great Depression, regardless of whether he deserves the credit.

Some suggest that the New Deal failed to strike the balance between the extreme left and right, and may even have slowed economic recovery. Particularly, this position is argued by UCLA economists Harold L. Cole and Lee E. Ohanian in their report "New Deal Policies and the Persistence of the Great Depression: A General Equilibrium Analysis," as well as in other articles. They contended that FDR's policies prolonged the Great Depression by seven years.

The greater number of economists and historians believe that Roosevelt restored hope and self-respect to tens of millions of desperate Americans. Most would agree that his administration's support of labor unions and upgrades of the national infrastructure greatly helped the struggling workforce and curbed economic decline, if not completely reversing it.

Some would even say that FDR saved capitalism in his first term, when he could have destroyed it by going to the extreme of completely nationalizing the banks and the railroads. While many of the New Deal initiatives were foolhardy and were quickly abandoned, others are so widely recognized as necessary that it would be political suicide to mess with them even today. Particularly, the Securities and Exchange Commission (SEC), the Federal Deposit Insurance Corporation (FDIC), the Social Security Administration, and the Federal National Mortgage Association (Fannie Mae) are responsible for greatly improving the economic health and growth of the nation for the last fifty years.

The engineers of the New Deal were not all of the same ilk and ideology. Some were political idealists, and others were hypothesizing economists who used the administration in order to experiment with the economy. As is common with scientific processes, some results were entirely unexpected. I believe that FDR just wanted to end the Great Depression, and would have been completely content with a return to the economy of the turn of the century. What he actually did was create the circumstances for the working class of twentieth-century America to live at the standard of the wealthy gentry of the past. Working people would no longer be peasants, as they'd been as recently as a generation earlier. Minimum wage and maximum hours; the elimination of child labor; weekends; the increased economic output started by World War II; labor unions backed by the power of the government in the form of the National Labor Relations Board; and other reforms all combined to cut the labor supply and raise wages and the quality of life for millions. The modern middle class emerged as a major force, which then drove the creation of new industries and a service economy.

So remarkable was the recovery that many of the bigheads chalked it all up to the American way, as if it were inevitable that we would create the world's largest middle class and highest standard of living. Between the '50s and the '90s, the median income nearly doubled during each successive decade. Through bubble and bust, this persistent progress has fostered the belief that this is just the way it is and will always be.

Nevertheless, with the exception of a few cornerstone programs, the New Deal has been dismantled piece by piece ever since. Worse still, the thinking of Roosevelt has been demonized progressively to such a degree that re-creating or reenergizing the factors that created this economy is politically unviable. It seems that President Obama would like to be the next Roosevelt, but the political positions that developed in opposition to the New Deal have calcified to such a degree that, beyond revisionist economists like Cole and Ohanian, there is powerful institutional opposition to anything that remotely smacks of socialism. Between 1970 and

2000, there has been a slow-moving wave of deregulation, reversing not only the policies of the New Deal, but reversing its very philosophy.

This deregulation reached a crescendo on November 12, 1999, with the Gramm-Leach-Bliley Act, which effectively repealed provisions of the Glass-Steagall Act that prohibit a bank-holding company from owning other financial companies. Many experts claim that this repeal directly led to the housing crash and thereby the global economic collapse that followed it.

Deregulation gained momentum in the 1970s, influenced largely by Chicago School of Economics theorists Ludwig von Mises, Friedrich von Hayek, and Milton Friedman, among others. Picking up on this, political think tanks in Washington, the Brookings Institution, and the American Enterprise Institute enthusiastically held seminars and published studies advocating deregulatory initiatives throughout the 1970s and 1980s.

What followed? Deregulation of transportation, energy, communications, and banking. The Railroad Revitalization and Regulatory Reform Act of 1976 was the first in a series of acts that deregulated transportation in the United States. It was followed by the Airline Deregulation Act of 1978, the Staggers Rail Act of 1980, and the Motor Carrier Act of 1980. The Emergency Natural Gas Act, which was signed on February 2, 1977, in an effort to contend with OPEC price hikes and the 1973 oil crisis, deregulated a significant area of energy production. The Telecommunications Act of 1996 was a major overhaul of United States telecommunications law that had remained relatively unchanged since 1934, aside from the breakup of AT&T. The act was claimed to foster competition, but it actually continued the historic industry consolidation begun by Reagan, whose actions reduced the number of major media companies from around fifty in 1983 to ten in 1996. By 2005, that number fell even further, to only six. For obvious reasons, we should all be concerned about concentration of media ownership resulting from the deregulation of controls that were designed to safeguard diversity of viewpoint and open discussion across society.

Yet, of all the economic sectors that were intended to be addressed by New Deal reforms, the most important were those focused on the financial sector. The conservative movement successfully dismantled many of these controls, as the nation forgot the lessons learned in the crash of '29 and the Great Depression. The junk bonds and M&As of the '80s and the booms and busts of the '90s ultimately climaxed with the crash of 2007–8.

All of this deregulation and the profiteering that followed has decimated the middle class. It is ultimately cannibalistic, because the many industries that subsist on the consumerism of the middle class are ultimately undermined. The harder it is to feed your kids, the less likely you are to use hard-earned money on anything not absolutely necessary. If the middle class isn't supported—or rather, promoted—the contraction of the economy will exceed the nightmares of those who have taken for granted that the way things have been is the way things will always be. Is it time to plan or still trust in the invisible hand?

While the middle class is the victim, it is a complicit victim, even if the complicity is based on ignorance. Everyone learns to read and is encouraged to do so. That so many don't is a pity, but hardly an excuse. The meritocratic elements of the system make it entirely possible for a person born into the modern serfdom to be elevated to the upper echelons of society. This is perhaps uniquely American.

For those who flow with the current of the system as it is, there is guidance to direct them where to go, what to think, and how to live. The status quo is well maintained. From early childhood, you are shunted into an education based on memorizing rules and compliance with the system. It's not too hard to sum up what people are conditioned to view as the ideal life. Think about what we have all been told. You know the rules. Walk in single file, memorize facts and patterns (after all, you will be tested and graded on how well you memorized those facts and patterns), get good grades, go to college, get a good job, work hard as a loyal employee, save your money in a bank, marry your high school sweetheart, buy a house, plan for retirement with a 401(k), and retire to a warm place before you die. In fact, many would sincerely feel that getting that all done constitutes a very successful life.

Yet rarely do the most successful people follow those rules. To the contrary, because of our preoccupation with sports and entertainment, some of the highest paid people were, as adolescents, class clowns or otherwise disengaged from academics. Some of the richest men in the world, including such billionaires as Microsoft's Bill Gates and Oracle's Larry Ellison, are college dropouts. As we discussed in the previous chapter, "good jobs" don't really cut it. Loyalty in the workplace is generally a one-way street, demanded from employees but rarely shown by employers. A typical savings account pays less than 1 percent interest, and even the best certified-deposit accounts rarely pay more than the inflation rate. In other words, our savings constantly lose value. While we put our money in the banks for negligible interest, the banks leverage forty to one with our money to pursue risky investments, which in good times reap colossal returns and in bad times are covered with tax dollars. The divorce rate for first marriages is the best when compared to those of second and third marriages, but unfortunately, it is still at about 50 percent. So, while your best shot may be your high school sweetheart, your chances still aren't that good. The one thing that people have always thought they could count on is home ownership, but even that isn't as trustworthy as you would think. Need I go on?

There is no new deal. It is the same old raw deal. It is a system-wide scam to use the strong backs and eager minds of the masses as fodder to build up the rich and powerful. That they don't realize their commonality with the rest of us only makes them ignorant cannibals.

CHAPTER SIX

Your Own Opinion or Own Facts? Selective Morality

When Johnny Carson left late night television, a three-way ratings battle ensued. Jay Leno and David Letterman continued a much longer rivalry, but at its beginning, there was a third contender—Arsenio Hall. Other than such highlights as having Bill Clinton play the sax with the show's band during the 1992 presidential campaign, Hall's show failed to sustain the sort of content that the remaining kings of late night have become known for. Nevertheless, there was one bit that I often enjoyed. He called it "Things that Make You Go Hmmm." He would generally cite some irony of popular culture or satirize politics. A lot of what he would say would miss the mark, but now and then he would nail something or someone. Maybe it would offend, inciting a groan from the crowd, or maybe it would just provoke a hearty laugh, but when it was good, it did make you think. Much of what I am about to say is in that spirit.

Why is it that the very conduct we expect, in fact demand, from children is so rarely followed by us as adults, and certainly not by our institutions? Hmmm. Why do we choose political positions and parties based on unrelated social issues that may never come up, instead of factors germane to policies that are certain to come up?

Hmmm. Why is this melting pot of a multicultural, pluralistic society tearing itself apart over cultural identity? Hmmm.

Opposing Parties or Warring Factions?

It is noteworthy to recognize that most of the big debates of our day are not really argued consistently, honestly, or even logically. Political opponents will get up in arms, whine like children, fail to seek common ground, lie, and demonize each other over artificially drawn lines of conflict. Even when the lines are real, they are rarely relevant to the most serious matters confronting the nation. Everyone claims the Constitution and the moral high ground as they each verbally eviscerate one another. The most consistent victim of this rhetorical warfare is the truth. Collateral damage is done to the needs of the nation, which remain unaddressed in the midst of the fiercest political battles.

Sadly this cannibalism is moored to our tradition of freedom, particularly freedom of thought. While we cherish our freedom, we suffer with its unpleasant side effects—moral relativism and its attendant hypocrisy. There is no moral authority universally accepted, no "parent," so morality is subject to perspective. Morality that is flaccid cannot help but give birth to controversy, and controversy is something we have in a debilitating abundance.

Much of the political rancor and intransigence that immobilizes the democratic process can be traced to the immorality that certain groups decide to selectively ignore, while at the same time condemning other forms of immorality. The demagoguery that is so prevalent in today's news debates is most frequently based on selective moralizing. You're a villain for these "sins," but those "sins" are completely understandable. If you don't agree, there is something wrong with you, and all of your opinions should be devalued to nothing. The opposers should be devoured; it's as if politicians were like those cannibal tribes who felt that killing your enemies was not complete until you feasted on their corpses. This is the nature of our biggest, most controversial public debates. Matters with the greatest socioeconomic significance that are critical to the health of the nation are neglected, while we fight over irreconcilable social views tied to cultural identity. These socioeconomic fights have become so vitriolic, as the "socio" overwhelms the "economic," that to seek common ground with the opposition is akin to making a deal with the devil. Meanwhile, these battles provide space for the pirates who exploit the confusion to cannibalize the nation's wealth. Factions are economically aligned against themselves, while only superficially pitted against each other over matters of exaggerated importance.

Ironically, this social war is rife with hypocrisy and inconsistent logic. Each side does precisely what it hypocritically accuses the other of doing with respect (or rather disrespect) to the facts. It is this hypocrisy that often creates inexorable rifts after the debate. Unrelated subjects become the basis for political identity. With a democratic process that relies on the organization of coalitions, the hypocrisy borne of moral relativism divides even those with common interests, making enemies of socioeconomic peers. These divisive issues undermine the pursuit of common needs. Will we ever see how self-destructive it is to devour the "others" who are none other than ourselves?

Hypocrisy of Moral Relativists

Theoretically, adherence to moral relativism should disqualify one from moralizing. Think about it. If you believe that truth is discovered in an individual's life course and that what is true for you may not be true for me, how can you condemn anyone for what he believes, even if it violates your moral sentiments? If you believe that right and wrong are subject to perspective and circumstances, how can you moralize about what other people do? Unfortunately, very few see it that way. Instead, most are perfectly content to hypocritically condemn certain wrongs while supporting or even committing other wrongs.

For instance, as the nation divides itself politically, you find some groups that focus intently on sins of a personal nature, and yet, inconsistently, will attack anyone who points out national sins. At the same time, others' priorities are the absolute converse. In

Harvard professor Michael Sandel's course "Justice: A Journey in Moral Reasoning," students are engaged in thought-provoking discussions on some of the most hotly contested issues of the day, including abortion, affirmative action, income distribution, and same-sex marriage. The careful analysis of these topics reveals that, very often, accepted standards of morality are not applied consistently, and in some cases opposing views are both valid and could thus never be reconciled. The very concept of consensus is nearly implausible in an environment of moral relativism.

So, how can we work together to build a "more perfect union" when the parameters of the world in which we each live are subjective? Moreover, when irreconcilable conflicts perpetually displace meaningful discussion of the serious problems that threaten our progress, but are otherwise solvable, how could we ever halt our economic attrition? Yet we continually allow ourselves to be driven by emotional inconsistencies, by hypocrisy. We need to take a more honest look in the mirror if things are to improve.

What inconsistencies am I talking about? Many who would proudly sing "my country right or wrong" would impeach a leader for marital infidelity. Some even criticized the president for merely mentioning regrettable American actions before foreign audiences, such as in President Obama's heralded June 2009 Middle East speech. The hypocrisy can be particularly overt if shrouded in patriotism. Patriotism can justify torture, napalm attacks, nuclear weapons, preemptive war, oppression of minorities, overthrowing governments, and many other atrocities, just as assuredly as it can unify a people, provide a sense of identity, and urge sacrifice and service for the greater good.

Nor is it consistent to lament public plights while completely ignoring personal morality. The very ones who weep over the plight of the poor also vehemently oppose any who would suggest a connection to moral conduct. Leftists who cry out for the legalization of marijuana completely ignore the proliferation of drug-related violence and prisons full of convicts who started down their dark path by smoking pot. They use the spurious reasoning that since everyone who uses recreational drugs doesn't become a criminal, drug use is not to blame.

Many bleeding hearts who have disavowed eating meat, who protest against cruelty to animals, and who may even go so far as to attack those wearing leather or fur, rarely show such concern for fellow humans beyond mock sympathy. Many will still wear diamonds mined by oppressed people, don clothes and other products produced in sweatshops, and subscribe to an overall system that destroys lives. Among those who find it very politically correct to decry animal abuse, it is not very politically correct to consider an unborn human life as anything more than a condition of the pregnant woman. On the other side, you have vigilante anti-abortion activists who consider themselves a sort of child-protective service while they bomb women's clinics. Inconsistencies? It's all crazy.

No one enjoys getting into the hard stuff, but let's take a stab. Our culture promotes sexual freedom while utterly failing to see how sexual immorality is the root cause of countless societal ills. Even those who publicly decry sexual promiscuity rarely practice what they preach. There have been far too many sex scandals among conservative politicians to give any weight to the right's professions of moral superiority in sexual matters. Whether politicians are rhetorically or physically hypocritical, as a matter of empirical fact, sexual promiscuity has its negative impact on society.

Premarital sex leads to ill-advised relationships. In turn, such relationships lead to bad marriages, single-parent families, or even abusive relationships, all of which degrade society by adding to stress and economic hardship of those involved. Extramarital sex undermines committed relationships. Even the prospect of adultery creates stress inside of a marriage, but when divorce actually occurs, the psychological, emotional, and economic turmoil is undeniable. As incendiary as it may be to say so, from a dispassionate, biological, and anthropological perspective, recreational sex, whether heterosexual or homosexual, does nothing to promote—and if practiced exclusively actually inhibits—healthy population development. Just because no one may have the right to dictate what you can or can't do in the privacy of your bedroom doesn't negate societal implications. One should ask what the crime rate would be if every child were born into a loving family with a committed father and mother. What would the divorce rate be if all marriages were based on deep compatibility instead of good sex had while dating? The implications of sexual morality are real. But who wants to mess with people getting their freak on? It is easier to be a hypocrite, even if the hypocrisy on all sides leads to a cannibal society where we all devour one another.

It is not to say that these and related matters could easily be remedied. They can't be. To the contrary, there is never a solution to a sensitive matter like any of these that would satisfy all. It is necessary, however, to recognize the damage caused to our system by the battles fought and lines drawn over these conflicting views. People demand their constitutional freedom to pursue happiness according to their independent views, but are not always content to permit others the same. Because of the absence of a central moral authority and thus the subjectivity of morality, social fragmentation is unavoidable in our society. Our founding documents may demand neutrality in matters of conscience, but conscience is hardly ever a neutral matter to an individual whose heart tells him strongly that something is right or wrong. One's convictions may be intensely powerful, shaping one's view of the world and one's view of those with conflicting opinions.

It's Intrinsic to Democracy

Many would take moral relativism as an axiom, in great part due to the lessons provided by centuries of abuse by moral authorities (particularly religious authorities) given absolute power. The famous quote "power tends to corrupt, and absolute power corrupts absolutely" was made with respect to a pope. Nevertheless, ubiquitous distaste for the concept of absolute right and wrong doesn't cause different people to prioritize and weigh morals in the same way. Various factions pick and choose from morals a la carte, giving some heavy significance in one context while completely ignoring violations to the same moral principle in other contexts.

Virtually every major issue that we debate in our country is rife with hypocrisy as we draw artificial lines with the ebbs and flows of common sentiment. Many of those who wish to present themselves as favoring small government and completely unfettered individual liberty, when examined more closely, actually seem to favor libertarian government for themselves and a restrictive, authoritarian government for the "others." Many of those who subscribe to a socially active form of government bristle at the notion of paying the taxes needed to facilitate such, but want someone else to pay for it. The only consistency is consistent hypocrisy. No particular faction has the monopoly on pharisaisms. The greater the controversy surrounding an issue, the greater the hypocrisy in the public debate of that issue.

Pundits and politicians conjure up the noblest-sounding phrases to define their political positions relative to their cultural views—pro-life versus pro-choice, marriage equality versus defense of marriage, equal opportunity versus state sovereignty, and individual freedom unhindered by small government versus government by the people that works for the people. All of these sound good. Why would anyone oppose any such ideals as they are packaged? It is hard to imagine that such labels are used by diametrically opposed positions in the most hotly contested debate of our modern era. And that's to say nothing of the pejorative expressions used to characterize the other side in these arguments. Representative Randy Neugebauer of Texas shocked observers of the passage of the health care reform on March 21, 2010, by shouting out "Baby killer!" as pro-life congressman Bart Stupak announced a deal struck with the president in order to vote in favor of the bill. It has become the norm to shroud one's side with a cloak of nobility while defaming the other side as the spawn of demons. Rarely does either side fully hold up to objective scrutiny as entirely free of inconsistencies.

The most acute areas of hypocrisy are seen in matters where religion asserts itself. The very concept of sin causes moral relativists to cringe. But fear not, because religion is where we find the greatest concentration of hypocrisy. Ironically, many religionists too subscribe to moral relativism.

Just look at all of the hoopla over gay marriage and gay rights. "Church folks" get particularly up in arms about homosexuality, and the Bible certainly does condemn homosexual sex acts, but no more than it condemns fornication, idolatry, lying, and many other acts that these people are all too ready to make excuses for. Moralizing about homosexuality while ignoring adultery and premarital sex is hypocritical. The hypocrisy is even more egregious when you consider the materialism, self-righteousness, discrimination, xenophobia, intellectual dishonesty, and intolerance that have come to characterize the stereotypical religious right.

Semantics of Social Warfare

Some of the fiercest arguments of our day boil down to semantics. Perhaps the two most divisive battles of the public dialogue hinge on the definition of "marriage" and "when life begins." In almost every case, the definitions to these terms given by candidates seeking public office are the most fundamental tests applied to qualify him or her in the eyes of the electorate. Elections have become proxy wars for social factions attempting to impose their menu of moral views on society. The social wars of abortion and homosexuality do nothing to advance the prosperity of the nation. Yet these battle lines determine who hold offices of leadership, the direction the nation takes, and the management of so many things that have nothing to do with marriage or abortion. Never mind competence, experience, or temperament; what is the candidate's view on…?

I am not making moral assessments here, and do not intend to suggest equivalency among all sides in all debates. I only suggest that there are problems with the framing of these debates and the distractions they cause. My complaint is not about the substance of any of these arguments. I don't care who or how people love. No one on earth has the right to interfere in the personal decisions of others. It's no one's business. If there is anything that is a fundamental right, it is the right to physical self-determination. The problem is the inconsistency and hypocrisy of the arguments, to say nothing of the way the arguments materialize into policy.

There seems to be very little interest in finding the proverbial happy median, even on the rare occasions when such exists. Interestingly, on the issue of gay marriage, when Bill Maher, social critic and host of HBO's *Real Time with Bill Maher*, made what may be the most balanced policy proposition to heal this breach to a panel of guests representing opposing political positions, he didn't get the response you might expect. He asked why *all* marriages aren't civil unions and why the government is involved at all in a religious institution. Neither his right-wing nor left-wing guests leapt at that suggestion. Really, do these factions actually want a solution or what? Probably not.

The issue of abortion is likely irreconcilable. It is not merely based on differences in lifestyles, but on contrary views of life. Instead of accepting the reality of these irreconcilable differences and focusing on matters where cooperation is possible, these issues have come to dominate political identity, often contrary to economic interest. Moreover, it is the nature of hypocrisy to want your opinion enforced against your opposition instead of compromising with them, and it is this sort of intransigence that locks us in a purgatory of economic torpor.

How can we as a nation deal with the issues of real importance, like war and peace, business and employment, health and welfare, or our place in the world in the era of globalization, when people are at each other's throats over bedroom politics? We fight to the death over God, guns, gays, and abortion, all while our leaders instigate these destructive fights to maintain power. Wall Street cannibalizes our real economy to drive their fake one, and China and the rest of the world gain economic advantages over us. These hypocritical fights are killing us.

Along this line, one of the greatest areas of utter hypocrisy is with regard to the role of government versus that of the free market. It is the ultimate left versus right debate, and even *it* is not argued honestly, consistently, or logically. Even libertarians who would say that government is the problem and should be excised from nearly every aspect of life would still expect a government-managed military, police protection, prisons, judicial arbitration, emergency management, basic civil services, and infrastructure. Those who do not tolerate such hypocrisy in their ideological views become intolerable to their political kin.

Take Rand Paul, who, as a senatorial candidate from Kentucky, felt compelled to defend private businesses' pre-civil-rights era "right" to refuse service to whomever they may choose. He told the *Louisville Courier-Journal* that the Civil Rights Act of 1964 should not apply to private businesses. While claiming that racial intolerance is abhorrent to him, his libertarian purity puts him in the position of supporting the notion of whites-only lunch counters, restaurants, or any other private establishment. The political sphere requires hypocrisy, instead of recognizing the inherent flaws in each and every corner of public debate.

The hypocrisy is apparent when we consider the arbitrary nature of the lines drawn and the self-interested selection of what should and should not be regulated; of what should be left to the invisible hand of the free market. Out of the 2007–9 U.S. economic crisis came what some call corporate socialism. The government ended up owning majority stakes in one of the world's largest insurance companies and what was once the world's largest carmaker. The expression "too big to fail" was the rationale for billion-dollar bailouts and the radical expansion of the government's role in the economy. Yet many long-time free marketers were silent about their handouts.

On the other hand, any assistance for "regular people" is a form of socialism that is unacceptable by this same lot. Debt financing of the wars in Iraq and Afghanistan is perfectly acceptable, while expanding the deficit for infrastructure, jobs, green initiatives, and health care reform is labeled as "plunging into Eurozone socialism" by the likes of Joe Scarborough, author of *The Last Best Hope: Restoring Conservatism and America's Promise*.

Most of these areas of institutional hypocrisy pit citizens against one another, degrading the civility of the civilization. There may even be damaging economic effects of duplicity in these areas. But there is one component of the system where hypocrisy routinely costs lives. It undermines countless businesses, threatens international competitiveness, and even threatens the solvency of the nation. The inability of a cannibal country to fully address health care honestly could prove fatal, in spite of the legislation Congress passed in 2010.

PART THREE:

WHERE ARE WE GOING?

The course is set: full speed ahead to self-destruction. But if this can be reversed or at least mitigated, it will require attention given to three important areas of our civilization: the health of the people, the education of the people, and the energy needs of the people. It will also require a realistic recognition of the function of the economy.

CHAPTER SEVEN

The Choice of Health

Whenever the words "health care" and "national" are combined, a third word invariably comes up,: "socialism." "Socialized medicine" has been a stinging, pejorative characterization of any involvement of the state in medical services, and that pejorative has helped maintain the status quo of the health care industry in the U.S. for more than a generation. This, combined with the isolationist tendencies of many Americans, makes it very easy to get traction with horror stories of problems with the health care systems in countries where the government is involved. Finally, add buzz phrases like "government between you and your doctor" and you have a formula to mount a serious battle against health care reform, which of course the cannibals did vehemently in 2009 and 2010. They all claimed to want to solve the health care crisis and even passed a historic bill, but any attempts to truly root out the systemic flaws of the American health delivery system were lambasted.

This self-defeating hypocrisy is a core characteristic of cannibal capitalism, and it has metastasized to all corners of our culture. Opponents eat each other alive, laying waste to the facts. While criticizing the health systems of other countries is commonplace, the facts don't speak well of the American system. You can't have an honest discussion without facing facts. What facts?

The State of Health

The U.S. spends more on health care per capita than any other U.N. member nation. It also spends a greater fraction of its national budget on health care than Canada, Germany, France, or Japan, all of which have national health care systems. Recent estimates put health care spending in the U.S. at approximately 17 percent of GDP. In 2008, health care spending in the United States exceeded $2.3 trillion (that's about $8,000 per person), and was projected to reach $3 trillion by 2012.[12] Health care spending is 4.3 times the amount spent on national defense.[13] In fact, the United States spends the most money on medical care of all advanced industrialized countries, but it performs more poorly than most on many measures of health care quality.[14]

The U.S. is 33 percent worse than the best country on mortality from conditions amenable to health care—that is, deaths that could have been prevented with timely and effective care.[15] The infant mortality rate in the U.S. is nearly seven deaths per thousand live births, compared with 2.7 in the top three countries.[16] Recent studies show that only a little more than half (54.9 percent) of adult patients receive recommended care. The level of performance is similar whether it is for chronic, acute, or preventive care and across all spectrums of medical care—screening, diagnosis, treatment, and follow-up.[17]

Underuse of care is sometimes a greater problem than overuse. Patients do not receive recommended care (as prescribed in national

---

12. Department of Health and Human Services, *National Health Expenditure Fact Sheet*, http://www.cms.gov/NationalHealthExpendData/25_NHE_Fact_Sheet.asp.

13. California Health Care Foundation, *CHCF Releases Annual Health Care Costs 101 Snapshot*, press release, March 2, 2005, http://www.chcf.org/media/press-releases/2005/chcf-releases-annual-health-care-costs-101-snapshot.

14. World Health Organization, *World Health Statistics 2009*, May 2009, http://www.who.int/whosis/whostat/EN_WHS09_Full.pdf.

15. Juan G. Gay, "Outcomes of Health Systems: Towards the Development of Indicators of Amenable Mortality," *Organisation for Economic Cooperation and Development*, October 9, 2009.

16. World Health Organization, *World Health Statistics 2009*.

17. Elizabeth A. McGlynn and others, "The Quality of Health Care Delivered to Adults in the United States," *New England Journal of Medicine* 348, no. 26 (2003): 2635–45.

medical specialty guidelines) about 46 percent of the time. Another 11 percent of patients receive care that is not recommended and potentially harmful, according to practice guidelines. Thirty percent of sick Americans report that their doctor did not review or discuss all of the medications they had taken in the last two years.[18]

Quality of care varies considerably by medical condition. People with cataracts receive about 79 percent of recommended care. Patients with alcohol dependence receive only about 11 percent of recommended care. People with diabetes receive only 45 percent of the care they need. Fewer than half of patients with diabetes have their blood sugar levels measured on a regular basis. Nearly a third (32 percent) of patients with coronary artery disease receive recommended care, and less than half (45 percent) of patients who suffer a heart attack receive medications that could reduce their risk of death by more than 20 percent. Evidence-based medicine indicates that when a patient has a heart attack, the likelihood of that person's dying from a second heart attack can be reduced by more than 40 percent through the use of beta-blockers.[19]

These sorts of statistics translate into very real, very preventable risks and even deaths. Since more than 40 percent of heart-attack patients do not receive beta-blockers, that noncompliance rate puts 450,000 Americans at substantially higher risk every day. Likewise, since only 65 percent of older adults are vaccinated against infections that commonly lead to pneumonia, nearly ten thousand deaths from pneumonia occur each year that could be prevented through regular vaccinations. Similarly, because patients with colorectal cancer receive only half (54 percent) of recommended care and less than two-fifths of adults are screened for colorectal cancer, nearly ten thousand deaths occur each year that could be prevented through routine screening and follow-up care. Patients with hypertension receive less than two-thirds

18. Elizabeth A. McGlynn, "Localize the Remedy: Community Efforts Can Ameliorate Poor Quality of Care," RAND, 2004, http://www.rand.org/publications/randreview/issues/summer2004/remedy.html.

19. RAND, "Landmark Study Finds American Adults Often Fail to Get Recommended Care, Posing 'Serious Threats' to Health," news release, June 25, 2003, http://www.rand.org/news/press.03/06.25.html.

of recommended care. Poor control of high blood pressure results in nearly 70,000 preventable deaths each year.[20]

I could go on with these details, but it would be easier for you to visit the web site of the National Coalition on Health Care. I do not share their agenda, but they have compiled a fairly comprehensive list of references. There are many other sources of the growing statistics demonstrating the flaws in the health care system. Pick your own. Whatever the source, the facts are facts.

Health Insurance Conundrum

From the early days of the Obama administration, despite other concerns gripping the nation, what to do about the quality, affordability, and access to health care was front and center. As always, the various factions came out in battle formation, and the rhetoric of those who either supported or opposed health care reform was often misdirected, if not disingenuous.

Unlike many subjects of public debate, health care is something everyone needs. It is a deeply personal matter that can, without exaggeration, even be of life-or-death importance. The importance of access to and affordability of quality health care cannot be overstated.

The cost of health care is one of the greatest impediments to job creation. From personal experience as a small businessman, I honestly can say that there were job roles that I outsourced principally to avoid the cost of health benefits.

Think about the numbers. At the time of this book's publication, a low-level office assistant typically makes less than $20,000 per year. That is about $800 per pay period, or roughly $1,600 per month. If such an employee is a woman of childbearing age, the monthly premium can cost up to $800 or more. Adding that to payroll taxes and other costs, and you will have nearly doubled the cost of a low-level employee. I actually used a company in India to do my bookkeeping to avoid these costs, as I am sure other businesses have. Universal public health care would be a boon to small

---

20. Ibid.

business and job creation, but then again, it would also decimate the trillion-dollar health insurance industry.

There has always been a lot of money to be made in the health care business. That means there are a lot of jobs and a lot of wealth to be protected. Depending on your perspective and proximity to the insurance industry, there were legitimate arguments against what some derided as "Obamacare," but to simply suggest that the government is incapable of paying for health care or that government involvement is worse than greedy corporate involvement is hypocritical propaganda made for political expedience. Health care, socialized or not, will be as good as its funding. There is the rub!

In our system, it seems that it is the job of the Democrats to create social programs and the job of Republicans to cut the funding to those programs, ensuring their failure regardless of whether they were well intended or well planned. Perhaps it is hopeless to expect a real solution to these real problems. We are, after all, a cannibal country where the good ideas of one side are decimated by the opposition. Compromise is both the greatest success and the greatest failure of the democratic process, as the health care legislation Congress passed in 2010 makes very clear.

During the 2009 health care debate, New York Congressman Anthony Weiner once left "Morning Joe" Scarborough speechless during a guest appearance on his MSNBC show with a simple question: "What value do health insurance companies add to health care?" His point was that while doctors, hospitals, pharmaceutical companies, and medical equipment manufacturers actually add value to justify their profits, health insurance companies profit merely due to their position between patients and health care, and not because of any value added to the system. It is a strong argument, and Morning Joe had no reply.

Truth be told, insurance companies do provide a very valuable service. They provide a social bureaucracy to aggregate wealth and use it to pay for the health care services needed by the participants in that bureaucracy. The extent to which health care is affordable to regular people is accomplished by health insurance. If there were no alternative to paying for health care directly without health insurance, then only the wealthiest would receive anything more than the simplest of medical care. The health insurance model does make health care (somewhat) affordable to the masses, at least theoretically.

Nevertheless, because nearly all American health insurance companies are now for-profit businesses, the interests of these businesses are not actually aligned with the interests of the greater public. The gamble these types of businesses make is that they hope to collect more revenue (premiums and other charges) than they have to pay out in benefits. This business model means that it is in the interest of the business to avoid covering sick people. Ideally, the goal would be to only pay enough in benefits to maintain credibility, retain healthy policyholders, sell new policies, and avoid paying anything more than that to anyone. It's funny how patients occasionally find services that were denied are suddenly covered when the public finds out through some news coverage (e.g., Alex Lange, a fat baby denied health care in 2009 due to the preexisting condition of "obesity," who was later covered after significant publicity). With trillions coming in, every percent retained means tens of billions pocketed, even though the moral implication of those retained earnings is that people may die from the lack of care. Though it can be sugarcoated and dressed up, the truth remains that every dollar *not* spent on overhead or someone's health becomes profit for someone. The incentive is to deny, deny, deny coverage.

Nevertheless, since everyone needs health care and the alternative of paying directly for medical services is unrealistic, the whole country is stuck with this system or nothing at all. Idealists have begun to ask if this is the best way. Is aggregating and redistributing wealth best handled as a capitalist enterprise? The stats above suggest not. Worse still, with our employer-based system, where health insurance is connected to payroll, the insurance companies take a piece out of every other business. These costs so weighed down General Motors that some called it a health plan that builds cars too.

Policy that was really in the national interest would seek to eliminate misaligned interests. Logic would indicate that you shouldn't have a health care system where the principal incentive is to deny health care.

Due to the fact that businesses in other countries are not burdened by the health costs that our employer-based health insurance system is, our international competitiveness would seem to require that we unshackle our businesses. The fact that we allow one sector of our economy to act as a parasite on every other business doesn't seem reasonable. The insurance industry is just one small segment of our economy, and health insurance is a subset of that. It's just not in the common interest to give so much for so little. Why must they get a piece of everyone's action? Why shouldn't this one niche, the health insurance companies, take one for the team?

Oh yeah . . . I almost forget. There is no team. It's every man for himself around here. This is cannibal country, after all. We are talking about hundreds of billions of dollars in profit raked in as these guys shuffle the money around and deny coverage. What capitalist would ever walk away from that kind of money for the greater good? No way! It's not gonna happen. The very notion is laughable.

The 2009–10 Health Care Debate

With the election of a Democratic president who had health care reform as a cornerstone of his national agenda, it was only to be expected that the health insurance companies would arm and align their troops for the battle that would precede any legislation. Reports indicated that in 2009, a half-billion dollars was spent on lobbyists, largely to undermine, if not prevent, any meaningful health care reform. That money was not funneled to just one party.

The way the debate took shape, it seemed that there was no earnest debate at all. You had to either believe that the pro-reform side was utterly inept at making a solid case for their agenda, or that at least some of them were in cahoots with their "opponents." Otherwise, what is the explanation for the reality that proponents never made—in fact, deliberately shied away from—the strongest arguments and best solutions? The best case never made prime time, but the most duplicitous opposition was given a broad audience. Instead, the pro-reform arguments were weakly framed from the beginning as "we have to do something" and "the status quo is worse," versus opponents' strong ideological tag lines, like "government takeover of health care," "moving toward socialism," or "unaffordable burden on our children." Some proponents took up the moral and nationalist arguments that it is unacceptable that this country has millions of uninsured and that we have fallen behind other countries, but these points fell flat against clearly focused opposition, whether or not grounded in reality.

Very few proponents of health care reform approached the matter economically, never mind that taking the burden of health care costs off of businesses would be far more significant than tax cuts. Tax cuts apply to profits. Health care costs are overhead. Lowering the cost of doing business is *much* more significant than just allowing a business to keep slightly more of its profit. Business financials include health care costs, and these costs are in the EBITDA (Earnings Before Interest, Taxes, Depreciation, and Amortization), which literally means that these are considered before taxes and many other economic factors. This accounting metric is used by businesses in capital planning, resource allocation, and pursuit of financing.

Worst of all was the ground given up in the public debate. When opponents said, "The government messes up whatever it touches," the point was allowed to stand. The premise that competition was the only way to lower costs was not only conceded, but actually embraced by proponents as the argument for why the public option was needed. This ridiculous approach actually created sympathy for the insurance companies, since it is not really fair for private enterprise to have to compete head-to-head against the central government, just as it is not fair for a mom-and-pop shop to have to compete head-to-head with a multibillion-dollar megacorporation. Instead of debating whether for-profit health insurance was best for the nation, the health insurance business was allowed to stand as a proxy for the entire free market system. Using free market rhetoric to promote a government health insurance program rang as hypocritical.

The problem in making dramatic improvements to health care a reality was that the *real* problems never reached the center of the debate. The environment was perfectly set for major health care reform, but those who promoted it showed apparent ineptness in connecting with the public and selling it. Democrats controlled the White House and both houses of Congress, and yet they lost the debate for major health care reform and had to settle for something that many considered so watered-down as to be almost worthless. Others have argued (with merit) that the final product was so riddled by political compromise that it could live up to the worst fiscal complaints levied against it in the debate.

Elimination of for-profit insurance in favor of what was commonly referred to as "single-payer health care" was off the table from the very beginning. This idea of centrally aggregating health care dollars transparently and without a profit motive was never compared head-to-head against the current system of aggregating health care dollars in the coffers of private corporations that get to rake a percentage off the top. That is not a debate that would have ended well for the private insurance business, and both sides moved early on to avoid it. Honest debate or hypocrisy—what do you think?

It may very well be by design that Democrats seem to have never come to grips with how to win the public debate. Some say that the left-wing party (Democrats) and the right-wing party (Republicans) are actually parts of the same bird. Each side feigns support for various segments of interests and ideologies, but thinly veiled is the more loyal support they maintain for big campaign contributors, most of which are common to both sides. Quips and sound bites rule the dialogue of the nation and do more to shape public opinion than the truth. People want chants, not nuance. When they really want to win, the left can use them as well as the right. "Yes we can" did far more for the election of President Obama than did his more professorial discussions. Yet the simple phrases like "the government between you and your doctor" and "socialized medicine" went largely unanswered, even when such statements were accompanied by hypocritical defenses of the "socialistic" Medicare and Social Security programs.

If so-called proponents of major health care reform had really wanted to win the debate, they could have done so with six simple tactics:

1. *Don't confuse them with the facts.* We all know that health care spending in the United States reached $2.4 trillion, and was projected to reach $3.1 trillion by 2012. It will likely reach $4.3 trillion by 2016. We know that we could go on about how health care spending is 4.3 times the amount spent on national defense. We pay far more than anyone else, and yet there are forty-six million people uninsured, and another one hundred million are underinsured. Yes, about half of the U.S. population has inadequate health care. It may be intellectually compelling that the U.S. is 33 percent worse than the best country on mortality from conditions amenable to health care—that is, deaths that could have been prevented with timely and effective care. If empathy were regarded as it should be, people would respond to the fact that, despite paying more than anyone else, the infant mortality rate in the U.S. is about seven deaths per thousand live births, compared with 2.7 in the top three countries. All of that is compelling and provides a sound basis for pursuing change, but it doesn't win the fight against the line "you want to nationalize health care!" In the sound-bite battle, numbers sound like a lot of blah, blah, blah. Yet proponents of health care reform never attempted to match rhetoric.

2. *Quip-for-quip.* When opponents said "socialized medicine," proponents of health care reform could have responded with "privatized medicine." When they said "government between you and your doctor," very few answered "greedy corporation between you and your doctor." When they talked about "nationalizing health care," proponents could have taken the moral offensive with "profiteering off the sick and dying." Quips and one-liners always win the day in this system, but all we heard was "we need to do something."

3. *Message sync.* By nature, progressives like nuance, intellectual depth, and individuality. Rarely will two progressives interpret the same view in the same way. Even when the entire movement is of one mind on a matter, the message comes through as confused noise, because everyone says things his or her own way. Any media-marketing expert will tell you that it takes consistent repetition to get a message across to the public. Proponents needed to say the same thing the same way. Perhaps they felt sullied by using this tried-and-tested Republican tactic, and refused to go with what works.

4. *Moralize, moralize, moralize.* As contrary as this may be to my earlier point about moral relativism, in the real world, assuming the moral high ground, whether or not legitimately, wins debates. Those in favor of caring for the health of the nation had the moral high ground, but didn't effectively use it. Arguments against health care reform were all financially motivated: the nation couldn't afford it, they would have to raise taxes, and it would squeeze private enterprise out of the market. Another missed opportunity considering that, down deep, most Americans are not comfortable with decisions being made just for money. Neither of the Iraq wars could have gained public support if it had been clear that it was all about the oil. At the very least, there must be a pretense of moral justification. People hate to been seen as money-grubbing even when they are, because most people are moored to a tradition that holds that money is the root of all evil and that those who do immoral things for money are bad. Shining the spotlight on the money-grubbers would have drawn a stark contrast. Packaged questions like "are corporate profits more important than a human life?" or "why should some people get rich off the sick and dying?" would have been quite compelling.

5. *Health care as a public safety issue.* One argument that consistently got traction was that the government shouldn't be involved in this or any private enterprise. In addition to the moral

argument against profiteering on the injured, sick, and dying, advocates could have drawn parallels to other government institutions that opponents would be disinclined to oppose as "government-run." Few would have argued that the military, police department, or fire department should *not* be run by the government. Why? They care for matters of life and death. So, what's the difference? Isn't health care often a matter of life and death? Who would tolerate a police force that only protected those whose security premiums were paid up? Would you stand for a fire department that would get your cat out of the tree but would not deal with catastrophic fire damage unless you could afford excruciatingly high costs? It is hard to even imagine a military that acted out of a profit motive. (It may be a little easier to imagine in the wake of the Blackwater scandal.) Yet that is precisely what happens in the realm of health and medicine. Recasting health care as a public service would have undercut arguments against government involvement.

6. *Insurance as the wrong model for health care.* When you really think about it, the business model of insurance is antithetical to health care. The term "health care" denotes taking care of your health, a constant, consistent need. Insurance is intended to mitigate risks, to deal with events that may or may not occur. While insurance makes sense for accidental injury or even the onset of a debilitating disease, it is not really conceptually appropriate for preventative or chronic care. People are shocked and disturbed that insurance companies only want to insure healthy people, but that is only indicative of their business model. It is based on actuary tables and the gamble that you won't need health care most of the time. That makes it the wrong system for a nation's health care, but no one really made that case. The insurance business was protected throughout the "revolutionary" health care debate.

Only fringe idealists came close to making these arguments, and perhaps that is why they are fringe. Honest arbiters are never invited to play. Contending parties are bought and paid for in advance. Was it all a fake debate?

In boxing, gambling interests used to pay favored fighters to intentionally lose high-stakes bouts to extend their control of the sport, avoid losses, and simply to make more money. The big health care debate looked a lot like a thrown fight; like the self-righteous supporters of health care reform deliberately lost the fight.

Insurers paid off both sides, and in return got a mandate in the congressional bills for millions of more customers, many paid for with government funding. Other than a few good-sounding but ineffective reforms, everything else stays fundamentally the same. It looked like a good fight. It went twelve rounds. Most are convinced that this was the best that could be done, but it was all an act. Billions upon billions of health care dollars will continue to line the pockets of people who don't provide health care, but merely shuffle the money around.

I don't have a dog in the fight, other than being an employer. I am not a member of any political party. As a neutral observer, it just looked like theater to me. It is the same show every time. One side stands up to proclaim advocacy for the little guy, whom they believe is best helped by free market capitalism and lower taxes; the other side professes their support for the little guy through the direct assistance of the government. Meanwhile, the little guy is being eaten for lunch by the cash supporters of both sides. It's a scam! Those who put their trust in these noble leaders are the dupes. Like gamblers on a fixed fight, the public picked sides, allowed their emotions to be manipulated by artful stagecraft, and, irrespective of the outcome, their hard-earned money lined the same pockets of the schemers behind the scenes. What is the difference?

Maybe Not "A Right," but an "Is Right"

There are the true believers who are convinced that the liberal notion of universal health care is a right of all. Others believe just as fervently that such a notion is not only wrong, but contrary to American values. Sadly, we hardly ever hear a symmetrical debate clearly contrasting the views of the true believers on each side. This is most likely because such a debate would undermine the rigging of the game. Misdirection from the facts most pertinent to the public, conflation of cultural biases with invented reality, and obfuscation of true motives driving the politics of the moment are easier to manage than a meritorious debate. Nevertheless, it is always very interesting to juxtapose antithetical arguments.

At the end of 2009, Jacob Sullum, a nationally syndicated columnist for *Reason* magazine, which is a monthly magazine geared toward a libertarian perspective, lucidly argued against the idea that health care should be considered a "right" of all. It certainly has been a rhetorical dictum of the left that health care should be a right irrespective of employment, wealth, or station in society. That may sound good in a speech or campaign rally, but is it really a "right" for citizens to have access to the *services* of the medical professionals, the *products* of pharmaceutical companies, and the *use* of medical equipment? Mr. Sullum argues that it isn't, going so far as to say that this suggestion is "a radical assault on the traditional American understanding of rights."[21]

In his article, he said that the Founding Fathers only had in mind "preexisting rights" that people have "simply by virtue of being human" and "can be violated (by theft or murder, for example) even in the absence of government." He asked, "Did Paleolithic hunter-gatherers have a right to the 'affordable, comprehensive, and high-quality medical care' that the Congressional Progressive Caucus says is a right of 'every person'? If so, who was violating that right?"

Building on this premise, he continued, "While liberty rights such as freedom of speech or freedom of contract require others to refrain from acting in certain ways, 'welfare rights' such as the purported entitlement to health care (or to food, clothing, or shelter) require others to perform certain actions." What actions? "They represent a legally enforceable claim on other people's resources. Taxpayers must cover

21. Jacob Sullum, "There Ain't No Such Thing as a Free Lumpectomy: The Folly of a 'Right to Health Care,'" *Reason*, December 23, 2009, http://reason.com/archives/2009/12/23/there-aint-no-such-thing-as-a. Unless otherwise noted, all references to Sullum in this section are from this article.

the cost of subsidies; insurers and medical professionals must provide their services on terms dictated by the government. A right to health care thus requires the government to infringe on people's liberty rights by commandeering their talents, labor, and earnings."

That last point bespeaks the motive of his argument and is the driving force behind many others on his side of the issue, but we'll get to that later. He ended his argument by contending that considering health care a right forces equivalency in the standard of care, even if that means a lowering of that standard for everyone.

While much of Sullum's argument served his political predisposition, his fundamental point is true. Health care is not a fundamental right. To suggest that it is for political expedience is nearly as hypocritical as the arguments of those opposed to universal health care along the same lines as Mr. Sullum. By definition, a right is a just claim or title, and no one has just claim to another's talents, produce, or property.

Hypocrisy is evident in the inconsistent application of this perspective of most in Sullum's camp. No one has a "right" to roads, police protection, national defense, any municipal or federal services, or anything at all that a government may do. For that matter, there is no right to even have a government.

Most people don't believe, however, that a government should refuse to do any and everything except that for which we have a natural right. When your house is on fire, you expect your government to have someone come to put it out.

Yet even fire protection is not without exception. In Obion County, Tennessee, if you live outside an incorporated city or town and do not purchase an annual subscription, you do not legally have any fire protection service. It may be hard to believe that there are places in the United States of America where, if you can't afford the subscription, the fire department will not respond—or if they do show up, they do so to protect the property of neighboring subscribers. This is the shocking end toward which the logic of Sullum and like-minded conservatives point.

No, rather than logical consistency, most conservatives prefer to pick and choose government services to support or rail against. Typically, they support the services they need or fear the absence of, and oppose those that could support or benefit their fellow citizens but for which they have no personal need. It is this myopic selfishness that undermines the potential strength of the nation.

Sullum's argument flies in the face of the very reason for the existence of government. Ancient hunter-gatherers may not have had quality health care, but they understood safety in numbers and the benefit of aggregating assets. Families became tribes, tribes became city-states, cities became nations, and nations became empires because of the mutual benefit of cooperative effort. This is the case made with the phrase "in order to form a more perfect union" of the preamble to the United States Constitution. The preamble states:

We the People of the United States, in Order to form a more perfect Union, establish Justice, insure domestic Tranquility, provide for the common defence, promote the general Welfare, and secure the Blessings Liberty to ourselves and our Posterity, do ordain and establish this Constitution for the United States of America.

As inconvenient as it may be to free market capitalists, libertarians, and conservatives, the words "general Welfare" appear right next to "common defence" (the British spelling of defense used in the original manuscript). Arguing over the difference between "provide" and "promote" is a more valid basis for discussion than the suggestion that developing a system to facilitate health care for all citizens is "a radical assault" on American tradition or contrary to the intent of the Founding Fathers.

Taxation in the interest of the general welfare is absolutely constitutional, even if distasteful to some. It is the cost of being part of a nation. The alternative is to buy an island and do everything yourself—defense, commerce, health, education, and the rest. Do you really think that you could create an equivalent environment for the "Blessings of Liberty," as the preamble puts it? Hardly.

Sullum may consider taxes to pay for health care that benefits all to be "commandeering" his assets, but then the same would have to be said for everything that the government does for the common good, even the things that he likes. No matter how much libertarians wish it were so, as the cliché goes, no man is an island.

Such shortsightedness is pitiable. In truth, social programs benefit everyone. What would the condition of our workforce be, if not for public education? Would your child be safe from smallpox, tuberculosis, and diseases that are far worse were it not for the Public Health Service and federally funded research for vaccinations? A healthy population benefits everyone and an unhealthy one hurts everyone.

Unfortunately, such a broad view doesn't really fit into the self-interest model of cannibal capitalism. If forty-five thousand people a year (the number estimated to die because of inadequate access to health care) were to die in terrorist attacks, the nation would be fully united, willing to engage whatever resources we could muster. Trillions in debt-financed dollars would be committed to the war against such terror. This is not hyperbole, for it is precisely what happened after 9/11.

Why is it so easy to commit trillions in response to the death of three thousand, and yet so hard to do so for the sake of many times more? Perhaps it is because the victims of terrorism are so random, affecting rich and poor alike. In the case of the attacks on the World Trade Center, many of the victims were quite rich.

Those who lack health insurance tend to be the working poor. People fail to see the urgency without the "it could be me" sentiment. If the poor all carried airborne, communicable diseases that threatened to kill the rich, the will would exist to end poverty, but short of that, we fail to make the connection between the risks to the few undermining the state of all.

Will we ever learn to subjugate politics to the best interests of the masses? I fear not. The system is based upon far too much shortsighted, selfish, contradictory, and hypocritical rhetoric. It is this sort of political self-mutilation that undermines any basis for hope. The ideologues in power refuse to admit any flaws in their views and deny any advantages of opposing ideologies, never mind that socialism is neither *all* bad nor capitalism *all* good. The process of consolidating power is at odds with solving problems, as constituents demand ideological purity. Even when some progress is made, you find that the pendulum swings both ways, sometimes even to the extreme. In our democracy, what is done by one side is sooner or later undone or undermined by the other. This would be innocuous if compromise (a fundamental tenet of moral relativism) always yielded the best results, but, more often than we'd like, one side is right and the other is wrong. We are thereby cursed to water down what is needed with what is not. And when compromise fails utterly, it fuels further furor in the ideological extremes. This is yet more of what makes us a cannibal country.

CHAPTER EIGHT

Miseducation of the Masses

Every loving parent takes a strong interest in the education of his or her children. We know that there is a direct link between a child's education and future prospects of success. Most want to see their children exceed their own achievements in life. They will sacrifice to ensure that their children get the best shot through good education.

But this ethic is not seen on the national scale. Our children are seen more as a market demographic to be exploited for profit than as the key to the future of the nation's economy and security. Toy and video game companies control the entertainment geared to the youngest. Children in their preteens have their tastes, self-image, and worldview shaped by the least worthy public figures. Magazine editors, merchandisers, and materialists show no restraint in exploiting our most vulnerable. The worst form of cannibalism is feeding on one's own young. We feed on the profit opportunities of their juvenile impulses, when we should be feeding their minds.

The State of Education

Despite the nationalistic pride in American exceptionalism and the fact that the U.S. spends more money per pupil on elementary and high school education than most developed nations, this country's standing with respect to the education of its young has fallen behind those of *all* of its major competitors—China, Japan, and the EU.

More surprising are the smaller or poorer nations that also exceed the performance of American children in math and science. According to the NCES, the United States falls below the international average in both science and math—*the average!* In fact, we are 25 points below the international average in math. That puts us behind Azerbaijan, Estonia, Lithuania, Latvia, and the Slovak Republic in math. In science, we fall behind such former Soviet bloc countries as Slovenia, Croatia, Estonia, and the Czech Republic.

The NCES reported:

> *On the 2006 Program for International Student Assessment (PISA), the average score of U.S. fifteen-year-olds in mathematics literacy was 474, which was lower than the Organization for Economic Cooperation and Development (OECD) average of 498 (table 403). (Possible scores on PISA assessments range from 0 to 1,000.) The average mathematics literacy score in the United States was lower than the average score in twenty-three of the other twenty-nine OECD countries for which comparable PISA results were reported, higher than the average score in four of the other OECD countries, and not measurably different from the average score in two of the OECD countries. In science literacy, the average score of fifteen-year-olds in the United States was lower than the average score in sixteen of the other twenty-nine OECD countries, higher than the average score in five of the other OECD countries, and not measurably different from the average score in eight of the OECD countries.*[22]

It doesn't take much imagination to see where these statistics point and what position it leaves the country in with respect to international economic competitiveness. In addition to international statistics, the internal statistics of the Department of Education are also not so promising. The national dropout rate stood at 8 percent in 2008.

22. U.S. National Center for Education Statistics, *2008 Digest of Education Statistics*, http://nces.ed.gov/pubsearch/pubsinfo.asp?pubid=2009020. In the following seven paragraphs, all statistics are from this source.

Among Hispanic children, the rate has been more than one in five. In 2008, the U.S. Bureau of Labor Statistics reported what seems at first glance to be a fairly good college enrollment rate. Of the 3.2 million youth who graduated high school from October 2007 to October 2008, 2.2 million (68.6 percent) were attending college in October 2008. Not bad, right? Look closer.

According to the Department of Education figures for 2000 through 2006, 30 percent leave in the first year, and an astonishing 50 percent never graduate. This trend only seems to be worsening. Putting together the dropout rates at each of the levels of education, we find that more than two-thirds of our kids never achieve a degree, even though college graduation is precisely what is needed to compete in the new global economy. In fact, some schools, like the University of Louisville, have targeted the dropout rate as a fiscal matter, and with good reason.

Unfortunately, as a country we don't invest much to ensure better results, even when it comes to qualifying young people to get into college. There are fundamental failings in the basic public education system. Many politicians and others pay lip service to the needs of the education system, but the facts don't lie the way politicians do. The NCES polled to determine the extent to which various environmental factors interfered with classroom instruction. Forty-four percent of public school principals reported at least some interference. Heating and air conditioning were the most frequently reported interferences, but respondents also cited physical condition of ceilings, floors, walls, windows, doors, and more.

And then there is the failure to provide a safe learning environment. In another NCES study, it was found that 29.8 percent of students in grades nine through twelve reported property stolen or deliberately damaged on school property; 28.7 percent were offered, sold, or given an illegal drug on school property; 12.8 percent engaged in a physical fight on school property; 9.2 percent were threatened or injured with a weapon on school property; and 5.4 percent felt too unsafe to go to school. It is not just the students who are at risk, either, as 9.6 percent of traditional public school teachers reported being threatened with injury in the past twelve months.

Declining academic performance, substantial dropout rates at various levels, poor environmental conditions, and even the risk of violence paint a troubling picture. What is going on in the world's only superpower?

We could go on and on elaborating on these statistics, but the most telling facts are revealed through an examination of the country's labor force. For your convenience, I've included the summary of the NCES report "Comparative Indicators of Education in the United States and Other G8 Countries: 2009," which shows that even the *value* of our education system is in decline:

> *In all reporting G8 countries, adults with a high level of education tended to earn more income than those with a relatively low level of education (i.e., those whose educational attainment was lower secondary education or below). Among U.S. twenty-five- to sixty-four-year-olds whose highest level of educational attainment was lower secondary education or below, 16 percent earned more than the country's median income in 2006. This percentage was lower than in all other reporting G8 countries, which ranged from 20 percent in the United Kingdom to 38 percent in Germany. Two percent of U.S. twenty-five- to sixty-four-year-olds with this level of education earned more than two times the country's median income. The corresponding percentages in the other G8 countries ranged from 2 percent in the United Kingdom and Germany to 7 percent in Italy. In contrast, 42 percent of such U.S. adults earned at or below half of the country's median income. This percentage was higher than in all other reporting G8 countries, which ranged from 17 percent in France to 39 percent in the United Kingdom.*
>
> *Among U.S. twenty-five- to sixty-four-year-olds whose highest level of educational attainment was upper secondary education, 38 percent earned more than the country's median income in 2006. This percentage was lower than in all other reporting G8 countries, which ranged from 42 percent in the United Kingdom and Germany to 56 percent in Italy. Italy was the only reporting G8 country where more than half of adults with this level of education earned more than the country's median income. Seven percent of U.S. twenty-five- to sixty-four-year-olds with this level of education*

earned more than two times the country's median income. The corresponding percentages in the other G8 countries ranged from 4 percent in Germany to 14 percent in Italy. In contrast, 24 percent of such U.S. adults earned at or below half of the country's median income; in the other G8 countries this ranged from 10 percent in Italy to 28 percent in Canada.

Among U.S. twenty-five to sixty-four-year-olds who had completed academic higher education, 68 percent earned more than the country's median income in 2006. The corresponding percentages in the other G8 countries ranged from 66 percent in Canada to 75 percent in the United Kingdom. Twenty-eight percent of U.S. twenty-five to sixty-four-year-olds with this level of education earned more than two times the country's median income. The corresponding percentages in the other G8 countries ranged from 27 percent in France and Germany to 32 percent in Italy. In contrast, 12 percent of such U.S. adults earned at or below half of the country's median income; in the other G8 countries this ranged from 7 percent in France to 18 percent in Canada.[23]

Decades of research reveals that one of the biggest problems with U.S. public schools comes down to ineffective teaching. As a nation, we have little regard for the profession of teaching children. This is evident not only in the pay, but in the entire system of education. In many colleges, those who take up teaching as a profession are cynically viewed as either rejects from tougher programs or idealists who will come to their senses after screaming, whining, undisciplined, unteachable reality shocks them to their senses. That cynical brand of reality is part and parcel of the education system's failure.

It's been more than thirty years since *Time* magazine displayed the cover "Help! My Teacher Can't Teach!" (June 16, 1980), and yet nothing has dramatically changed, at least not for the better. Far too often, teachers are unmotivated to do what should be done, and who

23. National Center for Education Statistics, *Comparative Indicators of Education in the United States and Other G-8 Countries: 2009*, http://nces.ed.gov/fastfacts/display.asp?id=71.

can blame them? In the extreme cases their classrooms are crammed full with unmotivated, cheating, rowdy, disrespectful, and occasionally violent people over whom they have no real authority. Their job may be thankless—but more damningly, it is also incentiveless. Pay raises are rarely tied to performance but more often to tenure. Instead of being viewed as the meaningful, world-shaping profession that it is, teaching is viewed as just another union job, where uniform mediocrity is valued over individual achievement.

One has to question the logic of a system that gives teachers lifetime job security after one or two years of work. The original intent may have been noble, since giving teachers tenure rights theoretically insulates them from the fickle political interests of school board members or other elected officials. However, it is hard to argue that this rationale outweighs the unintended consequence evident in the declining quality of education that tenure enables, especially when you consider the many federal and state laws protecting teachers from termination.

As things stand, schoolteachers are assessed before they are hired, not based on evidence of effectiveness as a teacher, but based on certification, degrees, and other pieces of paper that do not predict good teaching. To be fair, that is generally true when you hire anyone for any job. Nevertheless, the critical lack of quality teachers arises at least partly from the fact that there is no trustworthy, follow-through system to ensure that they are as good as they looked on paper; after they're hired, we pay them the same regardless of their effectiveness. School districts and individual schools are evaluated based on test scores; administrators generally evaluate teachers. No one ever asks the people who see the teachers at work day in and day out: the students. I don't suggest that children be given hire-fire authority over their teachers, but rather that their voices, together with their parents', the peer review of other teachers, test scores, and administrator evaluation should *all* be considered, backed up by full accountability.

The victims of this flawed system are the students, our children. It is not at all unusual to hear school-age children say that school is boring, useless, with the only benefit being the social outlet that it provides, including group sports. After early grade school, full intellectual engagement of our children is all but nonexistent. If you ask a kid what he or she learned in school on any given day, you will see the gravity of our failed system reflected in the blank stare and glazed eyes of this custodian of our future.

The workplace is where we see the greatest evidence of the damaging effects of the declining system of education. Employers frequently complain about their workers' lack of productivity, honesty, and integrity. Employees often are more interested in "getting it over with" rather than getting done with their work. Even when unemployment is high, the notion that a large pool of qualified candidates exists for any given job is a fallacy (except for unskilled jobs), especially when you consider the reality that the jobs needed in our modern economy require knowledge, skill, and judgment far above what our educational system typically confers.

One small-business owner told me that most job seekers he interviews are simply unemployable. It would be one thing if his business depended on highly skilled technical experts, but this was not the case. His business was selling auto parts, and he was looking for basic support staff. If an auto parts dealer is finding our workforce unqualified for such basic tasks, one must ask what that portends for the future.

As an employer myself, I have to concur with my friend's assessment. In fact, my experience has been more extreme than his. With my businesses, I have always outsourced tedious work. The people that I actually hire as employees are expected to be capable of thinking and making good judgments, but our education system doesn't teach how to think, and over and over I have found it necessary to create idiotproof processes for everything. The offensive term "idiotproof" is a common cliché among employers, managers, and those who create systems and procedures, but, really, who *wants* to hire idiots?

From every angle, the systemic failure of education in America can be clearly seen. Teachers aren't happy, students aren't happy, employers aren't happy, and, as we export unskilled jobs, we have to import educated technical professionals. These are not the signs of strength. Worse still, they forebode a collapse of the nation's dominance in the information age. How do we turn this around?

Redesigning How We Teach

Several years ago, I was in Britain teaching a group of educators how to better use technology, and I got into a discussion with a lifelong career teacher about the failings of the education system. Despite what the "bell curve" people preach, his theory was that all children are born with roughly the same potential, but vary in the timing of their development, be it physical or mental. It intuitively makes sense; the tallest child in first grade may not be particularly tall among his or her peers once reaching high school. Just as there are readily apparent growth spurts at varying times in lives of individual children, it stands to reason that mental development would be the same, meaning that not every child is ready for the same material at the same time. On the other hand, some subjects are belabored for so long that some students rebel against the tedium. Our system is so standardized that students are held back when they are ready to thrust forward, and are moved ahead when they need more time. Does this really make sense for distinct human beings?

Worst of all, our children are labeled early on and shunted into a particular path that may or may not be the best path for them farther along. Children who develop early physically are encouraged to be athletes; those who are earlier achievers in reading and math are heralded as "smart" kids, and those who are not yet ready for the so-called grade level are demoralized and set on a defeatist path. Who is really to say that these early categorizations are correct?

His point was that we need to eliminate the grade system altogether and match education to the developmental path of each child's mind. The grade system works against the best interest of each child by placing too great an emphasis on age. We expect every child to learn the same thing in the same way through some cookie-cutter curriculum, and to get to the same place at the same time, as evidenced by taking the same test on the same day. We end up pitting negative risks against negative risks, which leaves us to choose the lesser evil according to the politics of the day. For instance, we must either risk the self-esteem of some children or curtail the achievement of others. Imagine if you had been categorized and labeled for life based on the date when you were potty trained. While undermining the self-esteem of some, we discourage the achievement of the more capable. But this predicament is created by the system and is wholly avoidable.

There are points in a child's development where two or more grade levels could be covered rapidly, but during other periods, particularly the hormone-inflamed early adolescent years, there should be less emphasis on academics and more on socialization and physical development. Optimal educational effectiveness has been sacrificed in favor of the operational efficiency of a standardized educational system. This teacher's ideas are not far off from the consensus of many other education experts.

In small towns and rural communities, it has often been a matter of necessity to group children in ways other than by age. In some cases, the results have confirmed my friend's thesis. A report that summarized the findings of several studies noted,

> *Gutierrez and Slavin (1992),*[24] *Pavan (1992)*[25] *and Miller, (1990)*[26] *found that children in nongraded classrooms fare as well or better than children in single-graded classrooms on standardized measures of achievement. Pavan's review (1992) found that students in multigraded settings did as well as, or outperformed, students in single-graded classrooms. This is noteworthy because many have challenged the view that students in multigrade settings could achieve at a par with students in traditionally graded classes.*[27]

Some private schools, even in urban and suburban areas, seem to concur with the benefits, and practice multi-age grouping according to pedagogical criteria to maximize academic achievement.

Some researchers attribute the problems with the public education system to three fundamental flaws: (1) the failure to recognize and adapt

24. R. Gutierrez and R. E. Slavin, "Achievement Effects of Non-graded Elementary Schools: A Best Evidence Synthesis," Review of Educational Research 62, no. 4 (1992): 333–34.

25. B. N. Pavan, "The Benefits of Non-graded Schools," *Educational Leadership* 50, no. 2 (1992): 22–25.

26. B. A. Miller, "A Review of Quantitative Research on Multi-grade Instruction," *Journal of Research in Rural Education* 7, no. 1 (1990): 1–8.

27. Kathy Unrath, Tara Robertson, and Jerry Valentine, "Is Multi-age Grouping Beneficial to Middle School Students?" *National Middle School Association,* 1999, http://www.ncmsa.net/ressum15.htm.

instruction to facts of pediatric neuroscience; (2) the utter absence of a clear, understandable objective of education and its relevance to life in general for the individual who is being taught; and (3) the over-emphasis on memorization and the inadequate focus on developing critical thinking skills such as analysis, synthesis, and evaluation.

The ignorance of neurobiology cuts both ways, in that younger children's potential is often underestimated, while the effectiveness of group learning for young teenagers is often overestimated. Anyone with small children can attest to their rapid intellectual development, and yet in most elementary education programs we slow them down to a crawl of rote memorization and waste a period in life in which the mind is most receptive to new concepts.

On the other hand, with older kids we completely ignore the whirlwind going on within them. Institutionally we fail to recognize that the emotionally driven behavior of adolescents, including sexual promiscuity, angry outbursts, drug and alcohol experimentation, and even dangerous, risk-taking behavior, all have neurological causes. During this phase of neurological development, the amygdala, the center of the brain that drives emotional impulse and behavior, is more influential than the part of the brain responsible for careful judgment. Having peers around makes the situation worse.

My opinion is that, for most kids, there are a couple years in which a hiatus from school should be taken, preferably to live on a farm of some kind far from the emotionally charged and socially challenging environment of the twenty-first-century teen world. Since the serenity of farm life is hardly at arm's reach for most, at the very least, adults need to recognize the need to assist children in this period to develop control of themselves, which is one of the most important life skills we can ever pass on to our progeny.

Really, that is the point of education: passing on the knowledge and skills necessary for success for the next generation in a competitive world. It is pathetic that this meaning is utterly absent from the education we give our children.

It is a joke of late-night comedians to say that something they learned in school, like algebra for instance, has been useless in life—but this is no laughing matter. Think about it. After reading, writing, and arithmetic, what materials in the thirteen years of a typical K–12 education turn out to be indispensable in life? If you're honest about it, you'll struggle to identify one thing. Even when material has relevance in the real world, those real-world connections are rarely taught. This shows that even teachers are unclear about the mission of education. Everyone is mindlessly following rules and memorizing steps. There may have been efforts to redirect the education system away from this, but memorized learning is deeply seated in our system, which was designed for the industrial age, not the information age. Mindless repetition was a part of life for a turn-of-the-nineteenth-century factory worker. How, though, can that prepare the heirs of the nation to advance this technologically driven economy?

With so much time (more than 20,000 hours from kindergarten through grade twelve) wasted on meaningless, rote memorization, we are missing the more important things that would lead to a more prepared generation. Legendary education psychologist Benjamin Bloom classified how learning works in his renowned taxonomy, which is used to objectively measure whether a desired new behavior has or has not been acquired by the learner. The critical-thinking-domain classifications (analysis, synthesis, and evaluation), which are most important to the needs of the information age, are given very little attention in our education system, and most of that is in math classes that are taught without a practical context.

Analysis is the ability to separate materials or concepts into component parts, so that their organizational structure may be understood and one can distinguish between facts and inferences. Synthesis is the process of building a structure or pattern from diverse elements, thus building a whole from parts. Evaluation, often associated with analysis, is the ability to judge the value of ideas or materials. It is this faculty that allows a person to rationally decide between competing options based upon clear metrics.

Defenders of the status quo often cite improved standardized test scores, curricula, and multimedia resources to claim that the public school system has actually improved over the past fifty years. Yet this fails to recognize that the world has changed. The twenty-first-century economy depends on knowledge workers, and the education system must meet this challenge.

Needed Function of Public Education

The era of the rote job is over! There is little place left in the emerging economy for punching a clock, grinding through routines mindlessly, executing idiotproof policies and procedures, and still picking up a paycheck that meets American materialistic expectations. Computer automation and foreign labor just make too much business sense. Smart businesses will increasingly hire brainpower and outsource muscle. It is inevitable.

It is all about business now. We need people who can analyze situations and make smart decisions, who can piece together solutions, and who can prioritize accurately. We need people who can think. The problem is that our education system does not teach our children *how* to think. Thinking is relegated to the "means to the end" of memorization and repetition, when memorization should merely be the "means to the end" of assembling the tools and variables for applying logic to problems and synthesizing solutions.

The key to a better economic future will depend largely on our ability to conduct business in the developing world. We need people who can manage the process of opening new commercial channels, develop relationships with new trading partners, create and exploit new business opportunities, and bring the money home. The economic expansion of the second half of the twentieth century was driven by the growth and consumerism of the middle class in America. Now there are billions of people all over the planet who are primed to enter the middle class in their respective countries. There are trillions of dollars to be made, but will they be made by America or China?

China is already positioning itself to win such a contest. That really shouldn't be the case, though. China may be leveraging its liquidity to invest in the developing world, but the American way of life sells like no other. In 2009, reporter Maziar Bahari, who was held captive for 118 days in an Iranian prison, recounted his trying ordeal of a torture session in which his vicious interrogator revealed that he thought New Jersey was heaven on earth. Even our enemies have bought into the American dream. Yet this fact has yet to be fully leveraged to secure its profit potential.

Modern cities need to be built, followed by every conceivable business that we are familiar with in the more developed world. Global development will occur whether or not we participate in and profit from it. Transforming the developing world is not merely a humanitarian effort, but a way to rejuvenate the domestic economy. China has set the model for rapidly transforming a poor nation into a rich one. As the standard of living rises, there is a growing consumer base to profit from. The growth of the developing world (really, their purchases of our exports) is partly what staved off the Armageddon that the Great Recession of 2007–9 could have been. Instead of narrowly benefitting our economy, our populace must be educated to better capitalize on the needs of the global economy. Feeding off ourselves is just not adequate.

The economic cannibalism that threatens our posterity is attributable to a lackadaisical pattern of following the path to the easiest buck and grasping short-term gains irrespective of the consequences. Adding solid critical thinking skills to the can-do spirit of Americans is just the recipe needed to maintain economic dominance.

Early education is the crucial first step to developing a workforce better prepared for the twenty-first century. A study of schoolchildren in England, described in the article "Preschool Influences on Mathematics Achievement" published in the August 2008 issue of *Science,* found that the benefits of early education are "sufficiently large to be important for any government wishing to maximize educational achievement."[28] Findings also indicated that any type of preschool education was beneficial to children, but high-quality preschool programs were the most effective.

28. Edward C. Melhuish and others, "The Early Years: Preschool Influences on Mathematics Achievement," *Science* 321, no. 5893 (2008): 1161–62.

Next, the entire public education system has to be reengineered to produce a higher yield of qualified technical workers. To that end, a resurgence is needed in vocational training and a new standard of technical training within the public school curriculum must be established.

Finally, and this is the most important, college needs to be included as a part of free public education. Irrespective of how socialistic this may sound to many, it is a loss to the entire system whenever someone with the potential to be a great contributor to the economy falls short because he or she can't afford tuition. There would still be room for quality private schools, but a core of architects, engineers, doctors, scientists, and many other professionals could be produced in order to greatly benefit our international competitiveness. The reward would surely outweigh the cost.

A U.S. Census Bureau report titled "The Big Payoff: Educational Attainment and Synthetic Estimates of Work-life Earnings" estimated that over a lifetime, a college degree results in about a million dollars of additional earning power on average. The report stated:

[For] full-time, year-round workers, the forty-year synthetic earnings estimates are about $1.0 million (in 1999 dollars) for high school dropouts, while completing high school would increase earnings by another quarter-million dollars (to $1.2 million). People who attended some college (but did not earn a degree) might expect work-life earnings of about $1.5 million, and slightly more for people with associate's degrees ($1.6 million). Over a work-life, individuals who have a bachelor's degree would earn on average $2.1 million—about one-third more than workers who did not finish college, and nearly twice as much as workers with only a high school diploma. A master's degree holder tops a bachelor's degree holder at $2.5 million. Doctoral ($3.4 million) and professional degree holders ($4.4 million) do even better.

The difference in total economic productivity is undeniable. It is therefore in the general interest to see to it that the greatest possible number of students who are capable of achieving a higher education, and thus greater earning power, do so. No one should be forced to muddle through life short of his or her potential purely for economic reasons. It is not in the national interest. The less people earn, the less they consume, and the less they pay in taxes. When a person with the aptitude and desire to become a doctor, engineer, or scientist is restrained from this goal by money matters, it is a loss to all of us. It is also a painful disappointment on an individual basis.

I know the tragedy of the millions of smart young people who never get to college because of economics on a very personal level. I was not able to go as far in school as I had hoped because I needed to make money instead. But don't pity me for not getting my PhD in physics. I probably did better financially than I would have. No, I am talking about my mother. She didn't get to college at all.

When she told her mother and any of her eleven brothers and sisters who would listen about her college aspirations, they laughed in her face. Even though she earned a full scholarship, there was no way she was going to get the ancillary support she would need. She was one of twelve children born just two generations out of slavery. It didn't matter that she had a higher IQ than my father, who was a rocket scientist. But, really, don't pity her either. Pity the country, which lost out on the economic potential of someone who could have contributed so much more than she was able to, having never earned more than a $30,000 salary in her life.

The United Negro College Fund got a lot of mileage out of the slogan "a mind is a terrible thing to waste." In our cynical era, it now sounds like fodder for a joke. Yet it is very true. Unfortunately, instead of recognizing wasted minds and potential in terms of the incalculable national economic loss that they are, we relegate this reality to mere sentiment anecdotes in the realms of charity.

This is not a charity case. It is a matter of "promot[ing] the general Welfare" to again quote the Constitution. States are reducing their secondary school funding, and tuitions are rising, in many cases at faster rates than health insurance premiums. Reducing our intellectual output could easily result in a reduction in our economic output.

Even China has come to recognize its population as an asset to be leveraged to advance its national economy. Here, in contrast, we often exploit the uneducated in one way or another, even as we support some of them through welfare. There are innumerable schemes and scams to extract the limited amount of wealth from the poor, from high-yield payday loans to the lotto. Instead of driving upward mobility with the understanding that the more valuable we make people, the more they can contribute to the economy, cannibal capitalism seeks only to redirect public assistance funds into the hands of private enterprise. We expect little and get little. We don't even have the good sense to fatten up our turkey before Thanksgiving. We're just glad that many of the uneducated are spendthrifts who will blow much of the little that they have at Walmart.

Instead of a fragmented education system with twenty thousand separate boards of education and disparate outcomes, there is a need for unified effort and coordination with the goal of improving education across the spectrum. It is a national concern that requires a national effort.

Instead of cannibalizing our young, revolutionizing the education system would put the country back on the offensive. Instead of complaining about the loss of the middle class, the stagnation of wages, the trade deficits with other nations, and the outsourcing of jobs to the developing world, we could actually build the workforce needed for the times. This is not even to mention the social benefits of moving millions out of economic despair.

Unfortunately, this sounds too much like socialism. The reasoning that taxpayers shouldn't have to pay for poor children to go to college will most likely rule the day. The cannibalism will continue . . . and continue . . . unless . . .

CHAPTER NINE

Power to the People

Your electric alarm clock startles you awake. You reach over for a remote control to turn on your television, which is in standby mode (technically on, drawing power) just to be available for this moment. As you barely listen to and occasionally glance at the morning news, you muster yourself to your feet and, realizing that it is a bit chilly, you scurry over to the thermostat and crank the heat up to full blast. Without turning off the television, you make your way to the bathroom and fully open the shower valve to get the hot water going. The shower, together with the TV, becomes background noise as you brush your teeth. Just then you realize that, if you are going to be on time, you need to start the coffee. You flip on the light in your closet, grab a robe, and rush to the kitchen. While you fix the coffee, you flip on the kitchen TV, watch a few seconds hoping to catch the weather and traffic reports, before heading back to the bathroom, where the steam-filled shower is still running. After you and the rest of your family get dressed, you are ready to go. Your spouse takes one car, your teenager takes another, and you load the two youngest into the SUV. As you strap your toddler into the car seat, you reassure yourself that you turned off the lights and televisions, but forget that you turned up the heat. Off you go in your gas-guzzling behemoth, first to day care to drop off the toddler, then to the elementary school to drop off your middle child, and finally to work. You make your way through forty-five minutes of rush-hour traffic at twelve miles per gallon. This is just the beginning of your day.

Our Gluttonous Appetite for Energy

This is not an atypical scenario. How much energy was consumed? How much was wasted? How much did these questions even briefly enter the mind of the consumer of this energy? According to the U.S. Energy Information Administration, each person in America consumes 327 million BTUs on average each year. Our gross consumption of power is reflected in every aspect of the American way of life—where we live, where we work, how we entertain ourselves, everything.

The United States leads the world in electricity consumption at 3.873 trillion kWh annually. We lead the world in oil consumption at 19.5 million barrels (or 819 million gallons) per day, and we lead the world in the consumption of natural gas, at 657.2 billion cubic meters a year. We consume an obscene amount of energy in this country, using about one hundred quadrillion BTUs, and the majority of this energy is derived from fossil fuels. (Only about 15 percent of our energy is from nuclear and renewable sources.) Without even considering the environmental implications (which we will), the economic impact is nearly overwhelming.

Theoretically, there are many ways to provide the energy that we need, but practically, as the world now works, the energy issues primarily come down to one source: petroleum. That may seem like an overstatement when you consider that petroleum only makes up 40 percent of the total energy consumption of the United States and is responsible for only 2 percent of our electricity generation. Nevertheless, as important as electricity is, it is not the fulcrum of the energy issue. The world turns on transportation. Nearly all commerce depends on moving things from point to point, and, as obvious as this is, a realistic recognition of this fact is far too absent from the public energy debate.

Fuel for transportation is the point of vulnerability that can and has undermined the national economy. The generation of electricity is done by stationary power plants. We could transform our entire electrical infrastructure to clean sources like wind, solar, geothermal, and hydroelectric, and that would still do nothing for transportation. Despite laudable advances in battery technology, for the foreseeable future, most electric vehicles will be limited to small, lightweight, short-range, passenger vehicles used mainly for commuter travel. To traverse long distances and transport anything more than a couple of people, a more portable source of power generation is needed. It is no wonder that 90 percent of vehicular fuel needs are met by oil. Ninety percent is an improvement over what our dependence used to be, but it's still woefully inadequate. Our need for oil is a big problem.[29]

At 307 million, we make up just 4 percent of the world's population, but our oil demand is 25 percent of the global total. We consume well more than twice the oil that we produce, which leaves us with a significant dependence on foreign sources. Our entire economy and way of life is dependent on the accessibility of oil, and we are dependent on other countries to get it to us. You don't have be a conspiracy theorist to recognize that this is a precarious situation, to put it mildly.

At $80 per barrel, the country spends $30 billion a month on foreign oil, importing 13.5 million barrels a day. In 2008, when oil prices peaked above $147 per barrel, the nation spent nearly a half trillion dollars on oil from foreign nations, and this drove the Great Recession of 2007–9 as much as did any subprime loans. Yet, as bad as those oil prices were, with the continual instability of the nations that produce our oil, it could get that bad again or far worse. The implications are frightening, particularly when you factor in competition driving up the cost for this resource as China and India, each with populations over a billion, move closer to an American-like standard of living.

The combined population of these two emerging economic giants is over 2.5 billion. If the petroleum consumption of these countries were to equal ours (24.8 billion per year per capita), it would amount to sixty-two billion barrels of oil used per year. That is twice the world's total

---

29. For the official energy statistics from the U.S. government, see the web site of the Energy Information Administration at http://www.eia.gov.

production at its peak in 2005! The law of supply and demand suggests that we have seen nothing close to what the price of oil may soon be.

We're Addicted to Oil!

The implications of statistics like these have converted even life-long oilmen like T. Boone Pickens. Despite a career spent capitalizing on the importance and limited supply of oil and natural gas, Mr. Pickens has become a fervid advocate for alternative energy sources, such as wind and solar, and one of the most outspoken voices in the national dialogue for energy independence. In recent years, he has spent millions promoting his so-called Pickens Plan, which proposes replacing the 22 percent of the electricity that the United States gets from natural gas with wind energy, in turn enabling natural gas to provide 38 percent of the nation's fuel for transportation.

As T. Boone Pickens says, "America is addicted to foreign oil. . . . It's an addiction that threatens our economy, our environment, and our national security. It touches every part of our daily lives and ties our hands as a nation and as a people."[30] He goes on to state that this "addiction" has worsened over the recent decades.

At the peak price of $147.27 per barrel in July 2008, the weight of oil prices (reflected in gasoline prices) smothered the American people. You couldn't fill up an average car for less than fifty bucks. SUVs and other large vehicles could cost well over $100 to fill up. I remember spending $85 gassing up my four-door sedan. These prices literally put the issue of energy right between the eyes of everyday people.

Nevertheless, oil prices came down from those staggering highs, as did the short attention span of our people. As Pickens later said, "Lower prices have not reduced our dependence on foreign oil or lessened the risks to either our economy or our security. . . . We are in a precarious position in an unpredictable world." He has repeatedly been quoted as saying that if America continues on its current track of importing energy, "it will be the greatest transfer of wealth in the history of mankind."

---

30. http://www.pickensplan.com, accessed August 9, 2010. Unless otherwise noted, all references to Pickens in this book are to his web site.

Despite the gravity of the situation, it is not the nature of our cannibal country to effectively tackle long-term, systemic problems that call for radical change. There is little appetite even for the bipartisan Pickens Plan. Election cycles come along far too frequently for most politicians to be willing to risk short-term political losses for long-term national gains. Voters are unlikely to reward legislation that costs billions to fund a new energy infrastructure without recognizing clear and immediate benefits.

Even pain at the pump is ultimately short-lived once prices retreat from the highs. Prices that would have been thought of as intolerable a few years earlier are eventually tolerated and accepted because they provide relief from the highest prices. The urgency of the summer of '08, when gas prices peaked, was lost to the other stresses and effects of the recession. Restoring jobs and addressing the economy became the top priority of our nation.

Despite rhetorical attempts by some leaders, polls show that the public has not come to see the connection between solving this energy crisis and economic prosperity. In a Gallup poll published at the end of October 2009 (just over a year after record high prices), respondents were asked which matter should be treated as a priority by the president. The economy was chosen by 41 percent, 18 percent selected the situations in Iraq and Afghanistan, 17 percent indicated health care, 14 percent felt the deficit was the priority, but only 2 percent identified energy as the top priority. In the minds of millions of Americans, the energy crisis was over, at least as an overriding antecedent to all else. Sure, most would like to see gasoline prices back below $2 a gallon, but most are resigned to the higher levels.

Sadly, this thinking is suicidal. The reality, attested to by the facts, is that this period following 2008 of lower-than-peak oil and gas prices is merely a respite. Any recovery of the global economy is certain to be accompanied by increased oil consumption. The addiction has not been broken, and the inescapable increases in use will inevitably mean increased prices. Increased oil prices in turn will put downward pressure on the economy, trapping us in a vicious cycle of economic purgatory. Pickens says, "There is nothing more important to the present and future of our economy than energy. Any effort to address our economic problems will require a thorough understanding of this issue and willingness to confront our dependence on foreign oil and what domestic resources we can use." I have to agree.

Where Energy and Environment Collide

That is just the economic argument. Most advocates of shifting our energy infrastructure away from petroleum hold their position for environmental reasons. They may use the economic argument to curry favor and broaden political support, but this is revealed as insincere rhetoric whenever the subjects of coal and nuclear power generation come up.

Environmentalists' disinterest in the economic implications of energy costs are further revealed when you consider the support among Al Gore disciples for a carbon tax. The thinking is to use the pain caused by excessive energy prices to spur reductions in carbon emissions and innovations in alternative energy. This is nuts in my opinion, but I do understand that it stems from the frustration from years of their calls for change falling upon deaf ears.

Nevertheless, the environmental arguments are not to be ignored. If you have seen Al Gore's *An Inconvenient Truth*, then you know the basics. If not, the principal environmental argument against burning fossil fuels for energy is that it appears to be a significant contributing factor to potentially devastating planetary climate change, informally referred to as "global warming."

Scientists have studied the natural cycles and events that are known to influence the climate of our planet and have discovered a quantifiable pattern of global warming that can't be explained by naturally occurring factors alone. The empirical evidence strongly suggests that the climate is being changed by greenhouse gases emitted by human activity.

To establish the facts and build consensus, the United Nations organized a group of scientists called the International Panel on Climate Change (IPCC). The IPCC meets periodically to review the latest scientific research and report on global warming, documenting the consensus among hundreds of leading scientists.

From the outset, the IPCC's conclusions have been that mankind is indeed changing the composition of the atmosphere through the introduction of greenhouse gases produced by the combustion of fossil fuels in cars, planes, factories, and electricity production. Another human activity, deforestation, is also a culprit that raises greenhouse-gas levels in the atmosphere. Carbon dioxide (CO_2) is the gas most responsible for the warming. Deforestation effectively contributes to increased CO_2 levels substantially, though indirectly, because of the absence of plants, which absorb CO_2 and emit oxygen as a byproduct of photosynthesis, thus allowing otherwise-mitigated carbon dioxide to remain in the atmosphere. Additionally, the process of deforestation itself directly releases the CO_2 stored in plants and trees in various ways.

In addition to CO_2, there are other contributors, including methane produced through human causes like waste, nitrous oxide from fertilizers, and gases used for refrigeration and industrial processes. Some of these other greenhouse gases have more damaging effects than CO_2 when compared molecule-to-molecule, but because of the significantly greater concentration of CO_2 in the atmosphere, it is the greatest culprit behind global warming.

Greenhouse gases are at levels higher than at any time in the last 650,000 years, and the levels are still rising. As I have discussed throughout this book, the rest of the world is catching up with us in many ways, including energy usage and waste. In the last twenty years (since 1990), the same period in which China surpassed the United States as the greatest greenhouse-gas emitter, CO_2 levels have increased by 20 percent. It only takes common sense to see where that trajectory is leading.

Nevertheless, even these dramatic changes in the climate happen at an imperceptible rate and in inconsistent patterns. For instance, the decade of 2000–9, according to Michel Jarraud, secretary-general of the World Meteorological Organization, "is very likely to be the warmest on record."[31] Then 2010, a year characterized by heat waves in America, monsoons in Pakistan and India, and a huge glacier breaking off of Greenland, topped them all as the warmest year on record, but that is not to say that every year and every season in every region has seen a steady pattern of warming.[32] This is why many climatologists favor the term "climate change" over "global warming," even though the latter evokes a more visceral response and is therefore more politically expedient.

One has to step back to see the overall pattern and direction of warming. When you do, though, you see glaciers are melting, sea levels are rising, rain forests are drying, and wildlife is scrambling to keep pace. While I don't mean to endorse the position or agenda of Al Gore, to me, the most dramatic element of *An Inconvenient Truth* was not the lecture, rhetoric, or even the facts, but the comparison of pictures clearly depicting various landscapes changing over time. The fact that the deserts are growing, the glaciers are melting, and the seas are rising is incontrovertible.

The question of whether we are causing it is a bit tougher. The fact that warming happens when certain gases in earth's atmosphere trap heat has been understood since 1824, when Joseph Fourier calculated that the earth would be much colder if it had no atmosphere. We call this the "greenhouse effect" because, like the glass walls of a greenhouse, these gases let in light but keep heat from escaping. Without this effect, life as we know it on earth would not be possible.

However, the more greenhouse gases are in the atmosphere, the more heat gets trapped, and this is what forces us to look closely at man-made greenhouse gas emissions. Research confirms that greenhouse-gas levels have gone up and down over the earth's history. Nevertheless, for the past few thousand years, both global average temperatures and greenhouse-gas levels have stayed fairly constant, until recently. There has been no significant environmental or natural

---

31. Charles J. Hanley, "UN: 2000–2009 Likely Warmest Decade on Record," Associated Press, December 8, 2009.

32. Lulu Liu, "Global Warming: NASA Says It's the Hottest Year on Record," *McClatchy*, July 27, 2010, http://www.mcclatchydc.com/2010/07/27/98203/earth-bakes-worldwide.html.

phenomenon noted to account for the recent spike, other than the burning of fossil fuels and other man-made emissions.

The year 2009 ended as the fifth-warmest on record, replacing the year 2003. According to the U.S. National Aeronautics and Space Administration (NASA), the other warmest years since 1850 have been 1998, 2002, 2003, 2006, 2007, and 2009, all recent years indicative of a trend. NASA says the differences in readings among these years are so small as to be statistically insignificant. As I mentioned, 2000–9 was the warmest decade on record, and 2010 the warmest year of all. The U.N. panel reported that the global combined sea surface and land surface temperature for the January–October 2009 period was estimated at 0.44°C (0.79°F) above the 1961–90 annual average of 14.00°C (57.2°F), with a margin of error of plus or minus 0.11°C.

The Gore film depicted near-apocalyptic consequences of climate change, but even if the reality is far less severe, we cannot know all of the effects of the climate changing faster than some living things may be able to adapt to. The global ecosystem is far more complex, and in some ways far more fragile, than we can know. Unpredictable climate changes could pose unique challenges to all life on earth, if not threaten its existence.

The increasing rate of glacial loss is alarming, as earth's remaining ice sheets (such as those of Greenland and Antarctica) are starting to melt. The extra water could potentially raise sea levels, dramatically affecting (or destroying) habitable coastal cities, towns, and villages around the globe. Furthermore, changing the temperature and composition of earth's oceans would most likely change the climate in other unexpected ways.

Just based on current meteorological scientific knowledge, we can surmise that such changes would result in more extreme weather with more intense, major storms. This could include the extremes of more rain followed by longer and drier droughts, jeopardizing crops and undermining agricultural economies. Millions of people could be displaced, plants' and animals' habitual ranges could shift drastically…and entire ecosystems could be destroyed. The Internet is full of calamity-howlers who could further elaborate on the impending gloom and doom, but the sad reality is that scientists are already seeing some of these predicted changes occurring more quickly than they had expected.

In 1995, the IPCC issued a report that contained various projections of sea-level changes by the year 2100. They estimated that the sea will rise 50 centimeters (20 inches) with the lowest estimates at 15 centimeters (6 inches) and the highest at 95 centimeters (37 inches). The rise will come from thermal expansion (like all matter, water expands as temperature rises) of the ocean and from melting glaciers and ice sheets (melting ocean ice does not raise the sea level). Now the estimates appear in need of upward revision.

In 2007–9, the summer melt reduced the Arctic Ocean ice cap to its smallest extent ever recorded. Satellite imaging of the Arctic Ocean taken March 2009 (at the end of winter) revealed that the ice sheets were only slightly larger than the record low measured in 2006. *Science News* reported on May 9, 2009:

> *The spring melting of the Arctic Ocean's ice cap has already begun, and data suggest that the ice is more vulnerable than ever: The ocean area covered by ice is one of the lowest ever measured by satellites, and a record high fraction of that area is capped by thin, first-year ice that's more prone to melt than older, thicker ice is.*[33]

Of even greater concern are the ice sheets of Antarctica, Greenland, and other glacial land areas. Antarctica is covered with ice at an average of 2,133 meters (7,000 feet) thick, which equates to 90 percent of the world's ice and 70 percent of its fresh water. If it were all to melt, it would be enough water to raise sea levels a staggering 70 meters (230 feet). In the International Polar Year 2007–9 project, researchers found that Antarctica is warming more than previously believed. Almost all glaciers worldwide are retreating.

Various studies and data from NASA have shown that Antarctica's western ice sheet has been under siege from global warming for some time, with billions of tons of ice melting into the ocean each year and contributing to rising sea levels. Until recently, however, East Antarctica had seemed stable. *Discovery News* reported:

---

33. Sid Perkins, "Less, Thinner Arctic Ice," *Science News* 175, no. 10 (2009), 14.

Now a new set of satellite measurements indicate the East may have begun to succumb to warmer temperatures, losing as much as fifty-seven billion tons of ice a year since 2006. There is still a lot of uncertainty in the readings, but if the readings hold up under scrutiny, it would mark an important change in the world's largest ice sheet…The team's results in western Antarctica match up well with previous studies, which have found that the region is shedding around 196 billion tons of ice each year.[34]

The realities of global warming are clearly evident in zoology. The predictions of habitat loss and threatened species are already becoming reality.

Bill Fraser, an ecologist and penguin expert working as part of the Long Term Ecological Research Network, a program launched in 1980 by the National Science Foundation to chronicle environmental changes in twenty-six ecosystems around the world, travelled to Litchfield Island in the Antarctic, to see what remained of the once-thriving Adélie penguins, the classic tuxedoed penguin. Over the years, the number of Adélies had fallen to a few dozen breeding pairs on the island, and a census conducted earlier that season indicated that the colony was on the verge of disappearing. Fraser has personally seen their numbers decline from thirty-two thousand breeding pairs to eleven thousand in thirty years. With 87 percent of the nearby glaciers in retreat, Frasier cited the steady loss of sea ice along the northwestern Antarctic Peninsula as a principal cause of the decline of the region's Adélie.

Meanwhile, such destructive species as jellyfish and bark-eating beetles are moving northward out of normal ranges. More than just a nuisance, jellyfish are viewed as barometers of the ocean. "There is evidence of jellyfish explosions around the world that appear related to the adverse impact of human activities, and those include global warming," said Sarah Chasis, the senior attorney for the New York City–based Natural Resources Defense Council.[35] Evidence shows jellyfish species invade places where fish, coral, and other marine

---

34. Michael Reilly, "First Signs of Melting Seen in East Antarctica," *Discovery News*, November 23, 2009.

35. *Boston Globe*, "Jellyfish Flourish as Water Warms," July 2, 2002.

animals once thrived. They procreate more quickly in warmer water, tolerate pollution, and escape commercial fishing nets that decimate almost every other marine species. As the planet warms, "there are suggestions that the whole oceans are turning to jellyfish," said Larry Madin, the director of research at the Woods Hole Oceanographic Institution.[36] Across the globe in many tourist destinations, a plague of jellyfish has become the latest environmental hazard to be blamed on global warming.[37]

Spruce beetles have boomed in Alaska, thanks to twenty years of warm summers. Nearly four million acres of mature white spruce forest on the Kenai Peninsula in Alaska have been killed by a growing population of spruce beetles (*Dendroctonus rufipennis*) since about 1987. Scientists, including Dr. Edward Berg of the U.S. Fish and Wildlife Service and Dr. Kenneth Raffa of the Department of Entomology at the University of Wisconsin, attribute the beetle infestation to rising average temperatures in south-central Alaska in both winter and summer. More beetle larvae can survive, and higher summer temperatures allow the insects to mature faster and complete a two-year life cycle in one year. The trees, which previously lived in balance with the beetles, do not have enough natural defenses against this assault.

Beetles are not the only insects on the move; a study by the University of California, Santa Barbara, clearly demonstrated changes in species ranges as butterflies shift north to track a changing climate as the planet warms up. Camille Parmesan, who conducted the research while she was a postdoctoral fellow at the National Center for Ecological Analysis and Synthesis at the university, and her coinvestigators, found that out of fifty-seven species studied in Europe and North Africa (thirty-five of which there were data for both the northern and southern range boundaries), two-thirds had shifted northward.[38] She said, "This puts the nail in the coffin."

---

36. Drew FitzGerald, "The New Ocean Predator: Jellyfish?" *Global Post*, November 29, 2009, http://www.globalpost.com/dispatch/study-abroad/091022/the-new-ocean-predator-jellyfish.

37. Ibid.

38. University of California, Santa Barbara, *Butterflies Move North Due to Global Warming*, press release, June 10, 1999, http://www.ia.ucsb.edu/pa/display.aspx?pkey=312.

As climate change melts sea ice, the U.S. Geological Survey projects that two-thirds of polar bears will disappear by 2050.[39] Polar bears are not the only Arctic wildlife threatened by global warming. Scientists have discovered that Arctic foxes also struggle as the ice disappears, because they rely on the frozen seas to survive the bleak winters. Nathan Pamperin, a scientist at the department of biology and wildlife at the University of Alaska Fairbanks, who led the Arctic fox study, said: "With reduced access to sea ice, it is possible that, in the years when foxes would normally travel on the ice, they may face tougher conditions on land, and possibly lower survival."[40]

Other evidence of climate change is reflected in increased average precipitation (rain and snowfall) across the globe. There is also some evidence that glacier melt is encroaching on low-lying island states.

Some may cynically ask, "So what? What makes the extinction of Arctic foxes and polar bears a tragedy for us?" Some even believe the loss of Arctic sea ice could be a blessing in disguise, opening up the "Northern Passage" and allowing northern-hemisphere cargo ships to cross the globe in fractions of the time and expense. They may argue that the world has gone through changes before and we could adapt to this one. This is a change, not an apocalypse. Who is to say that that's not true?

We don't know. The loss of polar bears, as tragic as it may be, affects humans more sentimentally than directly, because we think they are cute, especially as cubs. In truth, we have lost many more species of greater importance to the ecology without any hoopla.

It's that we are losing species, losing habitat, losing rain forests, losing coastline, losing farmland to deserts, and we don't know what this all may do to life on earth. Life is a fragile thing, and the disruption of delicate balances could be catastrophic. Environmental changes to our planet in the past were in some cases extinction-level events. Even if changes were far less dramatic, the elimination of habitable regions of the world would have unfathomable economic and social effects. It's only common sense to try to avert such a disaster.

---

39. Associated Press, "Two-Thirds of World's Polar Bears Will Be Gone by 2050," Saturday, September 08, 2007.

40. David Adam, "Global Warming: Melting Ice Threatens Arctic Foxes," *Guardian*, Tuesday 15, July 2008.

The current warming trend is firmly in place. Even if we stopped emitting greenhouse gases today, the earth would still warm by another degree or so. But what we do from today forward will make a big difference. Depending on our choices, scientists predict that the earth could eventually warm by as little as 2.5°F or as much as 10°F. The latter could prove to be catastrophic. The difference between average global temperatures today and during the ice ages is only about 9°F (5°C).[41]

To mitigate the effects of global warming, a commonly cited goal is to stabilize greenhouse-gas concentrations at around 450–550 parts per million (ppm). This would amount to about twice preindustrial levels, which, according to the consensus, would avert the most damaging predicted impacts of climate change. According to the IPCC, greenhouse-gas emissions would have to be reduced by 50 percent to 80 percent of the current growth rate to reach this level.

Unfortunately, some of the global warming crowd have been put on their heels by controversy. The credibility of climate scientists has been called into question. The incident, dubbed "Climategate" by skeptics of anthropogenic climate change, came to light in November 2009, with the unauthorized release of thousands of e-mails and other documents obtained through the hacking of a server used by the Climatic Research Unit (CRU) of the University of East Anglia in Norwich, England. The University of East Anglia described the incident as an illegal taking of data. Allegations were made that the e-mails showed climate scientists colluded to withhold scientific information; interfered with the peer-review process to prevent dissenting scientific papers from being published; deleted e-mails and raw data to prevent data being revealed; and manipulated data to make the case for global warming appear stronger than it is. Even though the scientists were later mostly exonerated, this controversy produced the dark cloud of suspicion that skeptics had hoped for.

It is hard to gain momentum to conquer this colossal problem when science can be politicized and overzealous researchers give

---

41. Cynthia Rosenzweig and William Solecki, "How Does Climate Change Today Compare with Climate Change in the Past?" Columbia University, 2004–5, http://ccir.ciesin.columbia.edu/nyc/pdf/q1b.pdf.

credibility to the "flat earth" crowd who deny reality. Incomplete research is rarely conclusive, but the consensus of the broad scientific community is that global warming is real and that we are accelerating it, if not causing it. When you consider all of the interests at stake, consensus may very well be impossible. Someone once said that it is futile to debate with a person whose livelihood is dependent upon disagreeing with you.

It is only fair to state that this incident, as damaging as it has been to the public debate, involves only a very small percentage of the scientific community. By design, the IPCC draws from a large pool of scientists to develop the consensuses that they do. With or without the Climategate data manipulation, there is a preponderance of evidence demonstrating climate change.

Impediments to Breaking the Addiction

All of the foregoing shows that there are both strong economic and environmental arguments for shifting away from petroleum as our principal source of energy. Building a new energy economy would certainly create economic opportunities, and who can really argue against cutting air pollution dramatically? There are also security interests at stake. It certainly isn't a coincidence that nearly all of the national interest threats and engagements since the end of the Cold War have had a connection to the Middle East. Something has got to give.

So, what do we do?

Everyone agrees that we need to modernize our electrical grid. Most of our infrastructure is from the early post–World War II era, and some of it is much older than that. Updating this system is a no-brainer, though easier said than done. Also, there is a great deal of focus on improving efficiency and conservation of energy by improving electronics, appliances, and home and building insulation.

It is well understood that retrofitting homes and commercial buildings with proper insulation can dramatically reduce electricity use. Pickens cited studies that show that the equivalent of one million barrels of oil per day in energy would be saved, as proper insulation would slash both air conditioning costs in warm weather and heating costs in winter.

Transitioning to compact fluorescent lights, which use 20–33 percent of the energy used by equivalent incandescent lamps, is another practical energy policy that could cut electric power use by up to 7–10 percent, according to General Electric. But there is little new to talk about in this area; only a need to follow through. The Obama administration has already put forward many initiatives to conserve energy and promote these kinds of improvements with billions of dollars from the Recovery Act. These are laudable goals, which in time could make a measurable impact, and should by all means be followed through, but they miss the "elephant" that poses the greatest threat.

More than anything else, we have to bolster our weak spot and get away from petroleum-based transportation fuels. To this end, an uncomfortable alliance has been formed between political isolationists and environmentalists. The environmentalists are most concerned with averting the disastrous consequences of global warming, and the isolationists simply want to eliminate dependencies on other nations for critical resources.

Unfortunately, where there is a fault line in the alliance, political opportunists in favor of the status quo have fertile ground to undermine any substantive progress. In the spring of 2010, there was an earthquake on this political fault line when the domestic oil drilling mantra "drill, baby, drill!" collided with the reality of the catastrophic oil spill from a BP offshore drilling rig in the Gulf of Mexico. Any compromise on the subject of domestic drilling, a priority for the energy independence crowd, was arrested by the environmental disaster of millions of gallons of oil dumped into the Gulf off of the coast of Louisiana. BP, a cannibal capitalist corporation of the nth degree, was accused of cutting countless corners in their deep-well-drilling practices leading up to the Gulf disaster (accusations made even more convincing by the many media reports stating that BP has more safety violations than all the other major oil corporations combined). Yet, as horrendous as the effects of millions of barrels of oil gushing into the Gulf of Mexico have been and will yet be, none of this has really changed the course of oil production and consumption. As one of the largest oil companies in the world, BP's profitability and future prospects remained strong. The uncomfortable alliance between political isolationists and environmentalists was shattered, as the latter saw impetus to ban all offshore drilling, while the former feared the loss of domestic jobs and an increase in the dependence on foreign oil.

Score this as a win for the status quo. There are tremendously powerful economic forces that are interested in maintaining the status quo. The costs of buying land and pumping oil are relatively stable, but the potential price of this diminishing resource could well rise to astronomical levels. During the peak in oil prices, oil company ExxonMobil became the most profitable business in the history of the world.

Listening to the news, you'll hear oil company executives deny that there is any corollary between oil prices and their record profits, and you will hear some politicians even deny that the war in Iraq and the greater instability in the Middle East have anything to do with oil—none of which passes the smell test.

It has always amazed me that the most vigorously touted technologies for "going green" are the least viable for all practical purposes. It is as if there were someone leading us on a wild goose chase for the "perfect" plug-in electric car or a cheap biofuel to supplant gasoline. It is as if there were a concerted effort to only promote the technologies that are ill-equipped to truly supplant fossil fuels for combustion in the near term.

As we've already begun to see, ethanol would strangle agriculture. Even now, some denounce ethanol with the well-rehearsed line "burning food for fuel." Other biofuels have similar problems or would pollute just as badly as burning gasoline. Incidentally, all biofuels are hydrocarbons—emphasis on "carbons." While some may argue that biofuels are neutral because the sources of biofuels ultimately derive their carbon from the atmosphere, they are not a solution for reducing greenhouse gas emissions.

In short, electric vehicles are an overhyped crock! They might be viable for daily commuters who drive to work and back and run errands within a narrow radius, but not for the overall transportation needs of American families. All experts agree that only the smallest vehicles are feasible for plug-ins or even fuel cells in the reasonably foreseeable future. Electric engines are really weak on performance, and yes, that includes hydrogen fuel-cell cars. Although many would point to examples like the Tesla Roadster, let's keep it real. It's an extremely expensive, extremely small, and extremely lightweight vehicle. The Tesla Roadster is no family vehicle! What about the Chevy Volt? It's a sedan, right? According to Chevrolet, the Volt, like other new electric cars, is only good for 40 miles after an overnight charge up. Show me an electric vehicle today that I could use to take my family of six on a road trip from the Giant Forest, Sequoia National Park, through Yosemite, and down to the Grand Canyon. There is no such vehicle, even on the drafting table, and if ever there is, you can be sure that it will depend on a battery with extremely toxic and potentially explosive components.

Hybrids are a fake-out as well, especially the hybrid SUVs, which get only slightly better fuel economy than conventional SUVs. Doubling or even tripling gas mileage doesn't solve global warming, and it certainly doesn't end the dependency on oil. If anything, hybrids extend the dependence on petroleum.

Despite the fact that policy debate in our cannibal country tends to be argued from polar extremes, I am not an extremist. I would never suggest that we toss out hybrids and forget about plug-ins. We absolutely should continue to pursue the potential of electric-powered vehicles, but to tackle the transportation issues of today, we must be honest about the current limitations of these technologies.

We Need Hydrogen

Everything from lawn mowers to commercial trucks run using internal combustion engines that burn some kind of hydrocarbon fuel. The entire automotive industry and infrastructure is based on this reality. The most efficient and effective solution would be to put something else in the fuel tanks of our existing and emerging transportation fleet.

There are some out there, like T. Boone Pickens, pushing for a transition to natural gas, and to be fair, trucks, buses, or any other conventional vehicle could be adapted to run on natural gas, which is mainly methane (CH_4) as opposed to gasoline (octane, or C_8H_{18}). I don't mean to lose you in the science, but just looking at the chemistry, you see that hydrocarbons are hydrocarbons. The difference is mainly in the size of the molecule. It is the hydrogen that we want out of these fuel molecules. The carbon is the waste, and the problem of carbon is still there with natural gas. With four hydrogen atoms to each carbon atom, it may be slightly better than gasoline, but it is not good enough to really address climate change.

So I have to ask, what about just hydrogen? You know, the "hydro" without the "carbon." Hydrogen is only the most abundant element in the universe. It's the "H" in H_2O. It's the stuff that we launch rockets with. It's the stuff that, when burned, produces water as waste—no carbon. Hydrogen is found everywhere on earth: in water, fossil fuels, and all living things. Most significantly, it has the most powerful impulse in combustion of any element, which means that it has the potential of being the most efficient fuel of all internal combustion fuels.

We are usually so wasteful in our view of energy. We look for something to burn and couldn't care less what happens next. We put fuel in and pump out waste. We think of energy linearly, while the physical universe works with cycles of energy exchanges. There is no waste in these cycles; everything is recycled. Nature is an efficient system where what is waste to one component is fuel to another. Many of the most elegant cyclical energy exchanges found in nature are currently beyond our technology to reproduce, but not the cycle of water to hydrogen and oxygen and then back to water again. We know how to do this! We have the technology to design a closed-system, non-polluting, hydrogen combustion engine to drive our vehicles.

It amazes me that, with all of the talk of alternative fuels, there is so little talk of hydrogen outside of fuel-cell technology, a technology for producing electricity, which doesn't easily produce nearly the power of hydrogen combustion. Incidentally, NASA has been using hydrogen fuel cells for more than forty years, so this technology is far from new.

BMW has produced its Hydrogen 7, a seven-series sedan that runs on hydrogen combustion and maintains driving performance that is comparable to the gasoline-powered version. California has been quietly moving forward with its hydrogen highway, an infrastructure for hydrogen-powered vehicles. In the early 2000s, Airbus Deutschland announced a hydrogen-powered version of the A310 Airbus, also called the "Cryoplane." This information is out there if you look for it, but it is surprising that, given the mainstream media attention to the overall themes of gas prices and "going green" initiatives, there is hardly any attention paid to the most obvious and immediately viable alternative transportation fuel—hydrogen.

Hydrogen received a fair amount of hype in the early 2000s, due in part to the success of the best seller *The Hydrogen Economy* by Jeremy Rifkin. More recently, though, there has been a very broad campaign to discredit hydrogen as a solution. Frankly, I've noted more opposition to hydrogen than any other alternative fuel. Both ends of the political spectrum have united to tamp down any momentum toward realizing a so-called hydrogen economy.

One has to wonder why so much effort has been committed to opposing a theoretical solution to so many problems. It is certainly not scientific to shun a potential discovery and dogmatically preach a prejudiced disregard for a vast field of study. That is the modus operandi of corporate or political interests, not of science. On a scientific basis, hydrogen is the answer.

That's not to say that hydrogen is completely without problems. It may be the most abundant element in the universe, but it is virtually never found in its bare state. Because it is the simplest element, it bonds with other elements like carbon and generally has to be extracted from larger compounds. Also, because it is the smallest and simplest element, it reacts with nearly everything and can even pass right through larger molecules, making storage and transport difficult. And, right now, since its production is very limited and demand is limited mainly to scientific research, the current unit cost to purchase hydrogen is high. This problem, however, could be quickly remedied by mass production.

Despite what antagonists would have you believe, hydrogen can certainly be mass-produced. Instead of searching the world for an underground reservoir, dealing with fractious foreign governments, drilling while hoping to avoid another BP disaster, and finally refining oil, ready-to-burn hydrogen can be produced from water through a process called "electrolysis." In this process, passing an electric current through water separates the hydrogen from the oxygen (and the electricity required for electrolysis could just as well come from wind power or solar).

Hydrogen has been criticized as an inefficient and expensive replacement for gasoline, with some even citing the fact that there is more hydrogen in a liter of gasoline than in a liter of liquid hydrogen. For this reason, physics professor Richard A. Muller labeled hydrogen a "nonsolution" in his book, *Physics for Future Presidents*. He is certainly not the harshest critic and actually agrees that more research on hydrogen as a transportation fuel is warranted, particularly if fuel efficiency can be improved. He notes that hydrogen has "2.6 times the energy of gasoline per pound—but because hydrogen is so light, a pound of it takes up a lot more space."[42] That was a simple way of noting that liquid hydrogen has less than a tenth of the density of gasoline. In a way, you could think of gasoline as an efficient "suspension" for hydrogen. All else being equal, cars would need gas tanks three times larger and designed to store liquid hydrogen at the requisite –423°F. I agree that this is a problem, but not an inscrutable one. All other things need not be the same.

Yet while honest onlookers are confused and buried under a mountain of "facts" about how hydrogen is less efficient than gasoline and electric according to different metrics, no one remembers to restate the fact that we can "make" hydrogen from water. That's something we cannot do with gasoline, natural gas, or biofuels. This is the perspective that is so often lost as the "experts" argue in the weeds. Hydrogen is a

42. Richard A. Muller, *Physics for Future Presidents* (New York: W. W. Norton, 2008), 302.

high-energy fuel that we can manufacture in unlimited supply. Further, arguments against hydrogen are somewhat disingenuous, because when you look at all of the electricity that is wasted in transmission or during hours of underutilization of the power plants, there is also a great deal of inefficiency in our present method of power conversion. There is certainly wasted fuel and resources in every oil spill, in every political complication in the supply chain, and in the overall process from well to tank. The disastrous BP oil spill of 2010 certainly was not an ideal picture of waste-free conservation. Its costs were far more than the price of the lost fuel. Yet you still hear complaints about the inefficiencies in the power conversion of the most abundant element in the universe, one that we can obtain from water through a very simple process. Hmmm.

The thing is, all the problems with hydrogen can be solved with effort. Indeed, considering that hydrogen has three times the energy per pound as gasoline and produces high-pressure steam as exhaust, greater fuel efficiency in hydrogen engine cars is not only theoretically possible, it's already patented. So where is the effort? Even if you strongly believe that theoretical hydrogen fuel-cell technology is a better solution than the current hydrogen combustion model, why not start now, building the hydrogen infrastructure that both technologies need? Isn't the idea of leveraging our entire global energy infrastructure off of the most abundant element in the universe worth the effort of solving what are fundamentally logistical problems? Where is the media attention to create the political will?

Oh yeah, politics. I almost forgot that we live in the real world, and politics is at the heart of any real solution. There are massive economies based entirely on petroleum. Some say that the entire global economy is based on it. Didn't I just say that the most profit ever collected by a single company in the history of the world was by ExxonMobil, an oil company? People die every day for reasons that are, in one way or another, related to oil. So, I have to believe that there are people who would be willing to kill to prevent the obsolescence of gasoline any sooner than is inevitable.

I think that the greatest reason for ignoring the potential of hydrogen and hoping that people forget about it is its potential for destabilizing the economic status quo. After you build an infra-structure of electrolyzers and a distribution system, there is no way profiteers can centralize control of this infinite resource. How do you profit from a fuel that anyone with access to water and electricity could make? Just as many farmers abandoned cheap crops for so-called cash crops, energy companies lack a profit motive to pursue hydrogen.

Energy Cannibals

Is there no coalition powerful enough to counter this opposition and make hydrogen happen anyway? You would think so, with all of the groups clamoring for energy independence or an end to pollution. Then again, maybe that is another overriding problem: too many conflicting efforts supposedly attempting to do the same thing.

First, you have the purists out there; you know, the ones who can find a million uses for hemp and who are often at odds with the practical realities that people don't want to drive slower, use less power, or live in smaller homes. These are people who believe that you must replace gasoline with nothing less than a perfect solution. If that means everyone must drive small electric cars limited to a forty-mile range between charges, people should just suck it up, never mind the families with enough kids and pets to fill a GMC Suburban. (Incidentally, Professor Muller also listed electric automobiles as a "nonsolution.") These ascetics have been easily swayed by the critics and have thus been slow to embrace hydrogen combustion. They are typically not knowledgeable enough to see through the disinformation. The objections over hydrogen's inefficiencies seem reasonable enough, despite the reality that none of our energy sources are very efficient. The truth is that internal combustion engines capture only 15 percent to 20 percent of the energy in gasoline, and the conventional electric-power grid is only 33 percent efficient. The difference with hydrogen is that we can "make" it! If we make it strategically, we could actually increase the efficient use of our power plants.

Then you have contrarian scientists. You know, the ones hired to say that smoking is good for you and global warming is a myth.

They're out there programming people with the line that hydrogen is not a source of energy, but only an energy carrier, which is silly because all matter is such. Before buying that line, people should brush up on the law of conservation and the relativity of mass to energy. All matter has potential energy, whether or not we've discovered the technology to release it in a controlled process. Just because some matter is easily combustible and some isn't doesn't change the relativity of matter to energy; but I digress.

There are a plethora of reasons to replace petroleum fuels, and the most immediate, carbon-free alternative to gasoline is hydrogen. It is the unfortunate nature of cannibalism to only look as far as the next meal, never mind the long-term implications of obfuscating the best solutions.

Why is it a virtual secret that BMW has cars that drive on it, Airbus has a plane that flies on it, and California has fuel stations that pump it? If this is news to you, it's news for many others. It's time that these facts make the news.

Enter oilman T. Boone Pickens and his plan. This may be just the turn to make the dream of a hydrogen economy a reality. The Pickens Plan, like the rest, does not include hydrogen, but, as I mentioned, he wants us to switch our transportation fuel from gasoline to natural gas. The notion of converting to a natural-gas-based transportation system would lay the groundwork for the transition to pure hydrogen combustion as the alternative to gasoline. There are a lot more headaches in converting from gasoline to gas than from one gas to another. There is a good chance that converting a car from natural gas to hydrogen could be a shop procedure that could be done at the neighborhood service station. In the meantime, someone needs to push a plan to install electrolyzers at fuel stations across the country to make hydrogen on-site. Prices would drop, and the oil companies would have to focus on plastics.

Hydrogen is the only readily available resource that could completely replace gasoline, diesel, and jet fuel without compromising power and performance. The car companies could adapt to this *now*. The way the engines of today work would remain fundamentally unchanged. Cars, SUVs, trucks, and all other forms of transportation would still be in play. Then you'd have the potential for innovation that cannot yet be imagined.

Cleaner, Safer, Renewable Energy for All

As I have said, hydrogen is the most basic element in the universe, composed of one proton and one electron. It is everywhere. If properly harnessed and made from renewable sources, it would be what Peter Hoffman, author of *Tomorrow's Energy: Hydrogen, Fuel Cells, and the Prospects for a Cleaner Planet*, called the "forever fuel." Its only byproducts are heat and pure water. The simple circle of water to energy and back to water is as elegant as it is infinite. It just makes sense.

Some might be inclined to wonder whether water, something so essential to life, would then be commoditized to replace the revenue made from oil. In fact, water is already becoming a major geopolitical hot button. The United Nations and many new outlets have given a lot of credence to the notion of a global water crisis, despite the fact that we all know the planet is mostly water and water regularly falls from the sky. There is in fact no water crisis, but rather a *clean* water crisis. The process of electrolysis doesn't require clean water, just water. Industry wastes far too much drinking water for purposes that don't strictly require it and pollute far more water, rendering it undrinkable, but these issues are beside the point. Sure, we break the hydrogen out of water, but when we burn hydrogen, it reunites with oxygen, creating water. Hydrogen as fuel is no threat to the water supply. And where there is water, whether clean or dirty, there is potential fuel.

In 2009, when NASA bombed the moon, they were looking for water. Why? Water (H_2O) is the key to moon colonization, because, in addition to being drinkable, H_2O gives you hydrogen for fuel and oxygen to breathe. It is mendacious to suggest that hydrogen is perfect for supporting the operations of a permanent moon base, but all wrong for energy applications on earth.

As Hoffman writes in his book, hydrogen can "propel airplanes, cars, trains, and ships, run plants, and heat homes, offices, hospitals and schools…As a gas, hydrogen can transport energy over long

distances, in pipelines, as cheaply as electricity (under some circumstances, perhaps even more efficiently), driving fuel cells or other
power-generating machinery at the consumer end to make electricity
and water. As a chemical fuel, hydrogen can be used in a much wider
range of energy applications than electricity."[43]

There are some who speculate that hydrogen is simply too dangerous to ever be safely used for cars, but hydrogen may still be safer than
gasoline. Gasoline is a stable liquid, viscous enough to adhere to other
materials (like your skin and clothes), and it pools on surfaces, creating explosive risks. Hydrogen, however, is lighter than air, has to be
pressurized to be stored or transported, and immediately evaporates
if it escapes its container. When hydrogen is spilled, it doesn't puddle,
presenting an ignition hazard, but simply escapes upward. It's odor-
less, its flame is invisible, and its heat rises quickly, thus emitting very
little radiant heat. Unless you're in physical contact with a hydrogen
fire, it won't hurt you.

Yes, hydrogen burns, though. That is the point! But those who
attempt to invoke fear as a mechanism to obviate the hydrogen solution
are being disingenuous at best. The potential energy that we can leverage
from burning hydrogen is substantial, and fuel cells have tremendous
potential without combustion. Those who use images of the burning
Hindenburg are not making a logical case on scientific grounds, but are
appealing to ignorant emotion. Hydrogen is not more dangerous than
gasoline, natural gas, or a host of other common chemical compounds.
Producing and storing hydrogen effectively could usher in a real hydrogen economy, to the benefit of this nation and the rest of the world.

Of course, if we really did this, it would eventually put most of the
oil companies out of business and collapse the economies of certain
OPEC nations, which, I believe, is the actual reason why we never
hear this through mainstream channels.

Hydrogen may be the linchpin to resolving the transportation fuel
question, but, unlike fuels that merely need to be refined, hydrogen has

43. Peter Hoffmann and Tom Harkin, *Tomorrow's Energy: Hydrogen, Fuel Cells, and the Prospects for a Cleaner Planet* (Cambridge: MIT Press, 2002), 6.

to be produced from water or some other compound. It can be produced in a substantially centralized system (at major hydrogen plants), through a decentralized system (at neighborhood fuel stations), or via a completely decentralized system (most people could produce and store their own hydrogen at home). The real question, then, is one of costs, particularly the cost of producing hydrogen.

At present, the electricity needed to electrolyze water to produce hydrogen is more expensive than other methods of hydrogen production. In time, though, after a significant hydrogen infrastructure is developed, I believe the cost of hydrogen production could be nearly negligible. Some fear, though, that the carbon-emission benefits of hydrogen will be lost, because the cheapest way to produce hydrogen is from natural gas, at least for now. Improvements to the power grid are necessary to reduce the cost of electrolysis. Making electricity cheaper and more abundant is a critical component of solving our energy issues. Otherwise, economics will follow the path of least resistance, and dependencies on fossil fuels, with their greenhouse gas emissions, will continue. To complete the circle of clean energy, the cost of hydrogen production from clean sources must come down.

Wind, hydropower, and biomass power (generated by burning plant material such as wood waste and agricultural residue) are already cost competitive in many parts of the world and can be used to generate electricity for the electrolysis process. Wind power, for instance, is now the fastest-growing new source of energy; it averages 6–8¢ per kilowatt-hour at the wind generator, down from 40¢ in the early 1980s, though collection and transmission costs must be added. Photovoltaic (solar) and geothermal costs, however, are still high, and will need to come down considerably to make the process competitive with the steam-reforming process of natural gas now used most often in the production of hydrogen.

We need to design an overcapacity system for electricity generation, which would greatly reduce the cost of producing hydrogen or charging electric cars. Strategically located new power plants need to be built, together with an improved-efficiency transmission system.

Without compromise, the entire country can be powered without fossil fuels. This will, however, require a significant investment in a new energy infrastructure.

The geography of the country comes equipped with what some new energy enthusiasts call the great wind corridor. This area, the Great Plains, covers parts of Colorado, Kansas, Montana, Nebraska, New Mexico, North Dakota, Oklahoma, South Dakota, Texas, and Wyoming, totaling approximately five hundred thousand square miles. Windmills as a strategic energy solution may have seemed like a fanciful notion, but a 2007 Department of Energy study showed that developing the infrastructure to fully capture the estimated potential of the so-called U.S. wind corridor would produce as much as 20 percent of our needed electricity. Further political incentives are the estimated 138,000 new jobs that would be created in the first year of making this transition, and the more than 3.4 million new jobs that would be created over a ten-year period.

Similarly, our otherwise-barren deserts provide significant potential for solar power generation. Pickens predicts, "Building out solar energy in the Southwest from western Texas to California would add to the boom of new jobs and provide more of our growing electrical needs—doing so through economically viable, clean, renewable sources."

We also need to explore the use of geothermal energy production for our electrical grid. The term *geothermal* means "earth's heat" and is derived from two Greek words, *geo* (earth) and *therme* (heat); the earth's thermal energy is also called *geothermal energy*. As we learned in elementary school, the core of the earth is very hot, upwards of 9,000°F. The concept of usable geothermal energy is based on the principle that, if water descends to lower levels of the earth's crust through deep fissures, it will heat up and return to the surface, thereby transferring heat from inner layers to the surface. Natural instances of this process appear on the surface as geysers or hot springs.

The idea behind geothermal energy production is to mimic this natural process by drilling down to where the temperature rises approximately 17 °C to 30 °C for every kilometer deeper (50–87°F every one mile deeper), pump water in, and utilize the high-pressure, returning steam to drive electricity-generating turbines. With the hot water and steam used for initiation of generators, there's no combustion of fossil fuels. As a result, there are no harmful emissions of gases into the atmosphere. Only water vapor gets released. Generally, though, geothermal plants require strategically located sites at the borders of the earth's tectonic plates, where magma may leak into the upper layers of the earth's crust.

Some have suggested that geothermal energy has the potential to provide fifty thousand times the energy that can be gained from oil and coal across the world.[44] There are naturally occurring geothermal resources, from shallow, surface vents all the way to a couple of kilometers-deep reservoirs of hot water and steam, which could be brought to the surface and exploited. The most commonly considered disadvantage of exploiting geothermal energy is the fact that there aren't many areas of high volcanic and tectonic activity that are naturally suitable for exploitation. Actually, although volcanoes and hot springs are the simplest sources of geothermal energy, drilling technology is such that we could tap into the earth's heat in far more locations than merely where the crust is thinnest.

Perhaps what are most needed for our electrical grid are a few well-located nuclear power plants. Nuclear is clean, it can be produced anywhere, and it is virtually inexhaustible. Of course, ever since the Three Mile Island accident of 1979, the subject of nuclear energy has been rather controversial. Really, it could be said that there is an irrational level of fear surrounding nuclear for this reason. In truth, the opposition to nuclear energy has principally been rhetorical, symbolic, and largely without foundation; after thirty years of study, the actual harm done by Three Mile Island or even Chernobyl, the worst of all nuclear accidents, is markedly less than that of other energy sources.

The Paul Scherrer Institute in Switzerland found that, between 1970 and 1992 (a fairly narrow time frame including both the

44. Jeff Tester and Ron DiPippo, "The Future of Geothermal Energy: Structure and Outcome of the Analysis," Presentation at the Doe Geothermal Program Workshop (Cambridge: MIT, 2006).

Chernobyl and Three Mile Island incidents), nuclear power had the best safety record of all major energy sources, both in terms of total deaths and deaths per terawatt of energy produced each year. The results for the top four sources were: coal, with 6,400 total deaths and 342 deaths per terawatt per year; hydroelectric power, with 4,000 total deaths and 884 deaths per terawatt per year; natural gas, with 1,200 total deaths and eighty-five deaths per terawatt per year, and nuclear power, with thirty-one total deaths and eight deaths per terawatt per year.

This is not to suggest that nuclear energy is a panacea. There are very significant caveats. First, there are dramatic, long-term health hazards associated with mining uranium. Then, there is the matter of what to do with nuclear waste. The hysteria over these concerns, though, far exceeds the actual risks. It is really a matter of choosing the lesser of evils.

Compared with nearly any other system currently in use for generating power, nuclear is most equipped to provide the continuous supply of electricity that our civilization requires. Whether you burn coal, oil, natural gas, or the like, you are dealing with finite resources. Wind and solar solutions are inconsistent. Hydroelectric and geothermal are generally geographically bound. You can build a nuclear power plant virtually anywhere and produce power indefinitely.

Really, when you compare nuclear power to other power-generation systems in terms of the facts, it is hard to see why we don't use nuclear as our main source of electricity, unlike the French and others, who use nuclear almost exclusively.

Just considering our existing use of nuclear power, we find that its use substantially mitigates the emissions of greenhouse gases. A report, *The Keystone Center Nuclear Power Joint Fact-Finding*, published in June 2007 with funding from the Pew Charitable Trusts, the National Commission on Energy Policy, and nuclear industry representatives, reported that failing to replace existing nuclear power plants over the next half-century would actually increase carbon emissions by 12.5 gigatons. We have to consider the tremendous weight that nuclear is now pulling for the environment.

Nuclear fission energy actually has a lower greenhouse-gas emission rate than photovoltaic electric generation (solar power). Even cost effectiveness favors nuclear, which is nearly a third less costly in terms of operation, maintenance, and fuel per kilowatt-hour than fossil fuel, steam-power generation, and two-thirds less costly than either gas turbine energy or small-scale photovoltaic or wind energy.

Yet, according to the Department of Energy, only 20 percent of the electricity in the U.S. comes from nuclear plants, and "more than 90 percent of the power plants to be built in the next twenty years will likely be fueled by natural gas."[45] No new nuclear plants have been built in thirty years.

Why? The short answer is fear. The slightly longer answer is politics. The Cold War has given many the impression that all things nuclear are bad, but there is actually very little validity to most of the anecdotal indictments against nuclear power. Detractors will cite the expense of building nuclear power plants, the risks of nuclear meltdowns, the fact that the technology can be used for bombs, the toxicity of plutonium, or the unusual notion that it is bad for humanity to have an unlimited abundance of energy, because it would spur overutilization and waste. But the only substantive counterargument is that there isn't much of a long-term solution to nuclear waste. In most cases, nuclear waste can be reprocessed for future use, at least theoretically, but this is a complicated and politically charged issue.

In any case, there are several fully sustainable solutions for generating electricity without emitting so-called greenhouse gases. From these stationary generators, we can produce transportation fuels in the form of hydrogen and charged batteries for electric vehicles. Conserving and harnessing renewable forms of electricity not only has incredible economic benefits, but is also a crucial piece of the oil-dependence puzzle.

In addition to improving the volume of electricity generated, we need to enhance the efficiency of the distribution of energy with what some call a "smart grid." A smart grid would deliver electricity

---

45. U.S. Department of Energy, http://www.energy.gov/energysources/electricpower .htm. Accessed August 9, 2010.

using a bidirectional, digital monitoring system to keep track of all electricity flowing in the system, control appliances at consumers' homes, and thereby more efficiently use electricity. Theoretically, a smart grid should incorporate transmission lines that reduce power loss and integrate alternative sources of electricity, such as solar and wind, from distributed locations.

In our current system, electric utility companies are only concerned with delivering electricity to client sites. By adding data communications and application logic to the system, a smart grid could selectively turn on those home appliances and factory processes that can run at arbitrary hours (such as washing machines, in the case of home appliances) during off-peak hours. At peak times, such a system could selectively turn off appliances to reduce demand. And if appliance manufacturers worked with power companies on standards, they could eliminate the standby mode feature on countless appliances, thus avoiding drawing power to unnecessarily maintain a clock or respond to remote controls or electronic switches. The system would be capable of routing power in optimal ways to respond to a very wide range of conditions.

It may not be the "granola way," but we will continue to need more and more energy. We live in the Information Age. We have to accept that reality. Even the notion of all-electric vehicles requires more power. To concentrate national energies on energy, divide-and-conquer politics, which is cannibalizing our internal resources, will have to be replaced by a united effort.

Otherwise, energy costs will continue to bankrupt our businesses, immobilize our sprawling nation, pollute our planet, and fund our enemies. One step to avert the total disintegration of our cannibal country is to give the power to the people.

CHAPTER TEN

Bring the Money
Home to Momma

There was a time, now exaggerated by nostalgia, when there was generally only one breadwinner in a family. Sentimentally, we would like to believe that it was a time of solid family values, but that notion is contradicted by the troubled (sometimes repressed) childhood memories of millions. Infidelity was so common that the escapades of public officials with their mistresses would hardly raise an eyebrow.

The mother of twelve children knew that her husband was cheating. It was suspected that he had a secret second family. For all of the pain she felt, she had no place to go. As pitiful as her situation was, she was not entirely unhappy. And she never uttered a word of complaint. In fact, she taught her children to love and respect their father. When he would come home, she did everything you could imagine to make his welcome warm, because her husband had a key redeeming quality: he brought his paycheck home.

There was always food on the table. The children were always clothed and healthy. Through our lens of common, modern sentiments, it may be hard for us to comprehend the toleration of such lowered expectations. But, in the end, what was really more important to her? It was a different world. Things could have been worse. In fact, they surely would have been if he had left. No, he was bringing the money home at a time when there were few alternatives to putting up with the situation, so she could overlook the moral treachery and disrespect.

Many American corporations are like that husband, out philandering around the world, chasing easy money, cheap labor, and new markets. Hey, that is what corporations do. The question is whether they'll bring the money home.

Outsourcing services and exporting jobs rightfully arouses the ire of the American middle class, which once subsisted on filling those very same business needs. Yet it is impractical, if not absurd, to expect businesses not to pursue greater profits. The global economy is a reality, and the progress of Europe and Asia suggests that we need the global economy more than it needs us. Businesses have to be able to compete internationally, which means competing where the standards and costs of living are lower than our own.

Protectionism Won't Save the Middle Class

The bipolar debates over trade disparities and the unwanted effects of globalization usually come down to free trade versus protectionism. Both of these extremes make for entertaining discussions that go nowhere positive.

There are superficially reasonable arguments for protectionism. Outspoken, outlandish, and occasionally outrageous political activist Lyndon LaRouche argues that protectionism is the way to save the economy, based on the ideas of "physical economics," and he is not alone. Conservative Pat Buchanan has publicly made essentially the same arguments. They both contend that protectionism is fundamentally American, the policy of Alexander Hamilton, one of the chief architects of the U.S. Constitution, and that it was fundamental to developing the economy of America. Some have said plainly that protectionism is constitutional, implied in the Constitution, and more clearly described in Hamilton's "Continentalist" papers and his letter to James Duane. In the early days of this country, British free traders certainly didn't want the U.S. to become a competitive industrial power and used free-trade rhetoric to stifle the development of American manufacturing, which, at least initially, could not compete in pricing with Britain. Therefore, one could well argue that protectionist policies gave the country the breathing room to develop from an upstart experiment in democracy into the world's leading economy.

In 1850, a nearly forgotten economist by the name of Willard Phillips authored *Propositions Concerning Protection and Free Trade*, which argued in support of protectionism. This was, ironically, contrary to his original intent, as he stated in his preface: "I had the good fortune or misfortune, on investigating the subject anew, to convert myself to the opinions I had undertaken to combat."

In all, Phillips book put forth seventy propositions outlining the rationale for protective legislation. It is fascinating to note how many of his arguments for protectionism are still used 160 years later by economic nationalists. Consider his most long-standing arguments:

VI. Revenue laws will promote either domestic or foreign industry—Free trade is in favor of the foreign.

VII. The promotion of our own industry, or neglect of it, has momentous consequences.

X. Some kinds of foreign imports have a better influence upon the general welfare than others—Free trade says there is no difference...

XI. The whole world is not one community, to all intents and purposes, in respect to trade and industry—Free trade maintains that it is so.

XII. Men are to be considered as producers, as well as vendors and purchasers—Free trade considers them only as vendors and purchasers...

XV. The same amount of capital in a community can by protective legislation, be made to employ a greater amount of labor than would otherwise do—Free-traders expressly assumes the contrary...

XVII. In legislation, regard is to be had to the future as well as the present—Free trade considers only today...

XIX. Arts and manufactures do not spring up without encouragement—Disadvantages under which new arts and business labor—Free trade says, "Manufactures would encourage themselves as soon as the country was adapted to them."

XX. Low price, whether in money or barter, is not the sole criterion of the best economical policy—Free trade assumes that it is...

XXII. We ought not to depend upon any foreign country for such ordinary necessaries of life as the country is well adapted to produce...Free trade proposes to render us immediately and permanently so dependent...

XXVIII. Protection of our own domestic industry is no degree hostile to other countries—Free trade pretends the contrary...

XXXVIII. Protection favors the working classes; is for the benefit of both the many and the few—Free trade represents it be for only for a few...

XLI. Protection operates for the benefit of those in the interior in a far greater ratio than for that of those near the coast and ports—Free trade tends to make a few great commercial towns, and a thinly settled, poor, interior country...

XLVI. The object of protection is to make the interest of the public and that of the individual coincide...

XLVIII. Protection favors those who use capital—Free trade those who have it to lend.

LXX. A check to imports, and impulse given to our own production by duties, have always been followed by general prosperity; and an influx of imports, induced by low duty or however else, is always followed by general depression and distress, north, south, and west.[46]

It is almost uncanny how well some of Phillip's arguments have stood the test of time. This book predates not only the entire twentieth

46. Willard Phillips, *Propositions Concerning Protection and Free Trade* (Boston: Little, Brown, 1850), vii–xv.

century, but also the Civil War and expansion of the national territory. His prognostications of malaise in the Midwest and recessions and depressions following trade deficits have been repeatedly confirmed by history in the century and a half since. It is logical to argue that favoring important domestic industries with an eye on the future is a necessary role of central government in maintaining or improving a nation's economic position.

The thing about protectionism is that what makes sense at first look is undermined by modern realities. The early advocates of protectionism were mainly afraid of the economic power of the British Empire, but today we are "Britain" with respect to most of the counterarguments. Today, the arguments against protectionism are more substantive, even if they're counterintuitive. The seemingly common-sense claims that keeping out foreign goods will save domestic jobs, giving ailing domestic industries a chance to recover and prosper, and reduce the trade deficits are just not true.

Phillips argued that free trade favors the foreign, but with the dollar serving as the world's reserve currency, we are playing both sides. He argued that it is important to favor domestic industry, but many of our companies are now international, neither completely foreign nor domestic. Today, because of transportation and even more so the Internet, the world really is becoming one community, lending weight to the free trade argument.

The modern arguments against free trade are focused on lost jobs, when the reality is that protectionist policies can cause an even greater loss of jobs. By applying tariffs to imported goods or imposing quotas on the quantity of imports, the choice of consumer goods is restricted, thereby inflating the cost of goods and the cost of doing business. Free traders argue that protectionist policies suck buying power out of the economy, thus reducing consumer spending and ultimately destroying jobs. Some even argue that "according to the US Department of Labor's own statistics, 'protectionism' destroys eight jobs in the general economy for every one saved in a protected industry."[47]

47. Vincent H. Miller and James R. Elwood, "Free Trade or Protectionism? The Case against Trade Restrictions," International Society for Individual Liberty, 1988, http://www.isil.org/resources/lit/free-trade-protectionism.html.

The benefits of protectionist laws tend to be narrower than the broad national interests. There are certainly special-interest groups that benefit, such as big domestic industry corporations, unions, farmers groups, and certain domestic workers. Such groups reap higher profits by charging higher prices and getting higher wages than they could expect in a global free marketplace.

Jagdish Bhagwati, a professor at Columbia University and a senior fellow at the Council on Foreign Relations, stated in an article for *The Concise Encyclopedia of Economics* that "the fact that trade protection hurts the economy of the country that imposes it is one of the oldest but still most startling insights economics has to offer."[48] He was referring to nineteenth-century, classical liberal philosopher John Stuart Mill, who said that trade barriers, specifically duties levied upon imports, are "chiefly injurious to the countries imposing them."[49]

The father of modern economics, Adam Smith, outlined the argument for free trade in the eighteenth century by describing a world in which different nations would specialize in the production of what they did best instead of trying to be self-sufficient, and all would profit from free trade. The Smith rationale for free trade is to improve one nation's own welfare (the so-called national-efficiency argument). In our era of globalization, the prevailing argument for free trade is to improve every trading country's welfare (the so-called cosmopolitan-efficiency argument).

The reality of international economic growth, particularly driven in the past fifteen years by the Internet, is that, whether you view matters along the lines of the national-efficiency or the cosmopolitan-efficiency arguments, reduced impediments to trade have benefitted the world. Centuries of economic reasoning, historical experience, and empirical studies have repeatedly shown that, while free market economics are not perfect and produce a number of

---

48. Jagdish Bhagwati, "Protectionism," *Library of Economics and Liberty Concise Encyclopedia of Economics*, 2008, http://www.econlib.org/library/Enc/Protectionism.html. Unless otherwise noted, all references to Bhagwati in this section are from this article.

49. John Stuart Mill, *Essays on Some Unsettled Questions of Political Economy* (London: Longmans, Green, Reader, and Dyer, 1844), i.84.

losers as well as winners, on the whole the net benefit far outweighs that of protectionism.

Professor Bhagwati wrote, "Many economists also believe that even if protection were appropriate in theory, it would in practice be 'captured' by groups who would misuse it to pursue their own narrow interests instead of the national interest." This is emphatically confirmed by the conduct of lobbying interests in recent decades. Industries that would be in the national interest to protect are lost within a thicket of companies that seek protectionist policies for anti-competitive objectives that are not in the broader interest.

The cost of living and the cost of doing business have to be factored in. As Bhagwati said, "One clear cost of protection is that the country imposing it forces its consumers to forgo cheap imports." While improved wages seem exactly like what we should be defending, eliminating low-priced imported products from the shelves of Walmart and Best Buy would have far-reaching, negative impacts on the broader public. As we have all seen, when times are tight more people rely on the discount retailers for their needs.

It's a complicated issue, but free trade wins on purely economic rationale in a jet-set, Internet-connected world. The principal arguments favoring protectionism are sentimental, nationalistic, or at best moral.

Unfortunately for that perspective, even the moral arguments fall flat under the weight of the facts. Just consider a few. The $14 trillion U.S. economy depends substantially on free trade. According to the Office of the U.S. Trade Representative, in 2008, U.S. exports totaled $1.8 trillion, or a record high 13 percent of U.S. GDP, and supported 20 percent of U.S. manufacturing jobs. The potential economic gains from trade for America are far from exhausted. Roughly three-quarters of the world's purchasing power and almost 95 percent of world consumers are outside America's borders. The office's *2006 Trade Policy Agenda and 2005 Annual Report, March 2006* concluded that jobs directly linked to the export of goods pay 13 percent to 18 percent more than other U.S. jobs. As surprising as it may seem, even our farmers are greatly benefitted. That report showed that agricultural exports hit a record high in 2005 and account for around a million jobs.

The Office of the United States Trade Representative reported on its web site that "according to the Peterson Institute for International Economics, American real incomes are 9 percent higher than they would otherwise have been as a result of trade liberalizing efforts since the Second World War."[50] In terms of the U.S. economy in 2008, that 9 percent represents $1.3 trillion additional American income. Between 2005 and 2008, exports rose by 43 percent, accounting for 47 percent of overall GDP expansion.

Free trade is very important to us now, and will only become more so as the rest of the world advances in consumer buying power. The U.S. makes up only 4 percent of the world population and most of the rest of the world would like to live like Americans. It will take a lot of buying to get them there. Free trade treaties enable our businesses to do the selling.

Nevertheless, while free trade is extremely helpful for international business, it does create very real problems for domestic products and workers. Willard Phillips was exactly right about free trade concentrating wealth in a few cities and a few hands while large swaths of the country are neglected. The question is how to make free trade work for the people left behind. Like the philandering father, our international businesses need to be persuaded to bring the money home to momma. Just growing the national GDP doesn't automatically result in national prosperity, especially as that wealth is increasingly concentrated in the top 2 percent.

Embrace Globalization, Spread the Wealth

There is a solution. It is not a binary issue, as pundits sell it, of either free trade or protection. Protectionists loathe the notion of American jobs going overseas, but that's a small price to pay for the net economic benefits. By leveraging lower production costs abroad, we enable greater economic activity here and increase the buying power of American workers. Really, the solution is largely to be found overseas. While free traders view all

50. Office of the United States Trade Representative, *Economy & Trade*, 2010. http://www.ustr.gov/trade-topics/economy-trade.

economic legislation as anathema, it is in fact necessary to craft a national strategy to acknowledge, exploit, and bequeath wealth to the country through globalization. The solution is to increase the common benefit of export commerce, create business opportunities in the developing world for domestic small businesses, and adopt a national economic growth strategy. The political will to pursue such goals may very well exist.

The populist anger that was expressed in early 2010 over executive bonuses was unfocused, failing to connect with any meaningful remediation. Particularly offensive to many was the $16.2 billion bonus pool of Goldman Sachs. Those set-aside employee bonuses could have instead paid off eighty thousand homes in foreclosure, paid $2,700 to each unemployed worker when the unemployment rate was 10 percent, or given every household in the country $146. David Grant, a correspondent for the *Christian Science Monitor*, composed a list of ten possible uses of that money, not as a whole sum, but for the average bonus to each employee. He stated that the average bonus was enough to buy 3,240 homes in Detroit (presumably at fire sale prices), pay for four years of Harvard Business School, buy forty cars, take five luxurious trips around the world, and many other things.

Now, no one has the right to co-opt a private business's profits. Goldman Sachs defended their decision to pay out enormous bonuses as necessary for their business's continued success, but one must wonder if the accumulation of wealth by such narrow interests is the best distribution of capital. Depression-era Senator Huey Long argued there was enough wealth in the country for every individual to enjoy a comfortable standard of living, but that it was unfairly concentrated in the hands of a few millionaire bankers, businessmen, and industrialists. Many make the same argument today, if not to the same degree. Long promoted a draconian system of wealth redistribution. His "Share Our Wealth" movement, with its "every man a king (but no one wears a crown)" slogan, proposed legislatively prohibiting anyone from accumulating a personal net worth of more than 100 to 300 times the average family fortune, enforced through a progressive tax that ultimately would exact 100 percent from the wealthiest. The resulting funds would be used to guarantee every family a basic household grant of $5,000 and a minimum annual income of one-third of the average family income. By today's standards he would be regarded as a nut case, but at the time he was a nationally powerful politician who even had the potential to challenge FDR for the presidency. He was shot before that could happen.

In any case, was he wrong in his premise? The greatest wealth is still concentrated in the hands of a few. Perhaps a more market-oriented system could accomplish the same goal, but without such business-stifling measures as the "Share Our Wealth" platform.

Some of the best companies in the country use profit-sharing models to recruit top talent, build loyalty, and spread the wealth. It sounds a little socialist, and it might be, but it creates a sense of common interest, with everyone focused on the profitability and growth of the whole organization. Typically, a company contributes a portion of its pretax profits to a pool that will be distributed among eligible employees. The amount distributed to each employee may be weighted by the employee's base salary, so that employees with higher base salaries receive a slightly higher amount of the shared pool of profits. Generally this is done on an annual basis.

This model can and should be adapted on a national scale. All businesses profiting from global investments should be required to distribute dividends to the public. Instead of weighting the profit shares to higher income levels, compensation should be directed when possible to communities that are particularly negatively impacted by globalization. This would not be welfare, though. All recipients of dividends would have to be clearly contributing to the domestic economy. The capital distributions could finance or subsidize domestic small businesses in the form of grants. Instead of looking for jobs to return from overseas, we have to either help stretch the jobs that remain or drive new job creation. There are countless wannabe entrepreneurs who just need a little seed money. Whether subsidizing lower incomes or pouring the money into new business development, profit sharing could make up for all of the "damage" free trade creates. It is a classic win-win: reap the benefit while mitigating the damage.

Imagine for a moment that every time an American company opened a factory or some other operation overseas, it used the accompanying leverage and goodwill in that foreign land to negotiate a trading relationship between that community and the American community that was left behind. The presence of American businesses in the developing world elevates the standard of living and buying power of those communities, but rarely is the newly created buying power of these communities' consumers directed back in a concerted way. That's not to say that none of the wealth comes back indirectly, but merely that it is not ushered back strategically to create the best benefit.

A company intent on shedding the high costs of domestic production could go ahead and close operations in a town we'll call "Springfield" and open up in a village we'll call "Gualla" somewhere abroad. This makes business sense, because it will improve profitability by cutting the cost of labor facilities and providing tax benefits. It is a very good deal for Gualla, because as a result there is new industry and a significant source of employment that will drive the economic development of their nation. This is generally the end of the story in the real world, which leaves Springfield to fend for itself. Tough luck, Springfield, but that's the free market in a global economy.

Now, instead let's continue with the concept of "bringing the money home to momma." Imagine that the company builds a college in Springfield and pays the full tuition of their displaced workers. Then the company, now a hero to Gualla, negotiates on behalf of Springfield to buy products and services from Springfield businesses, even providing seed money to start new Springfield businesses. They finance and facilitate the opening of franchises in Gualla owned by entrepreneurs from Springfield. As Gualla begins to flourish, build infrastructure and homes, and start businesses of their own, the people of Gualla will buy a significant portion of their needs from Springfield. That is a win-win outcome.

We have to face the facts that it doesn't make sense for certain jobs to be done in lands where the cost of living is the highest in the world, when the work can be done for a fraction of the cost in the developing world. Here in America, high-paying jobs are being replaced by lower-paying ones, and this reality will continue. The ripple effect of this can be devastating to entire communities. At the same time, the companies that are shipping jobs to cheaper markets are reaping benefits. It only makes sense to return some of those benefits to those who have sacrificed, or rather been sacrificed. The key is to provide for the "general Welfare," as the Constitution puts it. Of course, there are those who would say that this is anti-American, but I don't think most Americans would mind any more than they minded the infusion of capital into the real economy caused by the housing bubble of the early 2000s. The difference here is that this cash infusion would be more sustainable.

If businesses brought home the money, it would make sense to completely unleash them to aggressively pursue the most profitable methods and strategies internationally. Open up markets everywhere, outsource to whomever, maximize profits in any way possible, but just make sure you bring the money home to momma.

Such a national profit-sharing initiative would change the political climate dramatically. Instead of a middle class that feels more and more like a Marxist proletariat, people would feel more invested in the success of the national business economics. It would be easier to overlook the indulgences of the super-rich; just like the wife at the outset, the middle class would have the things that matter most.

More is needed, though.

The consistently positive growth of the U.S. economy has been due to the growth of the consumer base, the economic elevation of the middle class, and principally, the entry of new households into the middle class. The "new" middle class will come from the developing world. There are a good three billion people seeking to enter it. There is much to be gained by investing in the developing world.

Henry Ford once said that he paid his employees well so that they could buy his cars. The common viewpoint that there is little market potential in the underdeveloped world because of rampant poverty and corrupt leaders is short-sighted. Holding to this viewpoint will only cause us to continually lose ground to China, which is working with a number of African and South American nations. It only makes sense to follow their creativity in developing these nations in exchange for their resources. We should add to this follow-up economic development, setting up small businesses patterned after our own Main Street businesses. The closer they get to Western-like buying power, the more their desires for Western-like lifestyles will result in consumer activity that profits our businesses.

To this end, we could enable American small businesses to establish peer-to-peer relationships with potential counterparts across the globe. After all, why should it only be the domain of large corporations to do business internationally? There is no good reason. This is just unfamiliar territory.

It will take cooperative effort with government support. It would be in our best interest to establish a consortium that enables small businesses to expand internationally. There are a few, anemic programs out there now to do this sort of thing, but these are woefully inadequate. It is time for the little guy to see the benefits of globalization instead of only its liabilities.

Everyone knows that small business and entrepreneurs are the engines of employment in this country, but the government gives virtually no support to the creation of new businesses. Yes, there is a Small Business Administration, and banks are always encouraged to lend to small businesses, but these measures don't *create* new businesses. Banks, whether or not guaranteed by the SBA, generally don't provide seed money to companies that don't yet exist. Most new small businesses are started with personal savings, credit cards, and home-equity lines. With that in mind, it doesn't take much thought to realize that when we most need to create new jobs (as on the tail of the Great Recession of 2007–9), we utterly lack the capacity. Savings were exhausted by unemployment and increased energy costs. The credit crunch resulted in limited access to unsecured credit lines, and the mortgage crisis killed home equity, not to mention loans against such equity.

Career politicians who have never created a business from scratch seem clueless about this reality. Rhetorically pushing the banks won't accomplish anything. General tax cuts won't cut it either. New businesses that aren't created out-of-pocket by the founder rely on venture capitalists. During the years of irrational exuberance, venture capital was widely available. More recently, it has dried up.

Subsidizing, providing incentives, and creating safe harbors for early-stage venture capitalists and angel investors are what we need. Legislation and administrative policies should be crafted to entice investors to fund new ideas. Without funding, a brave entrepreneur may start a company, but he will avoid every conceivable expense, even some that are actually needed, like employees. With funding, an entrepreneur has the elbow room to execute his business plan as intended. He will create new jobs and optimize operations. As counterintuitive as it may seem, it generally costs more in the end to run a business on a shoestring budget.

Real job creation will come if we make it easier to start a business. Making it easier and cheaper to get independent health-insurance coverage and facilitating readily accessible startup capital are the most significant ways to create jobs.

Henry Ford once said, "A business that makes nothing but money is a poor business." We have become a nation relying on businesses that just make money. Where most businesses are left to fend for themselves, the nothing-but-money businesses grow too big to fail. Because of the distorted emphasis on dollars and cents, real work, real products, and the whole real economy are devalued. It may look good on paper to have billion-dollar paper businesses, but it has resulted in an economy with too much wealth concentrated in the hands of too few. Ultimately, this will even hurt these few ultrarich captains of paper business, as the value of inflated money collapses under the weight of emaciated, formerly middle-class consumers. We can never forget that all of the exponential dollar figures of leveraged capital and trading multiples ultimately have to be backed by something real at some point. It is when traders forget this fundamental truth that the system faces existential threats.

We need to adopt a national plan to develop resource-oriented wealth development at every socioeconomic echelon of our society.

It can be done through equitable capital distribution, instead of always deferring to the trickle-down theory of trusting the biggest corporations to somehow magically trigger Main Street business development. Sharing the profits reaped from offshoring; developing new consumers and trade partners in the underdeveloped world; providing affordable health insurance; and generating accessible startup capital for the creation of new businesses can all elevate the national economy to a level never before seen.

Unfortunately, in a cannibal country where self-interest always outweighs the common interest, it will likely never happen. It sounds too "socialist" to pursue a national economic strategy, never mind that this is precisely what our international competitors are doing. Without dramatic change along these lines, America is doomed to eat itself to death, while China and the EU take their places as the economic engines of the world. Such is the fate of a cannibal country…unless…

CONCLUSION

Why Are We Promoting
Economic Cannibalism?

"Cannibalism" calls to mind images of some isolated South Pacific tribes or certain precolonial African cultures. In truth, the existence "of cannibalism among aboriginal peoples has been greatly exaggerated by the conquistadors and other colonialists to justify their aggression. Today, the social stigma against cannibalism is so ubiquitous that its practice is virtually nonexistent.

Cannibalism is universally viewed as an abominable evil. In mythology, cannibalism was attributed to certain malevolent characters to allegorize their utter wickedness. Though there have been spiritual motivations in certain cannibal cultures, most often cannibalism was used against enemies, and certainly not against members of the same tribe. It amounted to a sort of psychological warfare, instilling fear in rival tribes. Justification was possible because the enemy was not the same as you, and thus consuming him was not actually an act of cannibalism. It is this alienation of the other that justifies so much evil in the world, including a different sort of cannibalism right here, right now.

The modern form of cannibalism is not for spiritualistic reasons. It is not psychological warfare. It is not even a matter of survival in the face of starvation. It is practiced because it is easier than working for sustenance, and because the cannibals just don't care about their victims. It is easier to exploit than to create. It is easier to gamble than to invest (particularly when gambling with someone else's money). Cannibal capitalism is easier.

In this environment, the rewards for building an honorable business that creates wealth for the broader community are becoming fewer and fewer. Short-term gains are worshipped instead. I experienced this firsthand with my building business. There was every incentive to build cheap, prefabricated, cookie-cutter houses on cleared farmland or woodland that could be bought cheaply and clear-cut. There was no incentive whatsoever to build custom, environmentally conscious, high-quality housing on infill lots. (Infill development is, as the name implies, developing within broad areas that are already developed— filling in, before spreading out.) If anything, there were disincentives. Government officials would praise what I was doing, but did nothing to address the disincentives that drove the market toward cracker-box homebuilding. So, why not just go for the loot, building cookie cutters and getting rich? I just had no interest in that.

Cannibal capitalism encourages dreams of a better life, and then exploits every aspect of the lives of the dupes who believe in honest, hard work and ideals. Like any Ponzi scheme, you pay off a few to lure in the many. Some infinitesimal few see their dreams come true, enough to perpetuate the fantasy and keep the masses believing. The overwhelming majority is duped, doomed to serve as food for the cannibals or become cannibals themselves.

Consider the story of Herman. He played by the rules from the start. Herman was an excellent student, attended a top-tier university, and took a well-paying job at a Fortune 500 company. He paid his bills, saved his money, and protected his credit. However, in this system, expenses expand to exhaust income, so he never really got ahead.

To live his dream, he realized he'd have to start his own business, so he quit his job and started working fulltime to fulfill his ambitions. Herman went to his bank for a small business loan. Though his banker was impressed by his business plan, he regretfully informed Herman that, despite their two-decade relationship, there was nothing he could do to help. Perfect credit, thousands in paid interest, tens of thousands in savings on deposit, and when he needed a business loan, there was "nothing" his bank could do. After spending countless hours at the Small Business Administration, he eventually realized that there was effectively no such thing as an SBA business startup loan.

Herman persisted. He searched for private investors and found that brokers held the keys to the private investor market. He paid the fees and hired a broker, but the broker turned up nothing. Finally, he came to the realization that he was on his own. He took out all of the equity in his home, started filling out all of the credit card applications that came through the mail, and amassed just enough capital to get started.

He hired an attorney and accountant, spent money on marketing and stationary, leased an office, bought equipment and materials, hired employees, opened his factory, and gave sweetheart deals to lure in his first customers. For some time, everyone around him was making money off his dream except him, as he couldn't yet afford to compensate himself. His once-perfect credit was now stretched thin, but his business plan was working. His savings were wiped out, but the business started to turn a profit. He was succeeding!

Then came the mortgage crisis and credit crunch. The bank reduced his home equity loan to the current balance, making it useless for revolving cash flow. He faced some of the same from his credit cards. Not realizing the scope of the economic crisis, he poured his last personal reserves into the business operations account. He sought to refinance his home to free up more capital. In the process, he discovered that his credit score had tanked, not because of any missed payments (he had none), but because of the overutilization of credit. He also discovered that the value of his home was now 35 percent lower than the debt against it. He was personally insolvent, at least on paper.

Out came the cannibals. Even though he had never missed a payment or even paid late, his loan was called in. His principal supplier reduced the purchase credit-account limit for his business. The new limit would not be enough to support his operations level, and worse, the supplier refused to ship anything until the account was paid down to the new, greatly reduced limit. Having not received a key shipment, Herman missed an important deadline. A key employee got that sinking feeling that his future was far from certain and submitted his resignation. Everything was falling apart, but Herman remained persistent. Just as he juggled to compensate for these many disappointments, a customer served him with a lawsuit for that missed deadline. At this point, becoming a cannibal himself seemed like the best option. He could devour his customers, cut corners on his product, ignore factory safety standards, lay off his employees, bring in undocumented workers, and outsource to India. He could survive at the cost of his conscience. Eat or be eaten is the law of the land in cannibal country.

Perhaps the worst indictment of cannibal capitalism is the fact that, if Herman chose to become a shark and take the cutthroat path through this crisis, he would have been regarded as a success—as long as it worked. If, however, he held to a high moral standard and accepted the resulting economic downfall, it would make him a failure. People want to believe that the failures in the system come from immorality and that success is moral in itself. The truth is more often the contrary. Legal Madoffism is the ideal of cannibal capitalism.

People are content with the notion of survival of the fittest, but we have to ask, who's eating whom? You can't win a game fighting your own teammates. In our system, we devour one another, to our own demise. By tightening credit on Herman, his creditors and suppliers made their fear a reality. Like a novice skier so transfixed on a tree that he inevitably crashes into it, time after time the nation steers right into the economic disaster it is dreading. Instead of accepting the system for what it is, a perverse blend of fear, self-interest, and idealism causes the players in the system to pick each other to death.

Loose monetary policy is good…no, it's bad…oh, it's kind of good…but only without too much leverage,…no, there should be healthy balance sheets with assets marked to market level…uh… unless the market is really bad, and then we should just ignore that.

When a bubble is building, we sing "Happy Days Are Here Again," but when reality comes back to bite us, everyone starts cursing the sky. The system is schizoid, confused, hypocritical, and self-destructive. The concept of natural market forces is oxymoronic (or maybe just moronic).

Everything about our system of economics is artificial. Bubbles are not aberrations, but are inherent to the design. As I have said before, money is a bubble inflated by perception, collusion, and emotion. While some reminisce about the days of the gold standard, gold is also an illusion. There is just not enough gold on the planet to match the production and consumption of seven billion people. A service economy depends on the liquidity that is only possible with cheap money, but the problem is that liquidity creates subjectivity in the valuations of commodities, and worse still, the circumstances for arbitrage. Then we find that too many prefer to play around with the numbers than invest in the real economy.

Remember kwashiorkor? The victim consumes only empty calories, while the body eats itself to death. Inflating cash by trading derivatives and diluted equities, arbitrage, and the like may result in trillions of dollars of financial activity and may even make up a substantial portion of our GDP, but these are empty calories. The body is starving for real nourishment.

Nevertheless, the arbitrage economics of inflated markets, inflated currency, and paper wealth is the reality. Good, bad, right, or wrong, it is what it is. We can either watch this big bubble occasionally burst whenever our hollow market practices collide with reality, or we can use the "wealth" of the system to accumulate *real* wealth and build a more sustainable growth path. Our economy may be bloated with empty calories, but that is true of the whole world. The question is: what will we do? Bubble economics will only get us to a point.

We Have to Feed the Middle Class

The body of this country is the middle class. With the possible exception of minimal gains on retirement accounts, the middle class does not directly benefit from the empty calories of the paper economy. Middle-income workers cannot borrow against their man-hours to make exponentially more than their actual wages. It doesn't even make sense. No, the masses have to be in touch with realities. Thereby, they provide an anchor for the bubble economy. Labor productivity, commodities, and real estate are the only real things in our economy, and they must be tenaciously defended, not debased to prop up the artificial value of paper.

To maintain a vibrant domestic economy, the middle class must be restored, and more importantly, improved. One of the biggest problems with the modern middle class is that it is falling below the middle. According to a U.S. Census Bureau report, *Income Distribution Measures Using Money Income and Equivalence-Adjusted Income: 2008*, 50 percent of all income is made by the top-earning quintile (20 percent of the population), while the middle quintile earned only 14.7 percent (see Figure 11.1).

While CEO compensation has edged back recently, in the early 2000s, top executive compensation exceeded seven hundred times that of an average worker, as reported by the *New York Times*.

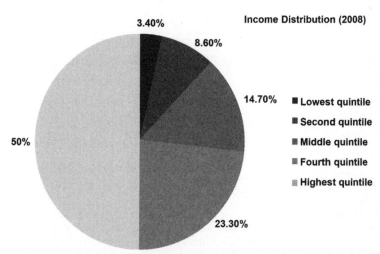

Source: U.S. Census Bureau report, *Income Distribution Measures Using Money Income and Equivalence-Adjusted Income: 2008*

Figure 11.1

But, oh yeah, upward wealth redistribution is regarded as success, but equitable distribution is socialistic or, the heavier pejorative, communist.

There is a logjam in our economy. Instead of healthy capital flows, there is stagnation in far too many sectors, most significantly middle-income wealth. It may feel good for the super-rich to look at a multiplicity of zeros on their personal financial statements while the middle class disintegrates, but the truth is that it is self-defeating. The rich need the middle class. The entire nation needs the middle class. The GDP doesn't grow in a healthy, sustainable way without a strong middle class. A more equitable distribution of the nation's wealth nourishes the economic health of the nation. The countries with the biggest gaps between the rich and the rest tend to be the poorest countries overall. Is that the way we want to go? It only makes sense that the easy money generated from arbitrage must be routed back to the real economy in ways that multiply economic activity.

It may sound socialist or even communist, but matters are becoming urgent. A January 2010 study from the Brookings Institution's Metropolitan Policy Program reported, "Suburbs saw by far the greatest growth in their poor population, and by 2008 had become home to the largest share of the nation's poor."[51] It described how, from 2000 to 2008, the number of poor people in the U.S. grew by 5.2 million, reaching nearly forty million, a rate that was twice the increase of the national population over the same period. Even as the economy showed signs of recovery, for many regular citizens the "labor market conditions...are the equivalent of a Great Depression-era," according to the Center for Labor Market Studies at Northeastern University.[52]

We have to remember that money isn't real. People, natural resources, manufacturing output, and salable services are real. Of

---

51. Elizabeth Kneebone and Emily Garr, "The Suburbanization of Poverty: Trends in Metropolitan America, 2000 to 2008," *Metropolitan Opportunity Series,* January 20, 2010, http://www.brookings.edu/papers/2010/0120_poverty_kneebone.aspx.

52. Andrew Sum, "The Labor Market Impacts of the Great Recession of 2007–2009 on Workers across Income Groups," *Spotlight on Poverty and Opportunity,* April 12, 2010, http://www.spotlightonpoverty.org/ExclusiveCommentary.aspx?id=12f13dec-535a-4586-872a-8abf5dc1c80d.

these, the most important component is the people. This is not only a matter of human compassion, but an economic reality. People should be educated, employed, and compensated. Resources should be conserved and used carefully. Manufacturing should be strategically supported both foreign and domestically. Trading the unreality called "money" for real things may be a colossal scam, but it is the game everyone is playing. You've gotta play to win. To do anything else is suicide.

It starts with human resources. The time is over for K–12 public education. Education tracks need to begin with prekindergarten and end with whatever achievable degree or certification an individual desires—for free. We need PK-Trade Certification, PK-Associate, PK-Bachelor's, PK-Master's, or even PK-Doctorate tracks. As far as interest directs and aptitude permits, our free public education should carry our children. There are many nations that set out far more career-minded exit points in their education system than we do. We have a generic precollege system with no guarantee that any student will ever go to college. A high school diploma is the most common educational level in our country, yet it is not geared to any trade, profession, or job. In fact, it's not geared toward a working environment at all. Does that really make strategic sense for a nation that wishes to be competitive in a rapidly changing, global economy?

There will always be a place for profit-oriented private schools, but it is not in the nation's interests to exclude otherwise-qualified Americans from reaching their professional potential. Leaving unrealized human capital undeveloped is not a sound strategy. Arbitrage traders make sure not to leave "money on the table" in our markets, and yet we leave vast swaths of our population out of the market, with all of the wealth this human capital represents.

After people, the most valuable commodities are natural resources. The unwise approach of exhausting one resource and moving on to the next robs future generations and destroys unknown future possibilities. Several whale species are still struggling to survive after two centuries of hunting reduced them nearly to the point of extinction. Whale oil supported the industrial revolution, and some would say that the decimation of the whales was a small price to pay for the prosperity that their oil endowed to humanity. Yet messing with the biosphere always has unknown, unwanted, and maybe even devastating consequences.

Loading the atmosphere with greenhouse gases, knocking off the tops of mountains to get to coal, poisoning waterways with industrial waste, dumping trash in our oceans, replacing mature hardwood trees with young pines or even deforesting entirely, encroaching on the habitats of countless species, and hunting endangered species are all generally opposed. Yet all of these things continue to take place. What will be the cost to the planet and to all of our lives? No one takes the long view in cannibal country, at least not enough to provoke real change. But strong, decisive change in man's stewardship of the earth is absolutely needed.

The resource whose exploitation has most undermined economic health and threatens the health of the planet is petroleum. Its costs—and the international dependencies it creates—pervert international commerce and equity flows. Some advocate decreasing dependency on this diminishing resource by raising its costs, thereby deterring its use. Unfortunately, this "solution" would only extend the mismanagement of and damage to our natural resources. OPEC would no doubt adjust supply and production to neutralize the intended effects. Meanwhile, businesses and consumers would further be strangled.

Petroleum must be supplanted and made obsolete, not priced out. The energy markets will gravitate to the cheapest, most accessible options, even if that inexpensiveness is the result of subsidies. Potentially, the biggest game changer for transportation fuel is hydrogen. Yes, hydrogen has problems, but so do such alternatives as biofuels, natural gas, and electric battery-powered transportation. As I discussed earlier, the problems with hydrogen can be mitigated. With technology we now have, we could totally transform the economics of transportation energy.

The difference between hydrogen and every other option is that we can mass-produce hydrogen from water. It's impossible to overemphasize this fact! Our internal-combustion-engine trans-portation infrastructure can be quickly adapted to this new fuel, because there would be no need for the development of significant new technology, as is the case with electric-powered transportation. If it were widely available, the cost could be pennies per gallon. Imagine what that would do for families and businesses.

For the economy to be best positioned for the twenty-first-century global economy, the focus must be on exports and international business development. The emerging markets in the far-flung corners of the world are the new wealth creators. Depending on an internal, consumer-driven service economy in an environment of trade deficits is unsustainable. The third wheel of manufactured goods and services must be used to grow the economy in concert with the growing global economy.

Unfortunately, the international strength of the dollar and the upward pressure on labor costs caused by the high cost of living in America undermine our ability to draw global wealth into the domes-tic economy. We want a strong dollar, we don't want suppressed wages, and so we can't match the labor costs of the poorest nations. (We shouldn't want to. Really, it would be grossly immoral to take away the only thing many underdeveloped nations have going for them—inexpensive manpower.)

So instead, we need to look at what equalizers can be achieved here that are not easily matched elsewhere in the world. We cannot match developing countries' labor costs, but they cannot match our technology, our sophisticated economy, and the buying power of the dollar, the reserve currency of the world. There are at least two domes-tic business sectors that need to take a bullet for the team: the oil industry and health insurance.

Looking forward to a hopeful future does not preclude living with current realities. People hated the bank bailouts and the concept of "too big to fail" institutions, but in this colossal global economy, we need international banks with thirteen-figure balance sheets, how-ever unpleasant that may seem. Believe me, we don't want to audit the Federal Reserve thoroughly and shine spotlights on all that they do and have done. Once the curtain is pulled back, the "great and powerful Oz" ceases to exist. The human psyche grants power to the mysterious, but quickly subtracts it from the familiar, because, as the cliché goes, familiarity breeds contempt. Because money is a materialized economic abstraction, you cannot predict how people will react to blatant revelation and repetition of that fact. Most likely people would soon forget, but not before another crash.

If the country were to invest heavily in a hydrogen-electrolysis infrastructure, the market would immediately respond with gasoline-to-hydrogen fuel system conversions. Every power plant and every fuel station could and should be equipped with electrolyzers. With production and storage costs subsidized, the costs of fuel could become negligible. The oil companies would still have their global market, because most countries would not be able to match such a hydrogen infrastructure.

Though widely feared as socialized medicine, a single-payer, "Medicare for all" health care system would greatly reduce health care costs and relieve families and business of a great financial burden. The opposition to such a system is almost entirely ideological rather than logical. Most health sector businesses would be unscathed or even benefit from the change. The health insurance corporations would take a big hit, but even they would retain a strong business in supplemental insurance and other types of insurance. Every other business in the country would enjoy tremendous relief. Profits would all rise, as would stock prices. The secondary economic benefits are innumerable. The increased buying power that comes with decreased health costs would certainly have multiplier effects throughout the economy.

The point is to strategically use the bureaucracy of the federal government to dramatically reduce the cost of living and the cost of doing business, so that domestic products and services can be sold more competitively in the global market. Instead of aggregating funds in the coffers of a few corporations, or worse, in the coffers of a few individuals with little or no benefits to the broader economy, it is more logical to aggregate and then redirect money spent for a general purpose to a general benefit. In fact, funds should be strategically used to maximize that benefit.

So, why not return to the commodity-based, gold-standard system, in which the total value of issued money is represented in a store of gold reserves? As I have said repeatedly, it won't work. Reestablishing gold as the basis for currency would especially devastate Western nations. There are some small nations that could theoretically back their currencies, but the large, complex economies of the G20 would be devastated by the constraints of a gold standard. Love it or hate it, we need fiat currency to keep up with global economic activity. This is especially true for nations like China, India, Brazil, and Indonesia, which continue to see broadening wealth distribution and middle-class growth.

Of course, fiat currency and dynamic markets inevitably and invariably lead to bubbles. This is the reality that no one wants to acknowledge, but is endemic to the system. In the February 2, 2010, *Forbes* article "Death, Taxes, and Market Crashes," senior editor Daniel Fisher stated, "You can add market crashes to the list of life's certainties." He was making a reference to the findings of the CFA Institute, a global, not-for-profit association of investment professionals. In one of their publications, *Financial Analysts Journal*, they reported:

> *The probability of a crisis can accumulate over a time horizon, which has a significant impact on long-run investments . . . Over a one hundred-year period, the probability of a crisis can be very large . . . Based on both simple and complex asset pricing models, such a rare event indeed has a high probability of occurring in a one hundred-year period (although just a small probability in a given year). In one hundred years' time, such an event is almost certain to occur, and investors should be prepared for it.*[53]

You may not want to heartily embrace this painful reality, but we need to accept the truth that there is no such thing as a moral immorality. The global economy is based on selfishness and exploitation and is driven by childish emotion. It will always bubble up and burst. These are characteristics of its artificial nature. You can even chart the

---

53. Guofu Zhou and Yingzi Zhu, "Is the Recent Financial Crisis Really a 'Once-in-a-Century' Event?" *Financial Analysts Journal* 66, no. 1 (2010): 24–27, http://ssrn.com/abstract=1462790.

consistent patterns of bubbles and busts. In fact, Hyman Minsky did it years ago in his theory of financial instability, laid out clearly in his 1986 book, *Stabilizing an Unstable Economy*. Minsky identified five stages to the bubble-bust cycle: displacement, boom, euphoria, profit taking, and panic. Others have built on and varied this description, but you can see this pattern leading up to nearly every major economic collapse the modern world has seen. Decades since Minsky's warnings, and despite the predictable nature of these patterns, history repeats itself time and again.

Whether we regulate the banks or not, the market will still crash again and again. Reinstate Glass-Steagall or apply the Volcker rule; it still won't matter. The course of history will always include the displacement of something old with something new. Excitement over the new will always result in some sort of boom, which, as people get rich, will lead to euphoria and irrational valuations as more and more want in on the action. Inevitably, profit taking will prick the bubble of irrational valuations, causing an accelerating decline as panic sets in. Soon enough, the news headline "Crash of ——" will ring out once again.

Given this inevitable cycle, the key is to use the excesses of the bubbles with a long-term view. "Tax and spend" is a long-time rallying cry of the political right against democratic politicians, but it needs to be reexamined. Conservatives have been known to say that you can't borrow and spend your way to prosperity, but that statement is antithetical to all business growth. Every business borrows and spends to build itself and its market share. During times of irrational exuberance in the market, it is critical to wisely spend as much money as possible on long-term infrastructure and other economic multipliers, because when the crash comes, these assets will remain. Tax and spend in the bubble, and shut it off the minute it bursts. Who would complain about taxes that are actually increasing wealth and the standard of living?

An investment expert once told me that the key to wealth building is the cycle of "cash to asset to cash." Our economy has been far too accustomed to transferring from assets to cash and then sticking to cash in one form or another. "Let your money make money" has become the axiom of the rich; they'd rather use financial tricks like interest-spread arbitrage instruments than reinvest in tangible things that build the real economy. People have been far more willing to give their money to a Madoff to build a house of cards instead of a solid house of real value.

As Professors Zhou and Zhu, the authors of the CFA Institute study, reported, crashes are inevitable. When the crash comes, infrastructure can be the key to recovery. As devastating as the Great Depression was, the industrial capacity built up before and during WWII laid the foundation for the subsequent economic expansion and burgeoning middle class.

Some economists have described the war spending, which is universally agreed to have ended the Depression, as Keynesian economics on steroids. While Keynes is often quoted as saying that, in an economic crisis, it is worthwhile to pay workers to dig holes and fill them up again, the war efforts of WWII created an industrial behemoth that enabled subsequent, major infrastructure projects like the interstate highway system. Expansion-related capital was used to nourish the body of the nation with solid food.

Somewhere along the way, however, we traded healthy, solid food for junk bonds. The 1950s infrastructure has been left as "good enough" for far too long. The service economy has displaced the industrial one, but we haven't bothered to retool for this reality. While coasting on our previous momentum, we've managed to sustain long-term economic growth by promoting materialism as a national ethic. We've defined the middle-class lifestyle through consumerism; the single-family home, the car, appliances, the television set, and the La-Z-Boy became staples of this new realization of the American dream.

Unfortunately, consumerism is a two-edged sword. Keeping up with the Joneses has demanded that ordinary people steadily increase their standard of living, resulting in a self-destructive, cannibal ethos. As a single income started to fall short of the demands of the upwardly mobile middle-class family, both parents began working. With the resulting absence of parents at home to closely oversee schoolwork, this in turn undermined the effectiveness of public education. And as families' double incomes fell short in their turn, households became more dependent on credit. Wall Street responded with ever-more-creative devices to juggle numbers and massage the national dependency on credit. Ultimately, even home ownership became dependent on creative financing. It was inevitable that the house of cards would collapse.

There has been a straight line from the cessation of infrastructure development and manufacturing of the fifties and sixties to the economic collapse of 2007–9. It has been economic kwashiorkor.

A major realignment is coming. In fact, at the time of the writing of this book, it is already under way. Will it be incidental or strategically guided? Will it be left to Smith's fantasy of an invisible hand?

It is not the nature of cannibal capitalism to fix itself. It is the nature of cannibal capitalism to follow the course of least resistance, even if that course is ultimately self-destruction. Its nature is to make money the easy way, even at the cost of jobs or broad economic development. The post-WWII boom is over, and a new boom must be engineered, or the attrition may be fatal. It must happen, and the proceeds must be invested domestically to trigger further growth.

I started this book to give a coherent narrative to the Great Recession of 2007–9 and provide a view of the way forward, but through my research, this book evolved into an examination of the more fundamental flaws in our whole commercial, financial, and political system. Matters are truly urgent, and correspondingly urgent attention must be given, particularly in the context of the rise of state capitalism as practiced by China. Toe-to-toe, a nation practicing state capitalism could obliterate a nation practicing cannibal capitalism.

It is all too easy to allow overly simplistic rhetorical devices to shape public debate. It is much harder to honestly look at a system that has created such wealth for so many and recognize where it is based on selfishness, greed, and delusion. Seem harsh? Think about it. Our markets—stock, bonds, commodities, and currency—are all based on the delusion of prognostication, a feat no human since biblical times has achieved. Nevertheless, we trade today based on tomorrow's values. We even use the term "futures" in some cases. Then, the world goes nuts when too many of these guesses about the future prove wrong.

We can repeat the standard line that the housing crisis was caused by people buying houses they couldn't afford. Yet the concept of affordability is artificial. What can be afforded is entirely enabled or disabled by lending standards.

The point is that the simplistic quips of popular opinion don't address the real problems. Worse still, they are generally wrong. A deadly combination—the general public's ignorance of the facts, the hypocrisy of the beneficiaries of the system who obscure the facts, and the ideology of politicians and activists who ignore the facts in order to score points of favor—perpetuates the economic cannibalism that is destroying America. The notion that everything would be fine if not for "this" or "that" economic factor is simply not true. Our artificial system is based on immorality, and you can't apply idealism to it. If you try to do the "wrong" thing the "right" way, you will often sabotage whatever made the "wrong" thing work, but you won't make the "wrong" thing into something else. Capitalism has to be capitalism to work. If you try too hard to change it, you will only screw up what works about it. Though limited, flawed, and volatile, the system does "work" to a point. We need to understand capitalism's limitations, allow it to work within those limitations, but force it to work for everyone. Capitalism *doesn't* have to be of the cannibal variety.

The housing bubble was generally viewed as a terrible thing that should have never happened and must be prevented from recurring, but it was perhaps the first bubble that created dramatic downstream benefits as it was forming. It stimulated countless small businesses and created jobs for plumbers, carpenters, electricians, material suppliers, and innumerable other middle-class workers. Though most would say that home equity shouldn't be used as a credit card, the bubble enabled consumer spending sprees that moved a lot of money through our economy, creating many jobs and covering many paychecks. It was both bad and good at the same time. Critics applied their moral arguments selectively.

It also spurred great economic activity globally. Who's really to say that popping that bubble was really any better than the alternative?

Imagine for a moment the "bubble money" being used to build schools, factories, or other long-term economic engines. Would it have been true to say that those things should *not* have been produced, just because the capital was generated through trading credit-default swaps? The problems arise when that capital stays only in the pockets of the traders. Then, it is all but useless to the broader economy.

There are undeniable benefits to a broad distribution of wealth. Personally, I believe that every stable, employed household should own a home, not out of some liberal ideology, but because home own-ership creates more economic activity. Developing a massive energy infrastructure could create an inestimable boom of innovation, enter-prise, and consumption. Expanding the broadband infrastructure to every corner of the country could deurbanize business and resurrect the American small town. Improving education, opening up markets while sharing the profits, eliminating or diffusing general costs that weigh down the economy, and building instead of just buying stuff could all propel the economy to greater heights. We need the middle class to be strong and growing stronger.

Unfortunately, sharing and spreading wealth, deferring short-term gains for the long-term benefit, and making investments with generational time horizons are antithetical to the ethos of cannibal capitalism.

People need to abandon the concept of the "other," recognize the commonality and connection that we all share, and then act in the interest of this larger whole of which we all are a part. It will probably never happen, though. History indicates that people will remain at each others' throats, and we could even lose this modern phenomenon called the middle class.

Without a change to human nature, the situation may be hope-less. In the meantime, however, misplaced idealism makes the bad even worse. To be indignant over the failures of a wrong system because it isn't right in its wrongness is to tryst with the absurd. The "let them fail" mantra of the bailout fatigue doesn't lead to greater prosperity. Eliminating the GSEs that created the modern housing market won't cure malaise in the housing market. Railing against monetary policies doesn't eliminate the need for liquidity in an expanding global economy.

The popular notion that the Great Depression was ended by World War II and that the war was funded by war bonds overlooks the factor of the diminution of the currency with the suspension of the gold standard. A bubble ended the Great Depression! Inflated money flowed into the real economy, triggering activity that created jobs and thereafter a wave of economic progress. Was that a bad thing? Only to an ideological purist who believes that money should be something that it has never been.

Instead of pulling at the loose threads of our tattered system and unraveling the whole fabric of society, we must leverage the positive to prepare for the future. Whether our currency is inflated "bubble money" or not, we must use it to develop a sustainable economy that's globally competitive. Using the fake (money) to acquire the real (land, commodities, and services) is the history of global economics, whether we like how that sounds or not. Accepting that reality and strategically following through only makes sense.

The twenty-first century is here. China has taken the place of Japan as the second-largest economy in the world, and there is no reason to think that they will be satisfied with that ranking. With its state capitalist system, China behaves more like a corporation than a country. The once-fractious nations of Europe have come together to form a union with the greatest gross domestic product in the world, despite the occasional failings of its weaker states. A cannibal capitalist country cannot compete with this. The virtual monopoly the U.S. enjoyed in the post-WWII era is a distant memory. There is real competition, and it is gaining on us.

It may very well be that the nature of democracy and free market economics precludes the possibility of strategically resetting the whole economy. Instead, the free market waits for some invisible hand to save the day, and democratic factions have become averse to compromise. "Eat or be eaten" may be endemic to our flawed humanity to such a degree that we are incapable of redressing it. The rifts between opposing ideologies may be irreconcilable.

Or maybe, just maybe, things could at least be improved. You can't legislate morality. Yet you can create incentives for good behavior and disincentives for bad behavior. Far too many people subscribe to the fallacious notion that, to win, others have to lose, and that success only comes on the backs of the losers. Such thinking is the essence of cannibal capitalism, and it runs counter to the fundamental principle of long-term investing: helping a business capitalize and then sharing in the subsequent wealth, a classic win-win situation. Shifting away from cannibal capitalism and expanding economic progress requires that we embrace win-win business development. Businesses can be encouraged to embrace responsibility for their impact on the environment, consumers, employees, communities, stakeholders, and all other members of the public sphere. In the past, at least some form of corporate social responsibility (CSR) was the standard.

As a Rotarian friend of mine described CSR, "This is the business owner who gives a hard-working employee a small bonus and a thank you. It's the local businessman who sponsors the Little League team. It's the local corporations that build parks, support the arts, fund academic programs, and otherwise make their hometowns better places. This is Pittsburgh's Heinz and Carnegie, Richmond's Philip Morris, Louisville's Brown-Forman, Chicago's Wrigley, Atlanta's Coca-Cola, and St. Louis's Anheuser Busch…it stands for companies that did right by the employees, and became corporate citizens. They are the presidents of their Rotary Clubs and fundraisers for the local children's hospital."

Muhammad Yunus, a Bangladeshi banker and professor of economics who won the Nobel Peace Prize for developing the concept of microcredit, believes that much more than CSR is needed. In his book, *Building Social Business: The New Kind of Capitalism That Serves Humanity's Most Pressing Needs*, he argues for the creation of corporations whose main objective is not to maximize profits, but to solve problems such as poverty, hunger, housing, and access to clean water. He believes that companies can be modeled after the best businesses of the capitalist system, but structured to serve the greater good instead of feeding off the needs of the greater number. His concept may strike some as overly utopian for our selfish world, but he confirms the need to turn away from cannibal capitalism.

The wealth that corporations extract from the public must be matched by the contribution they make to it. Not through token philanthropy, but through commensurate profit sharing. Companies cannot be permitted to offshore jobs, outsource services, profit from capital effectively extracted from the real economy, and give nothing back. If they don't voluntarily act as good corporate citizens, then maybe it's time to resurrect Huey Long and force them to through aggressive taxation.

The goal would be that no citizen of the wealthiest country in the world would die because of lack of access to health care. No able and eager child would be barred from higher education by economic limitations. Profits gleaned from the real economy would be invested back into the real economy.

Ideological dogma must be broken down. All human ideology is flawed, because all humans are flawed. The suggestion that the free market is all good and that socialism is all bad is ludicrous. Such thinking is just as absurd as the suggestion that communism works in practice. Accept the system for what it is, and take full advantage of what works about it. Then, use the central government to do what the market can't. The Western system of economics and politics is at best deeply flawed, but as Churchill said, it's better than the others.

What works in the free market? It is relatively easy to start a business in America if you can pull together startup cash. Access to early-stage capital for enterprising entrepreneurs needs to be augmented. Home ownership is an engine of economic activity in the real economy. We cannot let myopic arguments over mortgage products undermine rising standards of living and the ancillary businesses that those rising standards enable. Finally, regulation must not be so draconian that it unnecessarily impedes a business's cash-conversion cycle. Regulations should be limited to commonsense protection of consumers and the system itself. The free market can effectively pick winners and losers among businesses, but only if there is a truly level playing field and anticompetitive behavior is not tolerated.

On the other hand, the free market cannot do it all. There are far too many aspects of free market economics that are skewed toward monopolistic megacorporations. The popular board game Monopoly perfectly illustrates the ultimate outcome of a completely unfettered free market; although players start off roughly equal, in the end all the money flows to one winner. It is not the function of capitalism to serve the needs of the many, though it may be an occasional side effect. Rather, it functions to eventually concentrate more and more wealth in fewer and fewer hands, just like Monopoly. The populace has far too many needs than can be served by businesses pursuing their own interests. Self-interest must be married to common interest. Furthermore, there are needs of the market that offer no short-term profits, yet that must be initiated.

Instead of worshipping our ideologies, we have to recognize that, at times, we need to use measures taken from opposing socioeconomic ideologies. Sometimes a measure of socialism is needed. Children, the sick, the elderly, and the disabled often have little or no role in the free market. Their needs require the redistribution of some wealth. This can either be disproportionately borne by a few, or proportionately borne by all. It is logical to mitigate the expense of caring for these needs by distributing the weight generally.

In fact, there are many roles within the economy, beyond regulatory, which are better served by the government than by private interests. Early scientific research and infrastructure development need to be driven by the government, both to bear heavy expenses that offer little or no return on investment and to distribute benefits broadly. The Internet is a perfect demonstration of such development. The technology was worked out over time by the government, and when it was turned over to the private sector, the level, competitive playing field permitted the creation of thousands of new businesses.

Despite all the emotionally charged, irrational rhetoric to the contrary, health care insurance is a prime candidate for government centralization. Other Western nations have clearly demonstrated how superior health outcomes can be delivered at lower costs.

Health insurance companies are governmentlike bureaucracies. They aggregate money to pay for health care, but their profit motive precludes the potential for providing the lowest prices and broadest access to care. Where is the logic in ineffectually imitating a government function so that a narrow group may profit? Government is very capable of collecting money and writing checks without any profiteering. Some services are just better provided by socialistic programs, regardless of how unpalatable the concept may be in the abstract.

People need to get over it. This is your system, warts and all. Instead of crying over what should have been, you have to work with what you've got. The bubbles and busts of the early 2000s were the result of the free market, but unfounded idealism made the bust far worse. The Federal Reserve's idealistic response to the realization that there were millions of subprime loans in our mortgage system was to raise interest rates, triggering defaults, which in turn collapsed the whole house of cards. Millions of homes that were bought and paid for with these loans were foreclosed. Millions of construction workers who had been paid with proceeds from these loans lost their jobs. The idealism of tighter credit standards and fixed-rate mortgage loans cannot cover these homes or rehire these workers. While you can complain about the way the housing market overheated, it created a lot of downstream economic activity. Was that really all bad?

Coming face-to-face with unpleasant realities will require embracing necessities that run contrary to your ideological bent. If you are on the ideological left, you may have to give ear to the Cato Institute. If you are on the right, you may have to listen to the Progressive Policy Institute.

Alas, there is the rub. Instead of recognizing common purpose and dependency, and sharing in harmonious dialogue, these opposing factions are far more likely to engage in shouting matches and blame each other for all that is wrong with America. Like the schizophrenic with the gun screaming in the mirror, not realizing that what he hates is part of himself, the ideological factions can't see themselves beyond their insanity.

Perhaps the cannibal country is unredeemable. Most likely, the change people hope for, wish for, and vote for is out of the reach of our belief. Yet belief, even when futile, reaps its own rewards. The alternative—and the temptation—is to give up in the face of a bleak situation, but sometimes you have to deal with reality as it is, hoping for better until a real change does come. We have no choice but to carry on business with the best possible view. It doesn't matter that it is futile. It doesn't matter that a believable alternative is out of reach.

When I was sitting in bankruptcy court and my core business was in cinders, I refused to give in to that reality. It would have been easy to believe that if real estate is not sound, then no investment is worth pursuing. I could have recoiled into a defensive position, abandoning my entrepreneurial instincts just as the financial community did in response to the housing and credit crises. I did not.

I wrote this book to share my insights as a battle-hardened businessman. I rebuilt my war chest as a venture capitalist. After all, history teaches that market crashes give birth to tremendous opportunity. In fact, for a while I was tempted to forgo the real economy and just make money playing the stock market. Yet, as someone who rails against hypocrisy, I couldn't expect others to reinvest in our economy while I stood idly by, making my money via market trading. I accepted the environment for what it was, though. It was no time for upper-middle market housing, a market we now know was disproportionately dependent on loose lending practices. I instead opened up a boutique home-building business catering to the elite homebuyer. But this was not to be my core operation. I launched a new flagship business, Little Green Men, a green-technology business specializing in smart power management and automation systems. We are now developing and collecting intellectual property in anticipation of a major market launch, while our subsidiary, lgmtechnology.com, an IT service contractor, pays the bills.

I've spent twenty years in business and two years studying every aspect of the crash and recession of 2007–9 and the global economy. I now know how deep the rabbit hole goes. But this is an intervention, not a cure. The economy is on a suicide track, and the principals of the system need to decide whether they will do anything about it, and what.

I don't claim to have a solution that would allow us to make mutually exclusive principles coexist, and I don't believe anyone in the world has a total solution to the problems of cannibal capitalism. Nevertheless, there are some basic remedies that could make a big difference. The first step is to face reality, much as an alcoholic must first recognize his addiction before he can recover.

As horrible as it may sound to reinflate the bubble and let the foxes continue to guard the henhouse, it is doubtful that we could actually handle a total systemic realignment. Commentators and pundits have cried for a return to something that never existed. They have referred to a house of cards, as if the entire system of modern global economics isn't exactly that. It's not that I love things as they are; indeed, this book is a testament to the discontent I feel. It's just that, even though the inconsistent application of morality to a fundamentally immoral system is flawed (to put it mildly), it's what we've got—and got to work with. I still believe that my girls have a great future ahead of them. I believe that things will work out well. I believe that there is hope, albeit bleak now. A system based on calculated greed cannot work in the long run, and I don't claim to have an answer for exactly how to make a prosperous, new, world economy work. There is no one around here with the wisdom to pull that off.

We must simply *choose* belief. Our currency and markets depend on belief. An honest look at the facts and an honest debate of the issues is a starting point for those who believe that there is an answer. Some may believe in an entirely different system for the future. But those who wish to work with this economy need, at the very least, to deal with this fact: fighting over unrealities, decimating the ways and means of production, and letting cultural divisions undermine progress are not recipes for success. What will you believe?

In economics, suspension of disbelief may risk bubbles, but utter disbelief immobilizes completely. Even when you know that there are holes in what you believe, you still find rewards in believing. Even if you find yourself feeling stupid for having believed, you still were better off for a time because of that belief. That's not to say that a healthy level of skepticism is bad, for we cannot substitute credulity for plausibility, but in the end, utter cynicism is empty. No, we must always choose to believe and let our dreams carry us forward, because money and economics are based on nothing more than a consensus of belief. When that belief is optimistic, we advance. When it is pessimistic, we decline.

America does not have to lead the world, and if the cannibalism continues, it surely won't. The richest man in the world is now a Mexican whose wealth is derived from serving the developing world. China is slowly, surely, strategically gaining control of resources all over the planet. These realities tell us all that we need to know.

Educate our children! Invest in our small businesses! Export, export, export! Break OPEC with a transition to hydrogen! Use our inflated money to develop real things that build real wealth!

If we do, we will not only curtail catabolism, we will also emerge into the twenty-first century with the greatest surge of wealth creation we have ever seen. We had a good run in the wake of World War II, but the fat is gone. We are down to skin and bones. Instead of cannibalizing ourselves, we can bring in real nourishment by leveraging our current position as the largest economy in the world against the new realities of globalization. It's time to bring the money home to momma, to feed and not to eat ourselves.